MACWORLD™
MW
AUTHORIZED
EDITION

Macworld®
Mac®FAQs

Macworld
Mac FAQs

by David Pogue

IDG Books Worldwide, Inc.
An International Data Group Company

Foster City, CA ♦ Chicago, IL ♦ Indianapolis, IN ♦ Braintree, MA ♦ Dallas, TX

Macworld® Mac® FAQs

Published by
IDG Books Worldwide, Inc.
An International Data Group Company
919 E. Hillsdale Blvd.
Suite 400
Foster City, CA 94404

Library of Congress Catalog Card No.: 95-76834

ISBN: 1-56884-480-8

Printed in the United States of America

10 9 8 7 6 5 4 3 2 1

1B/SR/QX/ZV

Distributed by Macmillan Canada for Canada; by Computer and Technical Books for the Caribbean Basin; by Contemporanea de Ediciones for Venezuela; by Distribuidora Cuspide for Argentina; by CITEC for Brazil; by Ediciones ZETA S.C.R. Ltda. for Peru; by Editorial Limusa SA for Mexico; by Transworld Publishers Limited in the United Kingdom and Europe; by Al-Maiman Publishers & Distributors for Saudi Arabia; by Simron Pty. Ltd. for South Africa; by IDG Communications (HK) Ltd. for Hong Kong; by Toppan Company Ltd. for Japan; by Addison Wesley Publishing Company for Korea; by Longman Singapore Publishers Ltd. for Singapore, Malaysia, Thailand, and Indonesia; by Unalis Corporation for Taiwan; by WS Computer Publishing Company, Inc. for the Philippines; by WoodsLane Pty. Ltd. for Australia; by WoodsLane Enterprises Ltd. for New Zealand.

For general information on IDG Books Worldwide's books in the U.S., please call our Consumer Customer Service department at 800-762-2974. For reseller information, including discounts and premium sales, please call our Reseller Customer Service department at 800-434-3422.

For information on where to purchase IDG Books Worldwide's books outside the U.S., contact IDG Books Worldwide at 415-655-3021 or fax 415-655-3295.

For information on translations, contact Marc Jeffrey Mikulich, Director, Foreign & Subsidiary Rights, at IDG Books Worldwide, 415-655-3018 or fax 415-655-3295.

For sales inquiries and special prices for bulk quantities, write to the address above or call IDG Books Worldwide at 415-655-3200.

For information on using IDG Books Worldwide's books in the classroom, or ordering examination copies, contact Jim Kelly at 800-434-2086.

For authorization to photocopy items for corporate, personal, or educational use, please contact Copyright Clearance Center, 222 Rosewood Drive, Danvers, MA 01923, or fax 508-750-4470.

Welcome to the world of IDG Books Worldwide.

IDG Books Worldwide, Inc., is a subsidiary of International Data Group, the world's largest publisher of computer-related information and the leading global provider of information services on information technology. IDG was founded more than 25 years ago and now employs more than 7,500 people worldwide. IDG publishes more than 235 computer publications in 67 countries (see listing below). More than 60 million people read one or more IDG publications each month.

Launched in 1990, IDG Books Worldwide is today the #1 publisher of best-selling computer books in the United States. We are proud to have received 8 awards from the Computer Press Association in recognition of editorial excellence, and our best-selling *...For Dummies™* series has more than 17 million copies in print with translations in 25 languages. IDG Books Worldwide, through a recent joint venture with IDG's Hi-Tech Beijing, became the first U.S. publisher to publish a computer book in the People's Republic of China. In record time, IDG Books Worldwide has become the first choice for millions of readers around the world who want to learn how to better manage their businesses.

Our mission is simple: Every one of our books is designed to bring extra value and skill-building instructions to the reader. Our books are written by experts who understand and care about our readers. The knowledge base of our editorial staff comes from years of experience in publishing, education, and journalism — experience which we use to produce books for the '90s. In short, we care about books, so we attract the best people. We devote special attention to details such as audience, interior design, use of icons, and illustrations. And because we use an efficient process of authoring, editing, and desktop publishing our books electronically, we can spend more time ensuring superior content and spend less time on the technicalities of making books.

You can count on our commitment to deliver high-quality books at competitive prices on topics consumers want to read about. At IDG Books Worldwide, we value quality, and we have been delivering quality for more than 25 years. You'll find no better book on a subject than an IDG book.

John J. Kilcullen

John Kilcullen
President and CEO
IDG Books Worldwide, Inc.

Credits

Publisher
Brenda McLaughlin

Acquisitions Manager
Gregory Croy

Acquisitions Editor
Nancy E. Dunn

Brand Manager
Pradeepa Siva

Editorial Director
Mary Bednarek

Editorial Managers
Mary C. Corder
Andy Cummings

Editorial Executive Assistant
Jodi Lynn Semling

Editorial Assistant
Nate Holdread

Production Director
Beth Jenkins

Supervisor of Project Coordination
Cindy L. Phipps

Pre-Press Coordinator
Steve Peake

Associate Pre-Press Coordinator
Tony Augsburger

Media/Archive Coordinator
Paul Belcastro

Project Editor
Jim Grey

Technical Reviewer
Jeff Robbin

Project Coordinator
Valery Bourke

Production Staff
Gina Scott
Carla C. Radzikinas
Patricia R. Reynolds
Melissa D. Buddendeck
Dwight Ramsey
Robert Springer
Theresa Sánchez-Baker
Kathie Schnorr
Chris Collins
Angie Hunckler
Mark Owens

Proofreader
Henry Lazarek

Indexer
Liz Cunningham

Book Design
Jo Payton

About the Author

After graduating summa cum laude from Yale in 1985, Ohio-raised David Pogue spent six years conducting and arranging Broadway musicals. When it turned out that the world was hungrier for his writing skills than for his musical ones, he began writing and teaching about the Macintosh.

In New York, his computer students come from Hollywood (Mia Farrow, Gary Oldman, Natasha Richardson, William Goldman, Mike Nichols), publishing (Frances Lear, Gay Talese), the music world (Stephen Sondheim, Carly Simon), and so on.

David's column, "The Desktop Critic," appears each month in *Macworld* magazine. He also wrote *Macs For Dummies,* which, since its introduction in 1992, has been the #1 bestselling Macintosh book in all of its 15 languages. A sequel, *More Macs For Dummies,* debuted in 1994. For people whose thirst for Mac wisdom remains unslaked, Pogue also co-wrote the encyclopedic, 1100-page *Macworld Mac & Power Mac SECRETS.*

His first novel, a techno-thriller called *Hard Drive,* was called "a notable book of the year" by *The New York Times.* A new thriller is in the works.

David is a regular panelist at the Macworld Expo and user group gatherings nationwide. He's been profiled on *48 Hours,* in *The New York Times,* and in *USA Today.*

Acknowledgments

It took IDG Books CEO John Kilcullen about 3.5 seconds to green-light this book when I pitched it to him. I haven't stopped appreciating his confidence. It must have taken my editor, Jim Grey, about 3.5 man-years to whip the book, with all its 45 billion cross references, into shape. My thanks to him, too.

My gratitude also goes to the IDG Books team who brought this book, and my others, to high-quality life. This particular project benefited from special favors granted by Karen Bluestein, Brenda McLaughlin, Mary Bednarek, Diane Steele, Mary Corder, Nancy Dunn, Beth Jenkins, Jo Payton, Valery Bourke, Mark Owens, and Chris Collins.

Special thanks to two unsung collaborators: Leslie Jones, who drafted Chapters 28 and 29, and Gene Steinberg, who put together appendixes A and B.

The world should also know how much Steve Steele contributed to this book; he works at the Apple Assistance Center, and believe me, he's great at providing assistance. As a believer in this book, he made himself available for weeks on end to help find answers and confirm technical information. And if you enjoy this books's sidebars featuring hilarious true tales of Macintosh novices, we have Eric Hausmann (junkspill@aol.com) to thank; he collects those stories in his electronic newsletter, *Tech Support Tales*, and gave me permission to adapt them here. And then there's Jeff Robbin, Apple system-software engineer extraordinaire, whose technical review of this manuscript kept me on my toes.

Finally, thanks to the supporting cast: my 105-year-old grandfather, whose love of wordplay turns out to be genetic; my family, who put up with my seasonal disappearances when I go into book-writing mode; and, of course, the lovely Dr. O'Sullivan.

(The Publisher would like to give special thanks to Patrick J. McGovern, without whom this book would not have been possible.)

Contents at a Glance

Table of Contents

Part 2: About This Macintosh 83

Chapter 5: Look and Feel 85

Chapter 12: Scanning and OCR **157**

Chapter 13: Speech, Multimedia, and CD-ROM **167**

Part 3: Mac Models, Inc. 181

Chapter 14: Power Macintosh 183

Chapter 15: PowerBooks 193

Chapter 19: Frequently Cursed Glitches 233

Chapter 20: Startup Snarls 249

Introduction

What's FAQ?

It stands for Frequently Asked Questions.

I didn't make this up, by the way. The term *FAQ* is a by-product of the Internet explosion, when millions of first-time modem owners began to cruise that great worldwide bulletin board. (See FAQ 29-1, "What is the Internet?")

The Internet isn't exactly what you'd call user-friendly. You have to know all kinds of codes and protocols. You are required to refer to your own mother as *O_mother@worldx.umich.edu*. You have to know "netiquette" — unwritten codes of cyber-behavior. And above all, you're supposed to be *born* knowing all that stuff.

In fact, if you ask a veteran Internet inhabitant anything basic, you'll get the typed equivalent of a hassled sigh. "I learned that stuff the hard way, back in the 70s," is the unspoken submessage. "Why do you feeble-minded beginners bug me with the same dumb questions every single day?"

Before long, fed-up Internauts began preparing preventive defenses. They'd type up all the obvious questions with patient, beautifully explained answers. Each one- or two-page file of Q's and A's was called, of course, a *FAQ sheet*. They figured: Instead of answering the same questions over and over, getting snippier each time, why not answer all the questions patiently — *once*, in a FAQ — and *insist* that everybody read it before bugging the veterans?

That's exactly what happened. FAQ sheets began springing up faster than Boston Chicken outlets. At first, they were just Internet-related: Internet FAQs, Modem FAQs, E-mail FAQs. But the concept was so golden that FAQ sheets arose for other topics: White House FAQs, Seinfeld FAQs, Tax FAQs. You no longer had to be a modem junkie to appreciate the value of a FAQ sheet — just a computer owner.

What's Mac FAQs?

Of course, I run a great risk calling this book *Mac FAQs*. I mean, *FAQ* isn't as well-known a 90s term as, say, *O.J.* or *infomercial* or even *Internet*. At this very moment, somebody's in a bookstore somewhere asking for a book called *Mac Facts, Mac Fax,* or *Max Factor*.

But after tutoring hundreds of Mac users, conducting seminars, reading 50 e-mails a day from Mac fans worldwide for years . . . I, like those jaded Internet surfers, realized that millions of people have the same questions about the Mac.

Trouble is, there's no central place to go for the answers. Heaven knows that the Mac manuals don't provide them; Apple's manual-writers are like Stepford-wife robots, writing smiling, corporate prose. They're not permitted to acknowledge the everyday Mac glitches people encounter on one hand, nor the intense adrenaline rush of, say, morphing your face into Tom Brokaw's on the other.

Here, then, in one book, are the 500 most frequently asked Mac questions on earth.

Oh yeah — and the answers.

What's the plan here?

By their very nature, the *most* frequently asked questions arise in the first week of using the Mac. That's when you *really* need the answers.

For that reason, the first chapter of this book is dedicated to people muddling through their first Macintosh moments. Actually, you'll run across some very basic answers scattered through other chapters, too; my goal is to answer the *most frequently asked* questions, regardless of their technical level.

Parts 2 through 6 answer questions about the Mac in general, specific Mac models (like Power Macs and Performas), fixing things, buying things, and hooking up to things (like networks and the Internet), respectively.

There's one big problem with a book like this, though: Since you're turning to it because you don't already *know* the answers, how should it be organized? I mean, suppose you want to know: "Can I use Windows CD-ROM discs on my Mac?" Well, where should that question go — in the chapter on CD-ROMs or the chapter on IBM-Mac compatibility?

Fortunately, there's also one big solution for a book like this. And Apple came up with it. It's called *aliases*.

You know how you can make an alias of a Macintosh file, and stick duplicates of that icon in several different places? No matter which one you double-click, the *original* file, the actual one, opens up. In the same way, I've filed dual-purpose questions like that in *multiple* chapters. No matter where you happen to dip in your search, you'll be directed to the *sole* location of the answer. See? Just like an alias.

Do you get kickbacks from America Online?

OK, you're right. There *are* a lot of references to America Online in this book.

But the truth is, online services like America Online, e-World, and CompuServe are an indispensable part of Macintosh ownership nowadays. That's how you find out if Apple's about to introduce a faster, cheaper Mac model next week. It's how you get the little fixes, software updates, and patches that finally make your GeoPort work, or solve your color StyleWriter problem, or eliminate the sound dropouts when you use CD-ROMs. It's where all the experts hang out and can be hit up for answers.

It doesn't have to drive you to bankruptcy, either. If you're strapped, get an old 2400-baud (low speed) modem for $50 . . . or a used one for $25. Then call America Online at (800) 827-6364 and ask for a free ten-hour starter disk. Or call eWorld at (800) 775-4556 and ask for *theirs*.

Once you get their starter disk, you can use the service for free. For ten hours. After that, cancel, and you won't have spent a dime. That's totally 100% legal and fine. For ten hours — over the course of a month — you have access to the Internet; and 50,000 games, programs, sounds, and clip art files; e-mail; and all the other stuff those services offer.

If you *don't* cancel, you'll start getting charged $10 a month, and you'll be a member, which isn't such a bad state of affairs either. See Chapter 28 for details.

So, to answer the question: Nope, I don't get a kickback from America Online. But I *do* get a lot of free stuff — bug fixes, news, advice, utility programs, upgrades for the programs I already have.

And so can you.

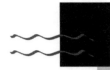

The David Pogue Pledge

As in all my Macintosh books, I make the following guarantee:

1. I will reply to every e-mail (except gratuitously nasty ones). My address is *Pogue@aol.com*.

2. I will not use trendoid terms in my writing: *the user* when I mean you; *price point* when I mean price; *performance* when I mean speed; *developer* when I mean a software company; *software package* when I mean a program; and so on.

3. I will never put an apostrophe in the possessive word *its*.

4. Each time IDG Books goes back to print some more copies, I'll make all corrections and make any other changes necessary to bring the book up to date.

5. Whenever I make changes to a book, I'll post those changes online — in the *Macworld* areas of America Online and eWorld — so that you can make the corresponding changes to the book you've already bought.

PART 1

Brave New
Mac

I still remember the day I unpacked my first Macintosh. Senior year of college, cramped little dorm room. I lifted the thing onto my desk, letting the white styrofoam blocks clunk to the floor. The solitary word *Macintosh* was painted on the front panel. I turned it on, took the tutorial, got excited.

Then I wanted to *use* it for something.

I turned back to the manual. It said: "Locate the application you want to use."

I sat upright, blinking stupidly. *Application?* Did I get one of those? Shoot, did I miss that in the packaging somewhere?

No kidding: I actually walked back over to the boxes and the styrofoam and started rooting through it, looking for one more plug, or add-on, or gadget — this "application" I was supposed to find.

The point is, nobody's there when you need 'em on the day you get your Mac.

This part of the book takes care of that little problem. You'll find all the questions most people have when they start using the Mac, plus instructions for accomplishing the most frequently-requested tasks. At the end of this section is a list of all the terminology you're likely to encounter in a typical reading of a Mac magazine or a computer article in the paper.

(Oh, and P.S. — *application* means *program*. I know that now.)

1

First-Timer FAQs

T his chapter won't teach you how to use your first Mac. (That's what Macs For Dummies is for.) But this is definitely the place to get the questions answered that everybody has at the beginning.

Help! I typed something, and saved it, but now I can't find it.

 It happens to all of us. Use the Find command.

1-1

The Mac's folder system works just like a real-world folder system: In the process of shoving a document away, you occasionally shove it into the *wrong* folder. You'll have a hard time finding it again.

On the Mac, finding something is easy. Make sure you're in the Finder (choose Finder from the application menu if you're in doubt).

Now use the Find command in the File menu. Type a few letters of the missing document's name, and click Find (see Figure 1-1). The Mac will show you the first file on your hard drive whose name matches what you searched for.

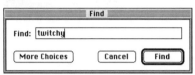

Figure 1-1: When you choose Find from the File menu, you'll see either the window at the top (System 7.5) or at the bottom (previous systems). Either way, get into this habit.

If it finds a match, but it's *not* the file you're looking for, choose Find Again from the File menu (or press ⌘-G instead). Keep doing that until you find what you *were* looking for.

System 7.5 note: If you're using System 7.5, you don't have to do that Find Again business. *All* the matches appear in one window — from there, you can double-click a file to open it.

See also FAQ 1-13, "Do I have System 7.5? What system do I have?"

See also FAQ 4-5, "What's the application menu?"

How can I avoid losing files in the future?

▽ **Always click the Desktop button before you save.**

Suppose you've just written a letter in ClarisWorks. When you choose Save for the first time, *click the Desktop button* before you click Save (see Figure 1-2).

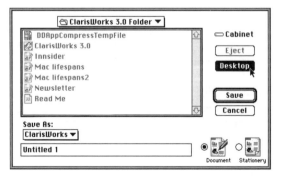

Figure 1-2: Click Desktop, and you'll never lose another file.

Then, when you quit ClarisWorks at the end of the day, the new file you made will be *sitting* right there in front of you (see Figure 1-3). Now it's a simple matter to drag it into an appropriate folder.

Figure 1-3: Your new file will be happily waiting for you, safely *not* buried in a folder somewhere. Put it where you want it.

Do this regularly, and you'll never lose another file.

Incidentally, if you use a Performa or System 7.5, you can *automatically* avoid losing things. Turn on your "Save new documents into the Documents folder" option in the Performa or General Controls control panel, and all new documents will go straight into your desktop Documents folder.

Should I leave my Mac on all night?

 Only for convenience or conscience; not to protect your equipment.

Engineers have argued both sides of this point for years. One school maintains that the heat of leaving the Mac on all the time weakens the components, shortening their life. The other school argues that the daily surge of electricity — from switching the machine on — is far worse.

There's an economic argument, too. Turning the Mac off at night saves hundreds of dollars' worth of electricity per year — and is better for the environment. On the other hand, Apple says that starting a computer uses many more watts than leaving it on.

The answer, then, is to do whatever's most convenient. Here's a handy compromise: Turn off the *monitor* at night. (It's perfectly OK for the computer to be on while the screen is off.) That way you don't have to wait for startup the next morning; no surge of power goes through the machine every day; a major power consumer is off; and your monitor's phosphor coating lasts longer.

See also FAQ 1-20, "Do I need a screen saver?"

Should I get a Mac now or wait for the next model?

▽   **Buy it now, unless Apple's coming out with a new model *next week*.**

Face it: *Any* computer is going to lose half its value and fall technologically behind-the-times in six months. The cycle *never* ends. If you wait for the ultimate "safe investment" computer, one that won't become obsolete or lose its value, you'll never own one!

This bit about ever-faster and ever-cheaper computers isn't specific to Mac, by the way. You'd fight the same technological dragon if you were an IBM fan. (If you want proof, ask your friends who bought now-discontinued Atari and Amiga machines!)

Therefore, the answer is: Buy the Mac now. In the time you would have waited for the next great thing to come along, you'll use it, have fun, and get a lot done.

On the other hand, you don't want to be dumb about it. Check to see if Apple's coming out with something newer and better *soon*. You *would* feel pretty silly if you had bought a Power Macintosh 7100/66 the week before the faster 7100/80 came out for the same price.

So how do you find out what's in the pipeline?

Way One: Ask the people at a computer store. It's free, but not totally trustworthy; these guys are often fairly clueless about Macs.

Way Two: If your newspaper is metropolitan enough to carry computer ads, watch the Mac prices as the weeks go by. When a certain model's price suddenly tumbles, it's because a new model is about to replace it.

Way Three: Sign onto America Online. Use keyword *Macworld* and leave a question in the message area: "I want to buy a ___. Is now a good time?" You'll get a good answer within a day. Or sign onto eWorld, where *MacWeek* magazine's articles are available for reading (keyword: *MacWeek*). That magazine almost always knows ahead of time what new models are on the way.

See also FAQ 28-2, "What's a keyword?"

Why is there so much more software for PC, DOS, and Windows than for Macs?

▽   **Because there are so many more PCs than Macs.**

If you visit your local computer store, you'll discover that most of the software for sale there is for IBM-type computers. Mac software is always crammed away on a single shelf somewhere.

It's perfectly logical for the store owners to do that. After all, 85% of the world's computers are IBM clones. So they fill their stores with 85% IBM-clone software, and only 15% Mac programs.

If that's what your local store is like, what are you doing there? You could be ordering your software from places like Mac Connection, (800) 800-4444, or Mac Warehouse, (800) 255-6227, which offer a *huge* selection, give deep discounts, generally don't charge sales tax, and deliver the stuff to your door overnight. Get your revenge that way.

Anyway, everything's going to change in the next three years. Now that Macintosh clones are on the market, more computers will require Mac software. And that means that the balance of power on those computer-store shelves will soon change.

See also FAQ 1-24, "Is my Mac IBM compatible?"

See also FAQ 4-53, "What's a PC?"

See also FAQ 23-2, "Should I get a Macintosh clone?"

So why are only 15 percent of the world's computers Macintosh?

▽ **Because IBM had a head start. And because of the Golden Law of Purchasing: Individuals buy Macs, companies buy PCs.**

IBM was selling computers before Apple was even a glimmer in Silicon Valley's eye. As a result, companies all across America bought IBM equipment. And once a company has invested millions in IBMs, IBM printers, IBM screens, IBM software, and IBM consultants, it's way too hard to switch. Even to something that's clearly better, like the Mac.

People aren't totally ignorant; almost everybody concedes that the Macintosh is simpler to set up, easier to learn, and more productive to use than IBM clones. So why do IBM clones still outsell Macs? Because when a *company* buys computers — and they usually buy IBMs, because of their previous investment — they often buy *lots* of them at once. On the other hand, when a family or an individual buys a first computer today, it's usually a Mac. Families and individuals only buy *one* computer at a time.

Once again, though, the times are changing. For years, a Mac's been able to read IBM disks, print on IBM printers, use IBM monitors, and even run IBM software. But recently, making it do all that stuff has become much easier and less expensive. Open-minded corporate buyers no longer face immediate dismissal for buying Macs — buying a Mac no longer means that the company has to junk its investment in IBM stuff.

Furthermore, the new Mac clones made by non-Apple companies will increase the Mac's presence in the world, too.

See also Chapter 26, "PCs and Macs."

How come Apple makes so many different models?

▽ **You would, too, if you had stockholders.**

See, Apple Computer doesn't just want to make the best computer the world has ever known. It also wants to keep its shareholders happy. These people *own* the company. They could get nasty and sell the whole place to AT&T if they felt like it.

To keep the shareholders happy, you can't just make the best computers the world has ever known. You also have to sell them. *Tons* of them. Profitably, too. Preferably more, percentage-wise, than people like Compaq, who make IBM-clone computers.

Apple has devised lots of ways to make sure it's selling the most computers it can. First, the very moment one of its engineers comes up with a clever new technology — stereo sound, or a PowerBook touchpad, or a faster new chip — Apple zaps it into a new model and gets it on the market. It's better to get that thing on the shelves, so that people can start using that new technology, than to keep it in the closet just to avoid angering everybody who *just* bought the *previous* model.

Second, Apple has discovered that there are different *ways* people buy computers. Business people still go to computer stores. But a college kid buys Macs through the college bookstore — and usually doesn't have the money for a sleek, jet-fueled PowerBook 540c. And Mr. and Mrs. America shop at places like Sears and Kmart.

So Apple sells Macs through three different channels. Computer stores sell Quadras, PowerBooks, and Power Macs. Schools sell the LC series. And department stores, superstores, and electronics stores sell ready-to-use Mac systems called Performas.

As a strange result, Apple started selling *the same* models under different names. For example, the Power Macintosh 6100 is also the Performa 6115. In general, the only thing different, equipment-wise, is the name painted on the case. In other words, Apple sells fewer models than you think.

The other part of this question's answer is, "They don't make as many as they used to." Apple has finally gotten the message that too many models cause frustration and confusion. As you can see by the chart, the number of different Mac models introduced each year has slowed down a lot recently (Figure 1-4).

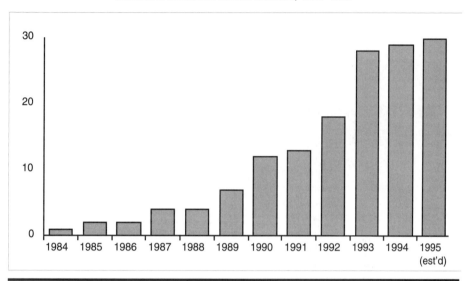

Number of Macintosh models available, 1984–1995

Figure 1-4: The number of different Mac models flooding the globe has finally slowed down.

 See also Chapter 23, "Gear Bought and Sold."

I have all these extra keys like F1, Del, and Esc. What are they for?

▽   "Future expansion" — or Microsoft programs.

When you buy a Mac and turn it on, those function keys (F1, F2, and so on) and other weird keys (Esc, Control, Help, and so on) don't do *anything*. That's why Apple also sells a keyboard (and a lot of laptops) without so many extra keys.

FA
Q
1-8

On the other hand, some programs, especially Microsoft ones, use those keys. F1 might trigger the Undo command, F2 might mean Copy, and so on. Furthermore, you can get a *macro program,* such as QuicKeys, that lets *you* assign meanings to those keys. You might program F1 to type out your return address, F2 to mean "launch ClarisWorks," and so on.

Finally, some of those extra keys aren't so oddball after all. The Esc key usually acts as a Cancel button in dialog boxes, the Page Up and Page Down keys scroll your windows up or down a screenful, Home and End often work to take you to the very beginning or very end of a document, and so on.

The power button on my keyboard doesn't do anything.

▷ See FAQ 17-9, "Is there any way to turn my LC on from the keyboard?"

It says "Not enough memory." Should I throw some stuff away?

▽ Nope — that won't help.

If you throw away files you don't need anymore, you'll make more disk space. But that won't affect your computer's *memory* at all.

See also FAQ 1-11, "What's the difference between RAM and hard disk?"

See also FAQ 6-1, "What should I do about these 'not enough memory' messages?"

What's the difference between RAM and hard disk?

▽ A file sits on the disk when the computer is *off.* It's in RAM, or memory, when you're *working on it.*

No wonder people get confused — RAM and hard-drive capacity are measured in the *same units* — megabytes! But they're completely different mechanisms.

The hard drive is like your VHS videotape library. You may have shelves and shelves of tapes, just as you may have hundreds of Mac files. Even when the TV is turned off, all your movies are safely recorded and put away.

When you want to watch, say, *Plan 9 From Outer Space*, you take that tape off the shelf, put it in the VCR, and turn on the TV. Now you can see what's on it; with the remote control, you can fast forward, record over parts of it, and so on. That's like double-clicking a Mac file, watching it open onto the screen, and making changes to it. It's now in *RAM*.

RAM is all electronic; without juice, your Mac's memory is erased. That's why you're supposed to use the Save command all the time. The Save command transfers what you've written on the screen — in RAM, get it? — back onto the much safer disk or hard drive.

Since RAM is electronic, it's expensive. That's why Macs have much more disk space then RAM. A typical Mac might have 8 megabytes of RAM, but 500 megabytes of hard-drive space.

 See also Chapter 6, "Memory."

How much RAM and hard-disk space do I have?

 **The About This Macintosh window tells you.**

To find out how much memory (RAM) your Mac has, choose Finder from the application menu. Then choose About This Macintosh from the menu. The resulting window (Figure 1-5) shows your Mac's total memory in the upper-left.

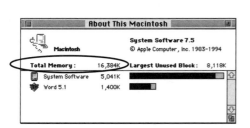

Figure 1-5: Here's how to see how much memory you have. Lop off everything after the comma to see how many *megabytes'* worth you have.

To see how big your hard drive is, double-click it to make its window open. Choose "by Icon" from the View menu. The window then shows you how much is in the disk, as well as how much free space is left (see Figure 1-6).

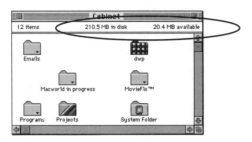

Figure 1-6: When you add the "in disk" and "available" amounts together, you get a rough idea of how big your hard drive is. The total won't come out to a nice round number, though, because there are a bunch of invisible behind-the-scenes files that these numbers don't show.

 See also FAQ 4-5, "What's the application menu?"

Do I have System 7.5? What system do I have?

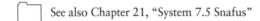

▽ Once again, the About This Macintosh window tells you.

Follow the advice in FAQ 1-12. In the upper-right corner of Figure 1-5, you can see that your Mac identified the system version you have.

See also Chapter 21, "System 7.5 Snafus"

What's all the stuff in the System Folder? Can I throw some away?

▽ Absolutely. Half of it is junk you'll never need.

Apple wants to make sure you're covered. In the event you'll want to hook your Mac to a network, buy a CD-ROM drive, or dial into another Mac a continent away, you've got the software for it.

In the meantime, if you're *not* planning to do all that stuff, get rid of the corresponding software. Trashing the useless stuff won't give you any extra *memory* to play with (see FAQ 1-10), but you'll gain plenty of *disk space,* which is valuable in its own right. And if you ever need any of this stuff again, you've got it — on your system disks or start-up CD. (If you have a Performa, see FAQ 17-1, "Hey! There are no system disks with this thing!")

Let's do this the quick way. Open your System Folder. Inside, you'll find an Extensions folder and a Control Panels folder. Open them up. Arrange the windows so that you can see their contents in a list view, as shown in Figure 1-7. (If you need help arranging windows, see FAQ 1-22, "What are the different controls on a window again?")

FAQ 1-13

FAQ 1-14

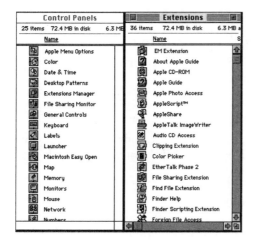

Figure 1-7: Arrange your windows, and prepare for a trashfest.

Ready? Let's start trashing.

If you don't have a CD-ROM player, throw these away:

Extensions folder: Apple CD-ROM, Apple Photo Access, Audio CD Access, Foreign File Access, High Sierra File Access, ISO 9660 File Access

If your Mac isn't networked to other Macs (and you don't use Remote Access — you know who you are), throw these out:

Extensions: AutoRemounter, AppleShare, Catalogs Extension, EtherTalk Phase 2, File Sharing Extension, MacTCP Token Ring Extension, Mailbox Extension, Network Extension, PowerTalk Extension, PowerTalk Guide, PowerTalk Manager, Printer Share, TokenTalk Phase 2, TokenTalk Prep

Control Panels: File Sharing Monitor, Network, Sharing Setup, Users & Groups

If you're not a programmer, toss these:

Extensions: AppleScriptLib, AppleScript, Object Support Lib, Scripting Additions

If you're not using a PowerBook, jettison:

Extensions: Assistant Toolbox, Caps Lock, PowerBook Guide Additions, PowerBook Monitors Extension

Control Panels: AutoRemounter, Control Strip, PowerBook, PowerBook Display, PowerBook Setup, Trackpad

These are files for Macs that take spoken orders (Power Mac or AV models only). If you're not using one of these Macs, pitch:

Extensions: My Speech Macros, Speech Guide Additions, Speech Recognition, SR Monitor, System Speech Rules

For the Power Macintosh only:

Extensions: ObjectSupportLib, PowerPC Finder Update, PowerPC Monitors Extension, QuickTime Power Plug, PowerAV Update, MathLib, Shared Library Manager, Shared Code Manager

Control Panels: Power Macintosh Card

Throw *all* of these away, *except* the ones that match your printer and your Mac model:

Extensions: AppleTalk ImageWriter, IIci/IIsi Monitors, ImageWriter, LaserWriter, LaserWriter 8, LaserWriter 300, LW Select 310, Personal LaserWriter SC, Quadra AV Monitors Extension, Quadra Monitors Extension, StyleWriter II Button Disabler (LC or Performa 500 series)

If you don't use disks from PCs (IBM clones), throw this away:

Control Panels: PC Exchange

If you use only American numbers and text, throw these away:

Extensions: WorldScript Power Adapter

Control Panels: Numbers, Text

These are help files; if you know your Mac cold, toss 'em:

Extensions: About Apple Guide, Apple Guide, Finder Help, Macintosh Guide, Shortcuts, Video Guide Additions

If you're not disabled, throw away these:

Control Panels: CloseView, Easy Access

Throw this away, period:

Extensions: A/ROSE

And *definitely* throw this away if you have a Power Macintosh:

> **Control Panels:** SCSI Manager 4.3

Each of the following is only for specific models; if yours isn't among them, aim for the trash. CPU Energy Saver, for example, can automatically shut off your Mac at a specified time — but it only works on Mac models that turn off completely when you choose the Shut Down command. (That rules out the LC series, the 6100, and so on.)

> **Extensions:** 630 SCSI Update (630-series only), AV Serial Extension (Quadra AV models), Record Button (Apple Adjustable Keyboard only)

> **Control Panels:** Auto Power On/Off, Brightness (Mac Classics only), Button Disabler (adjustable keyboard only), Cache Switch (Quadra/Centris models only), CPU Energy Saver, Serial Switch (IIfx only), Screen (LC 500's, Color Classic, Mac TV only)

That leaves the following, which you may as well keep; each adds a useful function to most Macs:

> **Extensions:** EM Extension, Clipping Extension, Color Picker, Find File Extension, PrintMonitor, QuickTime Musical Instruments, QuickTime

> **Control Panels:** Apple Menu Options, Color, Date & Time, Desktop Patterns, Extensions Manager, General Controls, Keyboard, Labels, Launcher, Macintosh Easy Open, Map, Memory, Monitors, Mouse, Sound, Startup Disk, Views, WindowShade

What's a Type 1 error?

▷ ☐ See FAQ 18-1, "What's a Type 1 error?"

What's "Application could not be found?"

▷ ☐ See FAQ 18-4, "It says, 'Application could not be found.' What gives?"

How can I get rid of the half-inch black border on my monitor?

▽ **You can't.**

Using the little knobs tucked somewhere on your monitor, you can make the picture fill more of the glass. But you won't get *more* desktop area (that shows, for example, *more* of a page at a time); instead, you'll only be enlarging the picture that's there. See Figure 1-8.

What you have now   What you want (more viewing area)   What you can get (same viewing area, larger dots)

Figure 1-8: You can blow up your picture, but you won't see any more.

Monitor companies say that if they made the picture fill the glass edge-to-edge, the picture would be distorted around the edges. (They also want to boost their sales of bigger monitors.)

See also Chapter 9, "Monitors."

Will I get cancer from my monitor?

▽ **Nobody knows for sure — but there's a precaution you can take.**

Several years ago, there was a considerable controversy among scientists. Computer monitors, like all electrical appliances, emit ELF (extremely low-frequency) radiation. Could sitting next to this thing all day long, all year long, increase your cancer risk?

Nobody's been able to prove anything conclusively. However, since those reports, most companies — such as Apple — started making their monitors *shielded* to prevent ELF emissions.

And besides: A *Macworld* magazine study found that by the time you're 28 inches away from the monitor, the amount of radiation drops to zero. So if you sit at arm's length from your screen, you're in no danger at all.

I've got all these old manuscripts. Do I have to type them all into the Mac again?

 See FAQ 12-5, "I have all these old manuscripts. Do I have to type them all into the Mac again?"

Do I need a screen saver?

 No — at least, not to save your screen.

If you leave the *same picture* on your monitor — that is, you never actually use your Mac — for two years straight, never turning it off, then you may begin to see a ghostly image of that picture permanently burned into the glass. Screen savers (such as After Dark) are supposed to prevent burn-in by putting moving images on the glass instead of a static image.

But most people don't leave their Macs on (and untouched) for quite that long. And second, a screen saver still lights up the monitor, which ultimately shortens the life of the phosphors that coat your screen. If you really want to protect your screen, there's a *much* better way: Turn the monitor *off* when you're not at your Mac.

That's right: Leave the computer on, but turn the *monitor* off. It's 100% safe; it's Apple-recommended; and it's a good way to save money, protect your screen, and save energy.

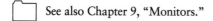 See also Chapter 9, "Monitors."

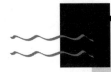

GUQ: Great Unanswerable Question

Why is it sometimes spelled *disk* and sometimes *disc?*

The *disk* spelling is used for floppies and hard drives. *Disc* seems to be reserved for shiny removable platters, such as CD-ROMs and video discs. Other than that distinction, there's no good answer — and not a great deal of point.

1-21

Do I need a virus program?

▽ **Not as much as you'd think — but it's free, so why not?**

Writing computer viruses — nasty little self-duplicating programs that attempt to mess up your computer — is a popular teenage programmer's prank in the PC world. In the Macintosh world, there *have* been Mac viruses, but almost none of them were actually designed to wreck your files. They did little more than make your Mac beep or act sluggish.

You can't get a virus from an online service like America Online. And you can't get a virus just by sitting at home working on your own stuff. In this day and age, the only opportunities for your Mac to get infected are:

1. You download programs from the Internet or a local BBS, or

2. You exchange floppy disks with other people.

You could buy Virex or S.A.M., two popular antivirus programs, but frankly I find them more annoying than useful. Every time you insert *any* floppy disk, even one of yours, they make a big time-consuming show of scanning it for your protection.

There's a free, less intrusive alternative: Disinfectant. If you have a modem, dial up any online service (such as America Online) and download away. You can also send away for it. Send a self-addressed, sturdy, stamped envelope and an 800K disk to John Norstad, Academic Computing and Network Services, Northwestern University, 2129 Sheridan Road, Evanston, IL 60208. (Of course, Disinfectant is also included with the bestselling Mac book, *Macworld Mac & Power Mac SECRETS.* End of plug.)

See also FAQ 28-25, "How do I sign up for an online service?"

See also FAQ 28-3, "How do I find a file I want to download?"

What are the different controls on a window again?

▽ They're at the corners and edges of every Macintosh window.

Here's a summary (see Figure 1-9).

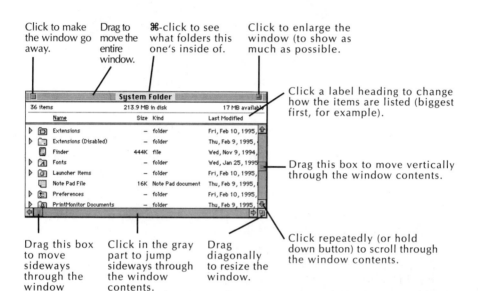

Figure 1-9: The various ways you can push, pull, or tug a window. Not shown: the View menu at the top of your screen, which lets you decide whether you want to see a list, like this, or regular-size icons.

The controls you'll probably use the most often are the **title bar** (lets you *move* the window), the **zoom box** (upper-right, which *expands* the window as large as necessary to see its contents), and the **close box** (upper-left, which *closes* the window).

If I have three Macs, do I really have to buy three copies of every program?

▽ **Depends on the program.**

We're talking about copyrights and licenses here. There's no *technical* reason you can't make as many copies of your programs as you want; copying a software program, like ClarisWorks or Microsoft Word, is easier than making a photocopy — and the quality doesn't degrade with each copy.

According to U.S. copyright law, you're allowed to install *one* copy of each program you buy, and make *one* safety backup. Fortunately, most software companies are a little bit more realistic than that; they *also* give you permission to install a second copy. This way, you can have one copy on your Power Mac and another copy on your PowerBook, or one copy at home and one at work. To find out what permission you're actually granted when buying, say, PageMaker, read the tiny 5-point type on the disk envelope, which is where the software license is usually printed.

If you work in an office, however, where several people use a program at once, you're supposed to buy a separate copy of that program for each Mac. Because this can get ridiculously expensive, most companies cut you a deal if you're buying more than, say, five copies of something.

Is my Mac IBM-compatible?

▽ **Yes. Sort of.**

Any Mac made since 1987 can definitely read floppy disks from IBM-type computers (hereafter called PCs). If you spend money on an extra circuit board or a program called SoftWindows, you can even run PC *programs* on your Mac.

📁 See Chapter 26, "PCs and Macs."

I ejected a disk, but the Mac keeps asking for it back!

▽ **And it always will, too, if you keep using the Eject Disk command.**

The Eject Disk command (in the Special menu) is one of the dumbest holdovers from the creaky days of Macintosh antiquity (1984). Do *not* use Eject Disk to eject a disk. If you do, the disk's ghostly image *remains* on the screen — even after you eject the disk. And the Mac stubbornly asks you to *re*-insert the disk before it lets you proceed with your regularly scheduled life.

Instead, highlight the disk and choose *Put Away* from the File menu. That pops the disk out. See Figure 1-10.

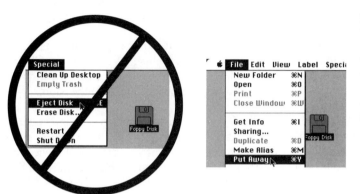

Figure 1-10: Don't use the Eject Disk command to eject a disk, weird as that sounds. Use Put Away.

Alternatively, you can drag the floppy-disk's icon to the Trash. You might *feel* as though you're about to erase the disk, but actually the disk pops right out.

What's this ".sit" file?

 It's been compressed to take up less space.

A file with a name that ends in *.sit* is a file that's been compressed into a compact form by a program called StuffIt. The point is, of course, to make it smaller. Making something small is useful if (a) you're using a pay-by-the-minute service like America Online, or (b) you're a software company who wants to pack your program onto fewer disks. That's why almost every file on America Online (and other services), and every program you buy on floppy disks, comes in compressed form. See Figure 1-11.

1-26

What the sender did

What you should do

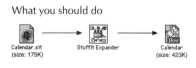

Figure 1-11: If you get a file that ends in *.sit,* it's compressed. You can't use it until you expand it to its fully inflated condition. For that, you need something like StuffIt Expander.

If you just got this stuffed file from America Online, eWorld, or CompuServe Information Manager (MacCIM), look around for the re-expanded version; those services normally unstuff this kind of file automatically when you sign off. (They usually leave the *.sit* file behind, though, so look for both the *.sit* and the expanded version.)

If the *.sit* file came from an online service but *didn't* expand automatically, do this. Launch the online service program (America Online, eWorld, or MacCIM). From the File menu, choose Open. Locate the *.sit* file and open it; it expands, and the program asks where on your hard drive you want to put the expanded version.

OK then: What if the *.sit* file *didn't* come from an online service, and you have no way of expanding it? You'll have to get the free program StuffIt Expander. You can get it from a user group, a friend, or — most conveniently — the online services themselves. (If you don't *have* one of those StuffIt programs, then double-clicking a *.sit* file gives you the famous "Application could not be found" message; see FAQ 18-4.) Anyway, to restore a *.sit* file, drag its icon on top of the StuffIt Expander icon.

See also FAQ 28-3, "How do I find a file I want to download?"

See also FAQ 28-25, "How do I sign up for an online service?"

See also FAQ 29-16, "What's .sit, .hqx, etc.?"

Should I get one of those Macintosh clones?

▷   See FAQ 23-2, "Should I get a Macintosh clone?"

1-27

How do I find a nearby Mac users' group?

▽   **Call (800) 538-9696, extension 500, and ask.**

1-28

That's Apple's user-group referral number. A user group is a great way to get all your *other* frequently asked questions answered — plus software, advice, discounts, and other artifacts of Macintosh culture.

How does the Mac know what time it is, even when it's off or unplugged?

 It has a tiny lithium battery inside.

This battery lasts seven years. That's right: If you're still using your current Mac seven years from now, you'll have to go out and find a new lithium battery somewhere.

You should *be* so lucky.

What's "The original could not be found" mean?

 See FAQ 18-10, "I'm double-clicking an icon, but the Mac says 'The original item could not be found.'"

How do I contact Apple?

 By toll-free phone, by modem, or by fax.

Apple is much easier to reach in recent years. If you're willing to sit on hold for up to 20 minutes, you can get a good, well-informed answer to almost any *technical* question. (You'll have a harder time finding somebody to yell at for discontinuing the Mac model you just bought last week.) The fax, eWorld, and Internet services are icing on the cake.

- ✦ Free technical help, repairs, problem solving by telephone: (800) **SOS-APPL.**

- ✦ Free technical help by overnight e-mail: On eWorld, click the icons as follows: Computer Center icon; Apple Customer Center; Apple Technical Support; Ask Apple, USA. Finally, click the correct category icon (Power Mac, Newton, etc.) and type your question.

- ✦ Free fax-back system for frequently asked questions: (800) **505-0171** (call by voice, and follow the instructions).

- ✦ Free downloading of fixes, software updates, product specs, and press releases by Internet: **ftp.support.apple.com** or **ftp.info.apple.com**. (These are generally available on eWorld, too.)

- ✦ Free newsletter containing advice, tricks and tips, announcements of software updates and fixes: **Information Alley** (available from any online service, most user groups, or by Internet at Apple.Support.Area of **ftp.info.apple.com**).

See also FAQ 28-3, "How do I find a file I want to download?"

See also FAQ 29-3, "What can you do on the Internet?"

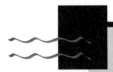

RAQ: Rarely Asked Question

Why does time begin on 1/1/1904?

There are several ways to find out that the Mac believes history began on January 1, 1904. You could try setting your Mac's clock as far back as possible. You could undergo a really awful system malfunction; when it's repaired, and your Mac is working again, its clock is likely to say January 1, 1904.

So why *that* year, of all things?

The original designers of the Mac chose that date for several reasons. First, in programmery terms, a *longword* (a piece of data 32 bits long — a handy size) has enough digits to specify about 130 years' worth of seconds. Second, they wanted to make sure that most Mac users' birthdays could be included; they figured 1904 was early enough. (That's too bad for my grandfather, who was born in 1890 and likes the Mac quite a bit.) Finally, they chose 1904 because it was arithmetically convenient — it was a leap year. (1900 wasn't a leap year because it was a century year.)

If you've got your calculator handy, you'll realize that the Mac's ability to recognize times will founder in the year 2030, on the Mac's 46th anniversary. At that point, the clock will reset itself to 1/1/04 again, and you'll have to buy yourself a new computer.

(Source: *HyperTalk 2.2 — The Book* by Dan Winkler, Scot Kamins, and Jeanne Devoto.)

Where do I get Apple software updates?

 From eWorld, America Online, CompuServe, the Internet, or from Apple.

Every couple of months, Apple releases one important software update or another. System Update 3.0, for example, solved a host of bugs and speed problems in System 7.1. System 7.5 Update 1.0 added several new features to every System 7.5 Mac, including the ability to turn it *off* by pressing the keyboard power key. And if you have a GeoPort, version 2.0 spelled the end of years' worth of compatibility headaches — and turned your Mac into a speakerphone, to boot.

The easiest way to get these free updates is by modem. Here's how:

✦ If you have an eWorld subscription: When online, click the following icons, which appear in this order: Computer Center, Apple Customer Center, Apple Software Updates, Macintosh.

✦ If you have an America Online subscription: Use keyword MOS. Then click the Software Library icon.

✦ If you are on the Internet (or can access the Internet from your online service): Go to the FTP site **ftp.support.apple.com** or **ftp.info.apple.com.** Burrow into successively deeper folders (directories), as appropriate — for example, Apple.Software.Updates brings you to Macintosh directory, which gives access to System.Software, which is a pretty good place to check.

Don't forget that you can access these FTP sites from America Online, CompuServe, or any other online service that offers Internet access. For example, use keyword Internet on America Online, click the FTP icon, click the Other Site button, type in the FTP address, and you're on your way.

✦ If you have no modem: For many updates, you can call the Apple Order Center, pay $10 or so, and ask for a particular update to be mailed to you. The number is (800) 769-2775.

See also FAQ 29-4, "How do I get connected?"

See also FAQ 28-2, "Whats a keyword?"

Seealso FAQ 28-25, "How do I sign up for an online service?"

 CHAPTER

2

How Do I Do It?

T*he mass media make no secret of what a personal computer can do. It just isn't very forthcoming on how you do it. Here are a few of the most frequently requested how-to's, from how to number your pages to how to send out a form letter.*

How do I start typing halfway across (or down) the page?

 Press the Return key to go down, or Tab to go across.

A word processor is funny that way: You can't just click in a convenient blank spot and start typing. Instead, it's pretty much how a typewriter works — you press the Tab key to move *across* the page before typing. And to start typing partway *down* a page, press the Return key repeatedly.

2-1

How do I number my pages?

 Depends on the program, but here's a summary.

Some programs offer several different methods of numbering your pages. I'll just give you the easiest.

2-2

Microsoft Word 5.1: From the File menu, choose Print Preview. Double-click the second icon (on the left side of the screen). The page number appears in the upper-right corner of every page.

Microsoft Word 6: From the Insert menu, choose Page Numbers. A dialog box appears; use the popup menus to specify a location for the page number on each page. Click OK.

ClarisWorks 2 or 3: From the Format menu, choose Insert Header. From the Edit menu, choose Insert Page #. If you want to center the page number or place the page number at the upper right, click the appropriate tiny icon on the ruler — the Centered or Right Justified icon.

Microsoft Works 4: From the View menu, choose Header. From the Insert menu, choose Page Number Field.

MacWrite Pro: From the Format menu, choose Insert Header. From the Edit menu, choose Page #.

WriteNow: From the Format menu, first choose Insert Header, then Insert Page #.

Nisus Writer: From the Insert menu, first choose Header, then Page Number.

WordPerfect 3: From the Layout menu, mouse down to the Header/Footer command, and choose New from the submenu. Click OK. In the header window that appears, click the third tiny icon on the ruler to pop the number into place.

FileMaker Pro: From the Select menu, choose Layout. Click the text tool (looks like an A). Click in the header area and type ##. When you print (or go to Select mode), that ## code becomes the current page number.

See also Chapter 22, "Frequently Used Software."

How do I make symbols, like ¢ and ¥ and ©?

▽ **Let Key Caps be your guide.**

There it is, right in your menu: the desk accessory called Key Caps. Open it. If you hold down your Option key, you'll see the complete map showing where all those useful symbols are hidden. (See Figure 2-1.)

By lifting your finger off the Option key as you stare at the symbol you wanted, you can figure out what normal letter key to type to produce it (when the Option key is down).

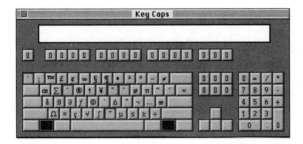

Figure 2-1: The Key Caps window. Press Option to see where most of the symbols are hidden. For example, Option-G turns out to produce the ¢ sign.

Don't forget to try Option with the Shift key, Option with the ⌘ key, and other combinations; symbols sometimes hide in funny places. Don't forget, too, that each *font* may have different symbols. Change fonts using the Key Caps menu, which appears when Key Caps is open.

And if it's too hard to remember that ⌘-Shift-Option-Caps Lock-7 produces some desperately needed Swahili diacritical marking, *click* the onscreen symbol when you see it. It appears in the text strip at the top of the Key Caps window, where you can select it, copy it, and *paste* it into whatever document you're working on.

How do I make accent marks?

 Use the Option key and press one of the magic keys: E, U, I, N, or ~.

2-4

These five "dead keys" are unique on the Mac. When you press one while holding down the Option key, you get *nothing* on the screen. The Mac now waits for you to press a *second* key, which then shows up on the screen — *underneath* the marking you wanted.

Example: To type the *é* in *fiancée*, press Option-e. Nothing happens onscreen. When you then type a regular *e*, the complete *é* will appear.

Same thing works with the other dead keys — Option-u, then a letter, makes the two dots, as in *über*. The Option-I creates the little circumflex, as in *maître*; Option-N makes the wavy thing in *Iñez*; and Option-~ (the upper-left key on most keyboards) gives you the accent grave, as in *crème*.

Note that the actual letter you put *under* the diacritical mark (which is what those things are called) doesn't have to be the E, U, I, or whatever; any vowel will do.

How do I put stuff in the menu?

▼   Hie thee to the Apple Menu Items folder.

Inside your System Folder is the Apple Menu Items folder, as Figure 2-2 shows. As you can see, all you have to do is open that folder; anything you put *in* there is suddenly listed in your menu. (See Figure 2-3.) Anything you take *out* is no longer listed there.

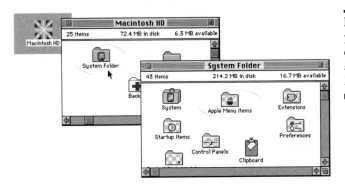

Figure 2-2: Double-click your hard drive, double-click the System Folder, and behold the Apple Menu Items folder.

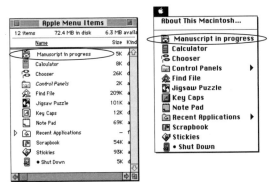

Figure 2-3: Anything you drop into the Apple Menu Items folder (left) shows up in the actual menu (right). Consider putting your current project there for convenient access.

Take two minutes to set up your menu now; it'll pay off in the future. For example, stick your favorite programs there — your word processor, for example. Next time you want to write something, just choose the program's name from the menu to launch it (instead of burrowing through a bunch of folders to find its normal icon).

Actually, for best results, don't put any *actual* files into the Apple menu. Put an *alias* of any file you want to list there.

See also FAQ 5-11, "What's an alias for?"

How do I transfer files between Macs?

 By disk, by hard drive, or by wire.

If you're only trying to move a couple of files, you can always copy them onto a floppy disk and *carry* them to the second Mac.

If you have a lot of files, it's a simple, inexpensive matter to connect the two Macs by a cable. You already own the necessary software to pull this off — *and* you already have the cable. See FAQ 25-1, "How can I connect two Macs?"

There is a third method, of course. If you have an external hard drive or a SyQuest cartridge-type storage gadget, copy everything onto *it* as a temporary holding tank. Turn off both Macs, move the drive or cartridge system to the second Mac, and copy your files onto the new Mac's hard drive.

How can I get my whole system to turn on with one switch?

 Buy a PowerKey.

The PowerKey is a multi-outlet, surge-protecting gadget. Plug everything into it: Mac, monitor, printer, CD-ROM. Then, when you turn on your Mac, the whole shooting match turns on.

 See also FAQ 17-9, "Is there any way to turn my LC on from the keyboard?"

Can I make the Mac turn itself on or off automatically?

 Yes, if you have one of the anointed Mac models. Or get a PowerKey.

If you have System 7.1 or later, you also have Auto Power On/Off, a control panel. It lets you specify when you want your Mac to turn itself on and off. That could be a useful feature if (a) you want your Mac to shut down by itself after a long modem transfer, (b) you want the Mac warmed up and waiting for you when you arrive at your desk each day, or (c) you're doing an elaborate, carefully timed magic trick.

Unfortunately, this magic only works with a weird selection of specific Mac models; some examples are listed here.

- ✦ Macintosh IIsi, IIvx, and IIvi
- ✦ Color Classic and Color Classic II
- ✦ Macintosh LC 520 and 550, 630 and 5200
- ✦ Macintosh Quadra 630, 840AV, 900/950
- ✦ Power Macs (except 6100-style models)
- ✦ Workgroup Server 95, 8150, 9150
- ✦ Performa 550, 575, 576, 578
- ✦ Performa 600 through 638

If your model doesn't work with Auto Power On/Off, you can get a PowerKey, as described in FAQ 2-7. It comes with a control panel that does exactly what Auto Power On/Off does — but on any Mac model (except the Mac Plus and the PowerBooks before the 500 models).

How do I connect the Mac to a TV or VCR?

▽ With a $250 adapter.

Mac models with the letters *AV* in their names, as well as certain Macs (such as the 630 or 5200 series) that can accommodate the optional Apple TV card, can hook directly to a TV or VCR. All you need is what's known as a male-to-male RCA cable (which probably came with your Mac) and hook it up to your VCR's Video In jack.

All other models require an adapter, known as an *NTSC converter*. Any mail-order place will sell you one; the LTV Portable (Focus Enhancements) is one of the best known.

This NTSC converter plugs into your Mac's monitor jack. (Of course, if your Mac doesn't *have* a monitor jack, such as the PowerBook 150 or the SE/30, you're out of luck.) Another wire goes to the VCR or TV, and a third gets plugged into a wall power socket. Your regular Mac monitor just sits there, gathering dust — unless you happen to have purchased one of the "Pro" converters, which have an extra jack for your monitor.

None of these methods makes your Mac's image look as good on TV as it does on its regular monitor. Don't forget that TV was invented over 50 years ago. The quality of the newer technology blows away the feeble offerings of a television.

Still, a TV is a handy (and common) large-screen appliance. For people making presentations on the road or using the Mac in a classroom, getting the Mac on TV might just be the ticket.

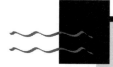

PRQ: Perfectly Reasonable Question

How can the Mac turn itself on — if it's off?

Good question: If there's no power to the Mac, how can it be keeping an eye on the clock — so that it will know when to turn on again?

As you know from FAQ 1-29, the Mac has a battery that keeps its clock going. As long as the machine is plugged in, a chip inside certain Mac models can communicate the time to the Mac's startup circuitry. (FAQ 2-8 lists those models.)

A PowerKey works similarly. It can read the Mac's clock because it's connected to your keyboard cable! When it's told that the time has come, it powers up everything plugged into its electrical outlets — such as your Mac.

P.S. — If you want sound, too, you'll need a cable that's *male RCA* on the VCR end and *male miniplug* on the Mac end. Visit Radio Shack; they know what to do. Plug the miniplug into the little jack on the back of the Mac marked by a tiny speaker icon, and the other end to the Audio In jack of the VCR.

 See also FAQ 23-17, "Where can I buy stuff?"

How do I make mailing labels?

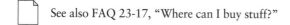 Use a word processor or a database. Buy Avery labels from an office supply store.

Avery self-stick labels come in different varieties, depending on your printer type and the shape of the labels you want. The most common by far are called Avery 5160, which feature ten rows of three stickers per sheet. These letter-size sheets go through a laser printer or a StyleWriter beautifully.

Then you have to set up your labels correctly on the Mac screen. Most word processing programs (Word, WordPerfect, and so on) come with ready-made empty documents — *templates* — into which you type your addresses.

More conveniently, database programs such as ClarisWorks and FileMaker come with templates all set up for specific Avery label sheet sizes, too. Figure 2-4 shows an example — FileMaker in action.

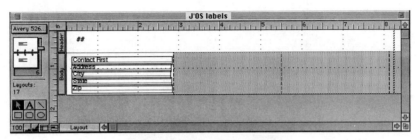

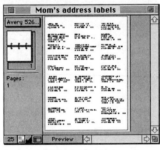

Figure 2-4: In FileMaker, go to Layout view. Choose New Layout from the Edit menu. Choose Labels; choose an Avery label type from the popup menu; and click OK. The result is shown at top. After you've typed your addresses (in Browse mode) and switched to Preview mode, the result looks something like the example at bottom. Print away!

What program should I use for my address book?

▽ **Your choice: a database or an address-book program.**

The latter is frequently (and annoyingly) referred to as a *PIM* — a *personal information manager*, especially when it comes with some kind of calendar program.

Use a database like ClarisWorks or FileMaker if you spend most of your day with that program running, or if you rarely need to look up phone numbers. (If not, it's too much trouble to launch a big slow program just to get a quick lookup of somebody's name or number.)

Use an address-book program like Now Contact if you look people up frequently. These programs, as shown in Figure 2-5, give you little blanks to fill in for each lucky member of your calling circle. An address-book program is quick to open, can print mailing labels, and can dial the phone number *for* you (if you have a modem).

Figure 2-5: In a serious address-book program like Now Contact, you have to type each piece of info into a separate blank. The payoff: Later, you can sort and print your list based on this kind of info — like a list of carphone numbers only.

Use an address-book program like QuickDex, InTouch, or InfoGenie if speed and dialing are your priorities. Even with 1500 names and numbers, it still takes less than two seconds to launch QuickDex (Figure 2-6), and only *one* second to find a phone number. This kind of program isn't quite so adept at *manipulating* your information — it's a hassle to print out only New York phone numbers, for example, or to sort by last name. But because it doesn't have individual blanks for first name, carphone number, and so on, it's faster and more flexible than PIM programs.

See also FAQ 23-17, "Where can I buy stuff?"

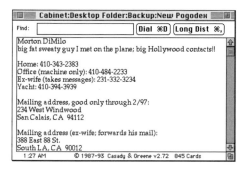

Figure 2-6: In a freeform address-book program like QuickDex, each person has a whole big page full of information. As you can see, you can be more flexible in what kinds of info you put there.

2-12

How should I keep track of my schedule?

▽ **The world is filled with good calendar programs.**

Now Up-to-Date is a good example. Not only does it have a nice full-screen calendar display, but it also puts its own little menu at the top of your screen, no matter what program you're using. Each day, you can pull down this menu to see the day's schedule.

For less money, you can also get the equally colorful, flexible Remember? program. It's *shareware*. Download it from America Online or get it with the book *Macworld Mac & Power Mac SECRETS*.

See also FAQ 23-17, "Where can I buy stuff?"

See also FAQ 28-23, "What are freeware, shareware, and so on?"

2-13

How do I print envelopes?

▽ **Patiently.**

This one isn't easy. Every printer, and every envelope-printing program, is different. Some printers do envelopes extremely well; others succeed only in mangling the envelope.

Setting up the printer

If you have a laser printer, you have no choice except to find the manual that came with it and follow the instructions. You're usually supposed to put the envelope into a special tray, in a certain position.

If you have a StyleWriter II, you have to make a couple of adjustments. First, you have to pull the lever on the right side toward the front of the printer (to the position marked by a tiny etched envelope icon). Then you have to open the front panel. See the two little blue tabs? Slide the top one, mounted on a black circular thing, to the far-right position — again, marked by a tiny envelope icon. Close the panel. Now put a single envelope into the paper slot. Flap side against the plastic. Top inward. Just set it there — don't try to push it into the slot.

Setting up the software

Now there's the issue of getting the address lined up on the screen. If you're using Word or an address-book program, use the envelope-printing feature; you'll have to experiment with the settings (Left, Right, Centered, for example), depending on your printer. (Just leave all the factory settings if you're printing on a StyleWriter II.)

If you have some other word processor, just play around with positioning the address on a blank document. Try printing onto an envelope. After about four tries, you'll finally have figured out how to adjust the address so that it prints out right — higher, lower, a little more to the right, and so on. Save that document as a template that you can use again next time.

ClarisWorks users: Your program came with templates for envelopes all ready to use. If you have version 3 or later, use the Assistant to create the appropriate envelope for you.

What if I want to mail out a form letter?

 It's called *mail merge*, and nearly every word processor can do it.

To prepare a mail merge, you have to type *two* documents. The first one contains the nonchanging part of your letter; the other contains just the names and addresses.

Every program's mechanism for creating form letters is slightly different. Here are the routines for the most popular programs, ClarisWorks and Word 5 (or 5.1).

ClarisWorks

1. Create a Database document; put all your names and addresses into it. Leave it open on the screen.

2. Open a new, blank word processing document. From the File menu, choose Mail Merge.

3. In the Select Data window that pops up, select the name of the database file and click OK.

4. Begin typing. At each point where you'll want the program to insert the recipient's name (or address, or whatever), double-click the corresponding field name in the small floating window (see Figure 2-7). It'll pop into your word processor document, surrounded by <<brackets like this>>. You can use the same fields more than once, if you want.

5. When it's all over, click the Print Merge button on the floating window. Watch as ClarisWorks prints out the finished letters, each with a different name and address.

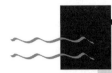

IAQ: Innocently Asked Question

What's this thing with the hole in the middle?

In a 1993 marketing ploy, the software company Computer Associates gave away 500,000 copies of its tax software. Perhaps it overestimated the computer-savviness of the recipients; one guy called up at tax time and said he was having trouble using the package to do his taxes. "What's this thing with the hole in the middle?" he asked.

This fellow had never seen a floppy disk before. And no wonder. He didn't even have a *computer*.

Word 5.1

1. Create a new document. This is where you'll type the body of your letter.

2. From the View menu, choose Print Merge Helper. A window appears; click New.

3. In the next dialog box, type the name for each blank (name, address, and so on), clicking the Add button each time. (See Figure 2-8.)

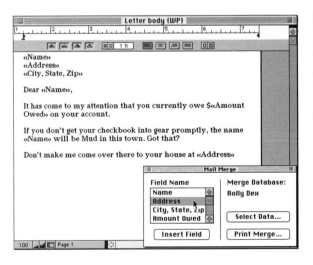

Figure 2-7: On the left: the document that contains your memo, minus the actual names. On the right: the name-and-address document.

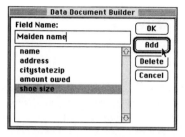

Figure 2-8: In Word, you begin by creating the blanks that the program will automatically fill in with each person's information.

4. When you're done creating the different pieces of info that will be spliced into the form letter, click Done. Word asks you to name this name-and-address document; call it something like Data.

5. Now you're back to your blank document. Type the body of the letter. At each place where you want Word to discreetly pop the person's name, choose *name* from the Insert Field Name popup menu on the ruler (Figure 2-9). It pops into your document surrounded by <<brackets>>.

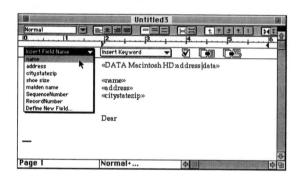

Figure 2-9: The final step in Word is to type the letter, using the ruler popup menu to supply the info that changes from letter to letter.

6. Finally, return to the document you first created — the one called Data. Click in the second row of the table and begin typing in the names and addresses, one per row. (Press Tab to move across the row, and press Tab again to begin the next name.)

7. When you finally print the body-text document, Word merges the names seamlessly into the body text of your document (*Dear Clive, Dear Felix, Dear Gertrude,* and so on).

See also Chapter 22, "Frequently Used Software."

How do I take a picture of the screen?

▽ **Press ⌘-Shift–3.**

You'll hear a satisfying camera-shutter sound. After a moment of frozen-cursor syndrome, you'll find a new file called *Picture 1* on your hard drive. (If you take more snapshots, they'll be called Picture 2, Picture 3, and so on.) Double-click the Picture file to open it in TeachText or SimpleText. At this point, you can do two things:

✦ Be confused. Be very confused. The menus and icons you're seeing now *aren't* real icons and menus — they're just a *picture* of them, in PICT graphics format. Resist the temptation to pull down these menus. See Figure 2-10.

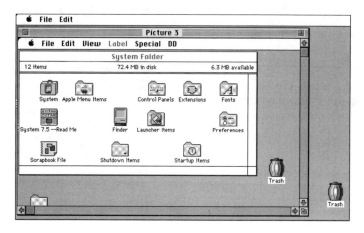

Figure 2-10:
Viewing a Picture 1 file (a *screen shot*) in SimpleText can be disorienting. You're looking at a *picture* of the desktop, not the real desktop. In *this* screen shot, the Trash can on the right is the *real* Trash — and the menus at the very top are the real menus.

✦ By dragging your cursor across the image and then choosing Copy from the Edit menu, you can grab a selected portion of the image and paste it into a word-processing document. (Incidentally, this is pretty much how I illustrated this book.)

Can I make my Mac into an answering machine?

▽ Yes, but it might not be worth it.

I can understand the attraction. It really does sound neat to have your Mac be your communications center, collecting voice-mail messages, acting as a speakerphone, and so on.

There are problems with that scenario, though. For example, the telephone software must be running at all times; if it quits, or if your Mac has a system crash, you have no answering machine anymore. Furthermore, sound files (such as the messages your callers leave) take up a lot of disk space. And, well, a *real* answering machine costs only $40, is more dependable, and uses a lot less electricity than your Mac setup.

If you're determined to try it, your best bet is the GeoPort Telecom Adapter Kit, version 2. Of course, only recent Mac models work with this odd, pod-shaped pseudo-modem (the GeoPort adapter): Power Macs and AV models, for example.

If your model can handle this *telephony* stuff, however, you're in luck. The GeoPort 2.0 software includes a program called MegaPhone that does indeed turn your Mac into a pretty formidable answering machine and speakerphone. You speak into the Mac microphone (perched, for example, on your monitor) and you hear the caller through your Mac speaker. The sound quality is excellent — unlike a real speakerphone, your Mac speakerphone doesn't cut out the caller's voice when you start to talk. And because this is an all *digital* answering machine, you can play, delete, or skip messages in any order.

The GeoPort 2.0 software is free (if you get it from online services); it also comes in the box when you buy a GeoPort adapter. If you decide to pay the extra $50 to upgrade to the full version of MegaPhone, you get a whole raft of additional features: You can retrieve messages by dialing in, integrate your existing programs with the dialing function, and so on.

See also FAQ 1-32, "Where do I get Apple software updates?"

See also Chapter 13, "Speech, Multimedia, & CD-ROM."

How do I set up an e-mail system in my office?

See FAQ 25-2, "How do I set up E-mail in our office?"

2-17

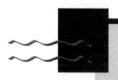

DAQ: Desperately Asked Question

Help! I have to use a Windows PC today!

Here are ten Windows 3.1 FAQs to help you get through the day.

(continued)

(continued)

How do I turn the computer on? — The switch is on the computer. The –
means on; the O means off.

How do I shut the computer down? — Quit your programs by pressing
Alt-F4 repeatedly, until you're told, "This will end your Windows
session." Click OK. Switch the computer off.

This mouse has more than one button! — Use the left button.

Where are my files? — To see your files, double-click the Main icon, then
the File Manager icon in the window that opens. You'll see all your files
and folders. Click a disk-drive icon (labeled a, b, or c) at the top of the
window to see its contents.

How do I delete or rename a file? — Launch the File Manager (see
above). To delete a file, click it and press the Delete *key.* To rename a file,
click it and choose Rename from the File menu.

How do I find a file? — In the File Manager, choose Search from the File
menu. Type what you're looking for (use a * for letters you aren't sure
of). In the Start From box, type **C:** to search the entire hard drive.

Why are there underlined letters in menus and buttons? — They're
keyboard shortcuts. To trigger one, type the underlined letter while
holding down the Alt key.

Where's the Option key? — It's called Alt. And ⌘ is called Ctrl.

What about those window controls? — This diagram should explain.

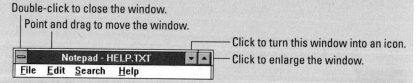

Double-click to close the window.
　Point and drag to move the window.
　　　　　　　　　　　　　　　　　Click to turn this window into an icon.
　　　　　　　　　　　　　　　　　Click to enlarge the window.

How do I see how much RAM and hard-drive space I have? — Choose
About from the Help menu to see how much free RAM you have. Then
go to the File Manager. The bar at the bottom shows how much free
space the selected drive has.

3

Protect Your Mac

*O*K, *so now you've dropped several thousand dollars on the most expensive appliance in your home. Before you go plotting DNA molecules or computing compounded interest on your Mac, consider protecting your investment. Fortunately, keeping your Mac safe and running doesn't require much effort on your part.*

I'm afraid if I do the wrong thing, I'll lose everything.

 It won't happen. This is a Macintosh.

That you might press one key and "lose everything" is one of those tales of urban folklore, handed down to us from the days of DOS computers. On those old machines, it was actually possible — type the wrong sequence of letters and symbols, and you could wipe your hard drive clean.

That is impossible on the Mac. You *know* how hard it is to get rid of something on the Mac! You have to drag something *manually* into the Trash can. Then you have to *empty* the Trash can. Then the Mac asks if you're sure — you have to click *OK*. And even *then* you can recover something you've just thrown away, using a program like Norton Utilities.

All right, I know what you're thinking: "But what if the computer just *breaks*?" This does happen — rarely. Hard drives croak, circuit boards fry.

Even if your Mac is completely wrecked — or dropped, or run over — it's *still very* unlikely that you'll "lose everything." A program like Norton Utilities, once again, can usually salvage your files from an ailing hard drive.

And if it can't, you still don't have to give up. Companies like DriveSavers, (415) 883-4232, use sophisticated, electronic/surgical techniques to get your files safely off your dead drive. It's expensive, but they claim a 98% success rate.

In other words, despite everything — user error, flaky equipment, natural disaster — you'll never "lose everything." *Especially* if you read the next FAQ.

How should I back up my files?

3-2

▽   **Manually or automatically; doesn't matter, just so you do it.**

To *back up,* of course, means to make a safety copy of the files you've worked on. If, because of an act of God or a child, something happens to your Mac, you have a spare copy that's in good shape.

The rule of backing up is very simple: If you don't do it, you'll wish you had. If you *do* do it, you'll wonder why you're bothering, because nothing will ever go wrong. Life's cruel that way.

By the way: If you're a Performa user, you already have a backup program. It's Apple Backup. Unfortunately, it can only back up your *entire* hard drive, or else just your System Folder — neither option is very useful. Do back up your System Folder and the free programs that came with your Performa — but thereafter, I'd use one of the methods described here for regular backups.

The simple, manual way

When you're starting out, backing up your work is simple. You don't need to back up your System Folder, and you don't need to back up your programs — you've *already* got all that on floppy disks. (Even you, Performa fans — as long as you followed the instructions that came with your Mac, and made a master backup the very first day.)

So, if you've written just a few letters and memos, here's a quick, easy guide to backing up:

1. Get a blank floppy disk. Insert it into the Mac. If you're asked to *initialize* it — because it's a brand new disk — do so.

2. Double-click your hard-drive icon. From the View menu, choose "by Name," so that you're viewing your stuff as a long list.

3. While pressing the Shift key, carefully go down the list. Click each thing that you want to back up. (The Shift key lets you click more than one file at once.) When you come to a folder that might contain something worth preserving, click its little triangle to see what's inside. See Figure 3-1.

Shift-click the files you want to back up.

Click a folder triangle to see what's inside.

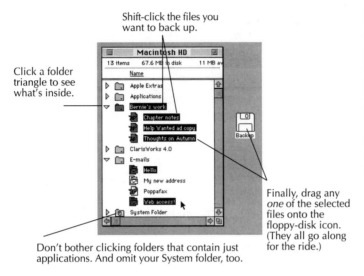

Figure 3-1: Backup made simple. This is the perfect way to back up if you use your Mac mainly for light stuff like word processing. Use the vertical scroll bar, if necessary, to see more of the list.

Finally, drag any *one* of the selected files onto the floppy-disk icon. (They all go along for the ride.)

Don't bother clicking folders that contain just applications. And omit your System folder, too.

4. If there's too much stuff to fit on a floppy, copy as much as you can. Insert another floppy and continue — and then consider using a real backup program, as described below.

5. Repeat this process according to your paranoia, but at least once a week.

The simple, automatic way

If that business of dragging files, by hand, onto a floppy disk is a little low-tech for you, here's another possibility. Use a program called CopyDoubler to do the copying *automatically.* (CopyDoubler comes free with another good program, DiskDoubler Pro.)

After you've installed the CopyDoubler control panel, set up your backup as follows:

1. While pressing the Control key, drag a folder you want to be automatically copied onto a blank floppy disk. (If you're using System 7.5, press ⌘ and Option instead of Control.)

   Instead of actually *making* a copy, you get a little window like the one in Figure 3-2.

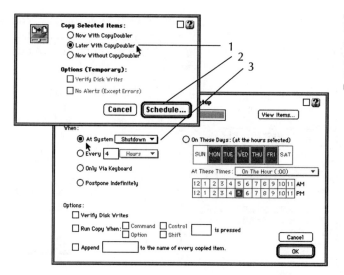

Figure 3-2: Answer a couple of questions, and you're on your way to automatic backups.

2. Click "Later With CopyDoubler," and click Schedule. . . . Now you see the *other* box in Figure 3-2.

3. Click the At System Shutdown button, and click OK.

From now on, every time you shut down the Mac, it'll ask for your backup disk — and back up your important folders automatically! Then it will shut your Mac down as you requested. As a bonus, CopyDoubler is smart enough *not* to bother copying stuff that hasn't changed, which makes the backing up faster.

The serious way

If your business depends on the documents you create, or if you work with QuickTime movies, graphics, or other stuff that won't fit onto a single floppy disk, you need something more serious. You need a program like Retrospect or Redux Deluxe, which can back up whichever folders you want at whatever time you want. And forget using floppies; get a backup hard drive, a SyQuest cartridge system, or a Zip drive to hold your backup files.

Of course, if you're Mac-savvy enough to set up one of those programs, you probably weren't the one asking "How should I back up my files?"!

See also FAQ 23-17, "Where can I buy stuff?"

See also FAQ 24-3, "My hard drive is full! What should I do?"

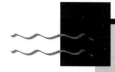

RAQ: Rarely Asked Question

Where can I get one of those cool Apple T-shirts?

From the Macintosh Catalog:

"Choose the classic white T-shirt in preshrunk 100% cotton. Printed on front with the six color Apple logo above a full chest imprint of the word *Apple* in black. Adult sizes S-XXL. $8.00.

"To order, call (800) 590-5005. Unless otherwise specified, UPS or best way will be used for all shipments. Add $10 for shipping and insurance for orders up to $50."

Do I need insurance for this thing?

 Possibly — but you're probably already covered.

Most homeowners' insurance policies cover your computer. However, your policy probably doesn't cover the *entire* cost of your system — software, cables, and so on. For complete coverage, you can get computer-specific insurance policies (such as SafeWare, (800) 848-3469 — about $120 for $10,000 of coverage, including theft of desktop equipment).

How do I keep my kid from messing everything up?

 Apple has already thought of that. Get At Ease or System 7.5, depending on the kid.

Having a well-meaning kid who needs Macintosh training wheels is one thing; having an out-of-control toddler or teenager is quite another. Here, then, are two degrees of Intrusive Child protection.

For mild protection

If only a mild dose of security is needed, install System 7.5 (if you don't already have it). (See FAQ 1-13, "Do I have System 7.5? What system *do* I have?")

Then do this:

1. From the menu, choose Control Panels. In the resulting window, double-click General.

2. Turn on the two checkboxes shown in Figure 3-3.

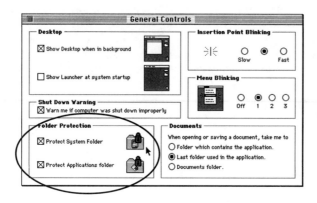

Figure 3-3: System 7.5's General Controls panel lets you protect your System Folder and your Applications folder to prevent the most serious disasters.

From now on, nobody can accidentally throw away anything from your System Folder (which could render your Mac nonfunctional) or from the Applications folder (which could render you broke and furious). If somebody tries to so much as *move* an item to the Trash, or even outside of the folder, a message appears: "You do not have enough access privileges."

Note: This only prevents icons *immediately* inside the System Folder and Applications folder from being moved. A diligent four-year-old is still perfectly free to trash individual *control panels,* for example, since they're nested in a folder *within* the System Folder.

For kidproof protection:

The System 7.5 Protection feature is only a minor deterrent. If you're trying to protect your Mac world against somebody who's truly interested in (or capable of) rooting through your important stuff, you need At Ease.

This program, which comes with the Performa and may be purchased for any other Mac, lets you set up different degrees of Mac access for different family members (or nonmembers). Once you've installed At Ease and then configured it using the At Ease Setup program, you see the message in Figure 3-4 whenever you turn on the Mac.

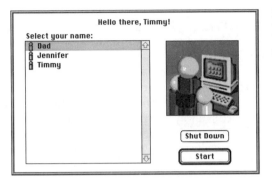

Figure 3-4: When you start the Mac, you select yourself.

It doesn't do you any good to pretend to be Dad — because At Ease can require a password for certain users.

After you identify yourself and click the Start button, you're in At Ease land. At this point, you discover how much access Dad (or whoever set up At Ease) gave you. In its most secure state, you can't go to the Finder, use control panels, or even save files onto the hard drive — you have to insert your own floppy. (That last option is useful in school situations.) Furthermore, you only have access to programs that the Dad figure set up for you (see Figure 3-5).

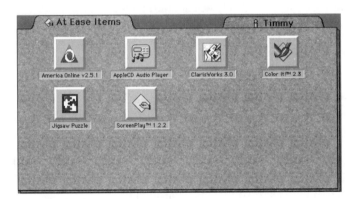

Figure 3-5: For kids, At Ease isn't so much a hostile set of virtual barbed wire as it is a streamlined interface. No folders to navigate — just big icons that launch when you click *once*.

What's nice about At Ease is that even mild hacking — such as holding down the Shift key while the Mac is starting up — can't defeat it. (Starting the Mac from a system floppy can, though.) At Ease, particularly version 2.0 and later, is a perfect solution for would-be kid-proofers.

See also FAQ 18-9, "'You do not have enough access privileges.' Why not?"

See also FAQ 23-17, "Where can I buy stuff?"

Is it OK to keep my Mac turned on its side?

▽ **Only if it's a IIci, IIcx, or Quadra 700.**

Those Mac models were designed for flexibility; you can set them on the desk either flat or standing up. Although Macs like the Power Mac and Centris 650 may resemble those other models, they shouldn't be turned sideways (resting on the thinner surface). Apple designed these later models with the horizontal position in mind; if you turn one vertical, the heat dissipation, air flow, and especially the CD-ROM drive (if there is one) won't operate correctly.

There's even an argument that says: Even if you do have an OK-to-tilt model, you shouldn't change the orientation once the the hard drive has been formatted one way. Still, I've never heard of any real person having trouble.

Can I put my PowerBook safely through the airport Xray?

▽ **Yes.**

An X-ray machine absolutely, positively will not hurt your computer or anything on it.

See also Chapter 15, "PowerBooks."

Can I password-protect certain folders?

▽ **Yes, but it can be a pain.**

What you want is FolderBolt, a powerful, very secure software program that lets you lock certain folders. Meddlers can't fool FolderBolt, either — none of the usual tricks (Shift key, starting up with Disk Tools) can get around it.

On the other hand, FolderBolt works by sinking its teeth deep in your Mac's hard drive and may interfere with file recovery (such as Norton Utilities) if the worst should happen. Keep good backups.

 See also FAQ 23-17, "Where can I buy stuff?"

How can I prevent my PowerBook from being stolen?

▽   **You can buy a cable kit. Or you could use common sense.**

Believe it or not, most stolen PowerBooks are *not* taken out of hotel rooms. They're stolen from airports and train stations. Thieves who are too dumb to know the difference between a Power Macintosh and a power drill are smart enough to know a laptop when they see one — or a laptop carrying case. Set your case down at the car-rental counter, in the airport waiting lounge, as you get your wallet at the train-ticket counter — and your PowerBook will be gone.

Learn to loop the carrying case strap around your foot if you're going to set the thing down.

As for cable kits: Kensington and others sell them. They let you lock the PowerBook to some heavy piece of furniture. Every PowerBook, even a Duo, has a slot in the case where this security loop attaches.

   See also FAQ 23-17, "Where can I buy stuff?"

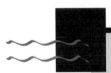

MAQ: Mind-Blowingly Asked Question

What makes a PowerBook slosh?

(A true story from a London computer technician. For your enjoyment.)

In December 1993, a customer walked in with a dead PowerBook 165. Problem description: hangs on startup. An additional symptom: While being carried from the customer's site to our service center, customer says he heard a *sloshing* noise within the machine.

"Has anything been spilled on this computer?" I inquired. No, no, nothing of the sort, protested the client. Taking this with a grain of salt, I went about filling in the repair order.

(continued)

(continued)

On the workbench, I started the PowerBook. Sure enough: an address error on startup, just after "Welcome to Macintosh." I lowered my ear to the keyboard, at which point I heard a crackling noise and became aware of a rather sharp odor that seemed to emanate from the inside of the machine. Flicking the computer off, I removed the battery from its compartment, only to observe that the entire battery casing was soaked in fluid. I also noticed that the same clear fluid was leaking out of the battery compartment onto my antistatic mat.

My first thoughts were that the battery had somehow leaked acid, which would account for the sharp smell (which reminded me of ammonia) — yet the battery terminals were dry.

Tipping the machine on its side, I watched more fluid run out onto the bench in a puddle about the size of a compact disc. I then unscrewed the computer and separated the two parts of the PowerBook.

The smell suddenly became a *lot* stronger. The hard disk looked like a solid lump of rust, and the daughterboard appeared to have about three barbecued chips. Although I was quickly forming my own opinions on what had happened, I invited several of my workmates in to take a sniff and offer an opinion. We were unanimous in our decision. I called the customer, who seemed surprised when I asked: "Do you have a cat?"

As it turned out, he didn't have a cat, but he *did* have a lovely fluffy bunny rabbit, who had been seen in the vicinity of the PowerBook only the day before. Yes, there was no doubt about it, little Fluffy had hopped up onto the keyboard and downloaded some incompatible data.

I checked the warranty form, but there was no provision for failure due to rabbit urine anywhere. I advised the customer to get in touch with his insurance company.

In the end, the PowerBook was unrepairable, and the customer upgraded to a 180c. I cleaned up the static mat and sprayed the service department with a healthy dosage of "Fresh Field of Flowers." I checked in with the customer a week later, asked how was he enjoying the 180c, asked if he'd managed to restore his data. And, of course, I asked how his rabbit was.

"Delicious," he said.

4

What is it?

The questions in this chapter aren't written as questions. I thought that making you read "What is . . . ", "What is . . . ", over and over again would be Chinese Water Torture.

Nonetheless, these are questions. This chapter is not supposed to be a complete glossary—you already know what mouse, Trash, and disk mean. Instead, these are new terms; modern terms, buzzwords, with an emphasis on computery abbreviations and acronyms (PDS, PCI, PCMCIA, and so on). These are words you read about, hear about, stumble across in the Mac magazines.

680x0

 When somebody refers to a 680x0 Mac, they mean a *non*-Power Macintosh. In other words, a Mac whose main chip is a Motorola 68000, 68020, 68030, or 68040 processor (such as the Mac Plus, the LC, the LCIII, or the Quadra, respectively).

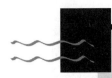

RAQ: Rarely Asked Question

What happened to the 68060?

It's true; there *is* a Motorola 68060 chip. It *is* much faster than the 68000, 68020, 68030, and 68040 chips used in Macintosh models. So how come no Mac model comes with an '060 chip?

By 1993, the 68000 chip series was mature; it was approaching the end of its expandability. IBM's newly-designed PowerPC chip, however, was already faster than the '060 — and had plenty of room for refinements and speedups.

Apple decided: As long as we're going to make our millions of Mac users go through a shakedown period of adjusting to a new chip (which had happened when Apple went from the '030 to the '040 chip two years before), we may as well make the leap to the newer, younger, faster chip — and do that leaping only once.

active matrix

▽ There are two kinds of thin, flat computer screens: *active matrix* and *passive matrix*. As seen on PowerBook laptops, active-matrix screens are crisper and clearer than passive; on an active screen, moving the mouse quickly doesn't make the cursor seem to disappear, as it does on a passive screen.

On the other hand, an active-matrix screen costs about $800 more than a passive-matrix screen.

☐ See also Chapter 15, "PowerBooks."

ADB

▽ ADB stands for *Apple Desktop Bus*, and it refers to the jack (on your Mac's back panel) where you plug in the keyboard. So why not just call it the keyboard jack? Because you can also plug in other stuff there: the mouse, drawing tablets, remote-control devices, and so on.

  See also FAQ 4-12, "What's a bus?"

AppleScript

AppleScript is a programming language. You can use it to create scripts — useful, ready-to-run, automated miniprograms — that perform certain multistep jobs for you automatically.

For example, one of the scripts provided with System 7.5 (in your Automated Tasks folder) makes an alias of a highlighted icon and sticks it into your menu. (And you don't even have to delete the word *alias* from the alias!) It's called Add Alias to Apple Menu. If you have System 7.5, try it!

If you're somewhere between an expert user and a programmer, you can create your *own* scripts to automate your Mac. Look up AppleScript in Macintosh Guide, read the help files that come with AppleScript, and study the scripts that come *with* AppleScript. If you're serious about learning AppleScript, you'll probably want to read a book — or buy the complete AppleScript programmer's kit from APDA, (800) 282-2732.

application menu

This menu is one of the Mac's most important features — yet amazingly few people know it by name. That's probably because its name doesn't appear on the screen, and its icon is always changing.

For the record: The application menu is to the right of the question-mark (Help) menu, as shown in Figure 4-1. The check mark always identifies the program that's in front; the rest of the menu shows what programs are running, even if they have no windows open.

application menu

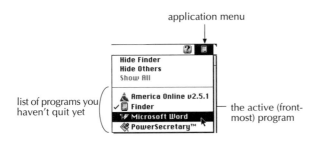

list of programs you haven't quit yet

the active (front-most) program

Figure 4-1: If you ever get an out-of-memory message, go straight to your application menu. Choose the name of a program you're not using, then choose Quit from the File menu to reclaim that RAM.

See also FAQ 6-1, "What should I do about these 'not enough memory' messages?"

ASCII

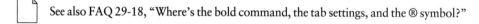

ASCII (pronounced *ASK-ie*) may *stand* for *American Standard Code for Information Interchange,* but it *means* a plain text file. TeachText, the stripped-down typing program that comes with every Mac, creates ASCII files — no boldface, no italics, no graphics; just plain, boring typing.

In the case of ASCII, however, boring is beautiful. Any word processor on earth, even on a non-Macintosh computer, can open an ASCII text file. (ASCII also refers to the set of 128 standard text characters that any computer can understand.) ASCII is the least common denominator in word-processor society.

See also FAQ 18-4, "It says, 'Application could not be found.' What gives?"

See also FAQ 29-18, "Where's the bold command, the tab settings, and the ® symbol?"

ATM

When I was your age, ATM stood for Automated Teller Machine — a cash machine. You may even have heard that ATM stands for Adobe Type Manager, the program that makes PostScript-type fonts look smooth on the screen.

But recent articles have brought us a *third* technology-related meaning for this acronym: *Asynchronous Transfer Mode,* a new technology for hooking up networks of Macs in an office. It's very expensive, but it lets voice, video, and other information move between computers at terrific speed.

baud, bps

See FAQ 27-6, "What's the difference between baud and bps?"

beta

When programmers write a new program, before they put it on the market, they persuade a bunch of people to *beta test* it for them — try it on their computers to help find all the bugs. "This is beta software," therefore, either means that the software *seems* like it's not, or actually *isn't,* ready for prime time.

binhex

4-10

If you have a modem, you can freely send typed messages from one online service (like America Online) to another. You can even send messages to the Internet (see Chapter 28).

But you can't send *files* — programs, graphics, or ClarisWorks documents, for example — to other services or to the Internet. At least, not directly. You first have to *binhex* a Mac file before you can send it: That means that you use a utility program to convert it into typed pages of gibberish — a pure ASCII text file. Your recipient uses a similar program to reconstitute your file on the other end. For instructions, see FAQ 28-15, "How do I exchange files with my friends?"

 See also FAQ 4-7, "What's ASCII?"

bitmap

4-11

 A computer knows two different ways to draw a graphic. It can represent the picture as a collection of individual screen dots; that's a bitmap. Alternatively, it can store the graphic as a series of behind-the-scenes instructions to the printer: "Draw a half-inch thick line, two inches long, starting here. . . ." These drawings are sometimes called *object-oriented*, *vector-based*, and *MacDraw-type* graphics.

Both artwork and fonts may be bitmaps, either intentionally or not. You might hear someone complain: "Oh, no! My brochure is printing out bitmapped!" — meaning that the lettering has jagged edges, as shown in Figure 4-2.

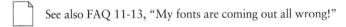

Chez Bruno

Figure 4-2: Two examples of printed type. The top example is a bitmap.

Chez Bruno

 See also Chapter 10, "Fonts."

See also FAQ 11-13, "My fonts are coming out all wrong!"

bus

4-12

 In computer terminology, a *bus* is a circuit, an electronic pathway for signals to follow. It's often internal — you might hear it used in the phrase *data bus* or *SCSI bus*.

cache

▽ Sure, it's important to know that a cache is a small piece of reserved memory that stores frequently used computer instructions (for the purposes of speeding up the computer). It's almost more important, though, to know how you pronounce it — *cash*. One syllable.

See also FAQ 6-2, "What's the right setting for my Disk Cache?"

See also FAQ 4-22, "What's disk cache?"

Chicago

▽ *Chicago* was the code name for Windows 95.

See also FAQ 4-80, "What's Windows 95?"

CISC

▽ The PowerPC chip (the one inside the Power Macintosh) is so fast because it's a *RISC* chip. (That stands for *reduced instruction-set computing,* whatever that means.) Suddenly the world needed a word to describe the *old* kind of chip — the one used in all computers *before* RISC. That's CISC (*complex instruction-set computing*). Every Mac model before the Power Macs has a CISC chip inside.

clock rate

▽ The clock rate is the speed — the heart rate — of a computer chip. The Mac's main processor chip, for example, has ranged over the years from 8 megahertz (the Mac Plus) to 120 megahertz (Power Macs) or more. Every year, you'll see chips with faster clock rates.

See also FAQ 4-45, "What's megahertz (mHz)?"

command key

▽ It's the only key on the keyboard that isn't labeled with its name — instead, the command key shows an Apple logo and the ⌘ symbol.

Copland

What makes a Mac a Mac, of course, is System, its operating system — the behind-the-scenes software that draws icons, puts the menu bar at the top of the screen, and so on. Apple improves System occasionally and slaps a sequential number on it; the latest is System 7.5. In 1996, we'll have System 8, code-named Copland.

According to Apple, this supercharged System Folder will offer dozens of new features. It'll let you change a file's name by typing in its window's title bar. You'll get a smarter, more helpful version of Macintosh Guide. Folders will temporarily pop open as you drag onto them, so that you can (for example) place a file deep inside a nested folder without having to open each successive folder manually.

Copland will also treat memory differently, separating applications from each other. When one program crashes, you won't need to restart your entire machine. In theory, a Mac running Copland will be stabler than today's Macs.

One of the juiciest changes will be the replacement of today's confusing Open File and Save File dialog boxes. When you use the new system, you'll see a "family tree" of nested folders, showing which folder you're looking in, instead of the popup menu you see now. Copland will also offer some powerful colorization and customizing options — and *native* (fast) speed on Power Mac models.

It looks like there will only be one downside: You'll have to get upgrades for all your programs — not to mention a Power Mac — if you want to use Copland.

> See also FAQ 4-32, "What's Gershwin?"

> See also FAQ 4-42, "What's Macintosh Guide?"

CPU

The *central processing unit* (CPU) is either the box portion of the Mac (as distinct from the monitor) or the actual main processor chip *inside* that box.

Desktop file

Every time you copy a new program onto your hard drive, the Mac stores basic information about it — its size, location, what its icon looks like — in an invisible file called the *Desktop file*. Every disk has one. For details on why anybody cares, see FAQ 19-3, "How come all my icons show up as blank pieces of paper?"

dialog

▽ Fast-talking computer jocks and writers of bad manuals say *dialog* when they mean *dialog box* (a box of choices the Mac displays, like the one that appears when you choose the Print command).

disk cache

▽ Ever notice that the *first* time you open a folder, it takes several seconds — but the *next* time you open it, it's much faster? That's because the Mac has stored the image of the folder's contents in a little piece of memory called the *disk cache*. (Cache, pronounced *cash*, is French for *hide*.) The disk cache makes your Mac faster. By storing information you use frequently in RAM (which is 100 times faster than reading it from the hard drive), the Mac has it ready to use faster the next time.

    See also FAQ 6-2, "What's the right setting for my Disk Cache?"

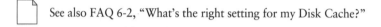

dpi

▽ You care about dpi, or *dots per inch,* in printing and scanning — it's a measurement of *resolution,* or quality. Your screen is 72 dpi; that's why you can see jagged edges on text and graphics if you look closely. But a laser printer is 300 or 600 dpi, the StyleWriter II prints 360 dpi, and this book was printed at 1250 dpi. The jaggies get harder to see the more dots you squeeze into the inch.

driver

▽ No piece of equipment you attach to your Mac — scanner, printer, CD-ROM player — will work unless it has a corresponding piece of *driver* software in your System folder. The driver teaches the Mac how to talk to that add-on gadget.

emulation mode

▽ A Power Macintosh can be amazingly fast — sometimes 12 times faster than a non-Power Mac — but only if it's running *native,* or Power Mac-customized, programs.

Fortunately, it still runs older, non-Power Mac programs, by impersonating a Quadra. When a Power Mac 6100, 7100, or 8100 does that — goes into *emulation mode* — it's no faster than non-Power Macs.

    See also Chapter 14, "Power Macintosh."

enabler

Used to be that every new Mac model required an updated version of the System Folder: System 6.0.3, System 6.0.4, System 6.0.5, and so on. With each release, Mac fans everywhere scrambled to get and install an entire new System Folder.

Finally, Apple got smart: "Let's just release *one* System for all models," they said. "If we need to make changes to accommodate a new model's particular features, we'll put the software changes into *one little file* that you drop into your System Folder." That's what they did. The universal System was 7.1, and the little file was the *enabler*. Each Mac model had a different enabler. Many Mac models won't work without this critical file.

System 7.5, by the way, includes the enabler-file information from all Mac models built before 1995; no separate enabler files are needed on those models if they're running System 7.5. But Mac models introduced after mid-1995 once again require enabler files.)

See also FAQ 18-12, "'System 7.1 won't run on this machine. A newer version is required.' What the —?"

EPS

An EPS (*Encapsulated PostScript*) graphic is known for two important traits.

+ It prints with stunning crispness and clarity on laser printers and professional printing equipment.

+ It's actually a two-part file — there's an invisible set of printer instructions that you never see, and there's a low-resolution screen image that gives you an idea of what the thing will look like. (This latter part is called a PICT file.)

See also FAQ 4-58, "What's PostScript?"

See also FAQ 11-18, "How come my EPS graphics print out jaggy?"

Ethernet

A system of cables and connectors for wiring Macs together into a network. It's faster, but more expensive, than LocalTalk.

See also FAQ 4-41, "What's LocalTalk?"

See also Chapter 25, "Network City."

extension

▽ They used to be called *inits*. You know those little icons that march across your screen when the Mac is starting up? Each is a little program that runs *all the time* you use your Mac — a screen saver or an antivirus program, for example.

Because extensions aren't aware of *each other*, they sometimes — OK, often — conflict with each other and give you Type 1 and Bad F-Line errors.

📄 See also FAQ 18-1, "What's a Type 1 error?"

📄 See also FAQ 18-2, "What's a 'bad F-Line instruction'?"

📁 See also Appendix C, "Troubleshooting Cheat Sheet."

fat binary

▽ Refers to a software program format in which the programming for both Power Mac and 68000 processors are combined into a single icon (file). This kind of program takes up more disk space, but has the advantage of running at top speed whether it's on a Power Mac or not.

📄 See also FAQ 4-47, "What's native?"

FPU

▽ FPU stands for *floating-point unit*, but it refers to a math-genius chip — a *math coprocessor*. For years, you'd mostly hear about the FPU because it was the main difference between Performas and other Macs. For example, the Quadra 605 has an FPU, but the otherwise identical Performa 475 does not. In techie terms, Macs whose main chip is a *68040* have the FPU chip, but Macs whose main chip is a *68LC040* do not. Table 4-1 gives a few examples.

Table 4-1

Mac models with and without an FPU

Have an FPU	Lack an FPU
Quadra 610	Centris 610
Quadra 630	Performa 630 line
Quadra 700, 800, 900	LC 520, 550, and 575

Have an FPU	Lack an FPU
PowerBook 170, 180, 180c	PowerBook 150, 160, 165
PowerBook Duo in Duo Dock	PowerBook Duo not in dock
Power Macintosh*	PowerBook 520 and 540 line
* but it's a new type that's not compatible with older, FPU-needing software	

An FPU does *nothing* to speed up word processing, database work, Quicken, games, online services, or other everyday tasks. It *does* speed up sophisticated heavy-duty math programs, pro drafting software, a few Photoshop filters, and three-dimensional modeling.

See also FAQ 18-6, "Why do I get 'No Co-Processor Installed' errors? My Mac *has* an FPU!"

Gershwin

If you've read FAQ 4-19, "What's Copland?." you know that Apple has lots of niftiness in store for the Macintosh operating system. In 1997, or even later, Apple will, according to gossip, introduce yet another new system, code-named Gershwin. It's still too far away to predict what new features it will offer. One of the primary missions of Apple's programmers, however, is to give it *preemptive multitasking* — a technique that lends greater speed and stability to the programs you're using (but requires that you buy upgraded versions of all of them).

FAQ 4-32

gig

Gig is short for *gigabyte*. Table 4-2 shows how a gig relates to *other* units of data storage.

A few points of reference: It takes one byte to specify one letter of the English alphabet. A floppy disk is 800 or 1400 kilobytes. A typical hard drive is between 200 and 500 megabytes. A CD-ROM disc holds 600 megabytes. The maximum Mac hard-drive capacity is 4 gigabytes.

FAQ 4-33

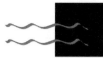

Table 4-2

From bytes to terabytes

These	Make one of these
8 bits	a byte
1024 bytes	a kilobyte
1024 kilobytes	a megabyte
1024 megabytes	a gigabyte
1024 gigabytes	a terabyte

high-end

In the computer industry, *high-end* always describes the expensive alternative — the hardware or software marketed to professionals, and the one with the most horsepower demands.

4-34

HyperCard

Macintosh software genius Andy Herzfeld invented this program. He called it a "software Erector set," meaning that you could use it to construct your own programs. They weren't fast, and they weren't fancy, but you could do it — you could make your own address-book program, recipe holder, calendar, kid's storybook, whatever. What was most significant about HyperCard was that it came free with every Mac, giving thousands of Mac fans the chance to try their hands at some easy programming.

Eventually Apple stopped giving away HyperCard — you had to buy it from Claris — and instead gave you something called HyperCard *Player*. The Player let you use *other* peoples' stacks, but didn't let you make your own.

Still, with the release of the much faster, much more flexible HyperCard 3.0 in 1995, Claris indicated that HyperCard isn't dead yet. It's a perfect training ground for novice or intermediate programmers.

4-35

IDE

Beginning with the PowerBook 150 and the 630 line of Macs (Performa 630, LC 630, Quadra 630), Apple introduced a different kind of hard drive. Instead of the usual SCSI internal drives, these models come with *IDE (Integrated Drive Electronics)* hard drives.

4-36

Because IDE hard drives are common in the PC world, they cost less, and Apple can sell Macs for a lower price.

Most people never even know they have an IDE drive. Life with one is identical to life with a traditional Mac SCSI hard drive — it has the same speed, size, noisiness, connectability to external SCSI gadgets, and so on. You may need to update your hard-drive utility software (Norton Utilities, Mac Tools), however.

And if you ever reformat the disk, you must use the special Internal HD Format software that came with your Mac. If you want to use other hard-drive formatting programs (Drive 7, SilverLining, FWB Toolkit), ask the software company if you need an updated version.

See also FAQ 17-7, "I have a 630-series Mac. Can any IDE drive be used for my computer?"

See also FAQ 17-8, "My hard-drive formatting program doesn't work on my Performa 630. How come?"

INIT

 The pre-System 7 word for *extension*.

See FAQ 4-29, "What's an extension?"

4-37

LCD

 PowerBooks wouldn't be very portable if they used the same kind of 25-pound glass screens that desktop Macs use. Instead, they come with thin, flat, low-power, *LCD (Liquid-Crystal Display) screens.*

See also FAQ 4-2, "What's active matrix?"

4-38

leading

This measurement (pronounced *LEDing*) describes the vertical distance between lines of type. For example, double-spaced type has twice as much leading as single-spaced. All of today's word processors let you freely adjust this setting.

4-39

ligatures

A ligature is a typed symbol that merges two adjoining characters, as in Figure 4-3. FL, FI, OE, and AE are the usual ones. Typographers of old used ligatures to add gracefulness and readability to type. Thanks to the Mac — and especially QuickDraw GX, which can automatically create ligatures when you simply type the component letters — this nice typographic touch is making a comeback.

Figure 4-3: On the left: what you type. On the right: the same words with ligatures.

LocalTalk

When you need to connect Macs, the least expensive option is a system of wires and connectors known as *LocalTalk*. The connectors, one per Mac, cost about $15 each; the cable is ordinary telephone wire, which is dirt cheap.

See also FAQ 4-28, "What's Ethernet?"

See also FAQ 25-1, "How do can I connect two Macs?"

Macintosh Guide

One of the major new features of System 7.5 is Macintosh Guide, a new step-by-step on-screen help system. It lists dozens of definitions, "How-do-I" questions, and even "Why-can't-I" questions — and walks you, step by step, to the solution. Figure 4-4 shows how you use it.

You might think of Apple Guide as Apple's version of this book — with all the discussions of unpleasant stuff (like error messages) edited out.

See also FAQ 21-1, "I heard that System 7.5 requires 8 megs of RAM and 20 megs of disk space. Is it worth getting?"

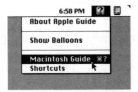

1. Choose Macintosh Guide from the Help (?) menu.

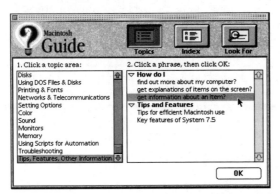

2. Double-click a topic. Or click the Look For button and type what you're searching for (such as Fonts).

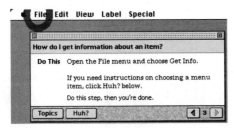

3. If all goes well, the ghostly red magic marker, and the gentle text on the screen, will show you what to do, step by step. (Click the little right arrow after each step.)

Figure 4-4: In a perfect universe, Macintosh Guide would be available no matter what program you're using. At the moment, only System 7.5 and a handful of applications offer it.

4-43

Mac OS

▼ Until recently, there was no reason for this term; the Mac was the Mac, and the operating system was just part of it.

In 1995, however, clone companies began making computers *not* called Macintosh that nonetheless run the Mac OS (our familiar desktop of icons, windows, and the Trash). Moreover, Apple is working on making computers that *don't* just run the Mac OS; these future computers will also run operating systems like DOS and Windows. Therefore, the world needed a term that referred to the system Mac fans have been using since 1984. The previously-unnamed Mac OS now has a logo, too; see Figure 4-5.

Figure 4-5: The computer you buy in 1996 may not be *called* a Macintosh, but if it has this logo, it's a Macintosh.

Mac™OS

4-44

math coprocessor

▼ 🗋 See FAQ 4-31, "What's an FPU?"

4-45

megahertz (MHz)

▼ The unit of speed measurement for a computer chip. Mac models' main processor chips have ranged from 8 to 120 MHz — with faster speeds on the way.

Incidentally, you can't compare the speeds of different chips by comparing their megahertz ratings. For example, a 60MHz PowerPC 604 chip might be just as fast as a 100MH z 601.

🗋 See also FAQ 4-16, "What's clock rate?"

MIDI

▼ Stands for *Musical Instrument Digital Interface* — the connection between a Mac and a synthesizer. MIDI lets the Mac record what you play — and play it back.

4-46

native

If a program has been specifically written to take advantage of a particular chip, that program is said to be *native*. In the Macintosh world, the term *native* most often refers to software written for the Power Mac's high-speed PowerPC chip. A native program comes with a sticker on the box that says "Accelerated for Power Macintosh." Contrast with 680x0 programs, which, on a Power Mac, run in *emulation mode* (more slowly).

See also FAQ 4-1, "What's 680x0?"

See also FAQ 4-25, "What's emulation mode?"

See also FAQ 4-30, "What's fat binary?"

NuBus

NuBus is a connector (slot) design found in many Mac models. It accommodates NuBus circuit boards, each of which adds a specific feature to your Mac. For example, one NuBus board turns your videotapes into digital QuickTime movies; another accelerates your screen so that images appear faster. Replaced in 1995, in some Mac models, by *PCI slots*.

See also FAQ 4-54, "What's PCI?"

See also FAQ 4-56, "What's PDS?"

NumLock

Of course, you know what this *is*; it's a key on every Mac keyboard. But few people know what it *does* — which, in the Mac world, is usually nothing. Microsoft Word is the rare program that uses this key. Pressing NumLock switches the function of your keyboard's number pad between typing numbers and navigating your document.

See also FAQ 22-6, "Why don't the keys on my number pad work in Microsoft Word?"

OCR

OCR stands for *Optical Character Recognition*, the process of turning a scanned *image* of text into actual word-processable text. This term is usually used to describe software, such as OmniPage, that analyzes each scanned-in (or even faxed-in) blob and decides what typed letter it is.

See also FAQ 12-6, "I have all these old manuscripts. Do I have to type them all into the Mac again?"

partition

FAQ 4-51

See FAQ 8-2, "Someone told me to *partition* my drive. What's that about?"

passive matrix

FAQ 4-52

See FAQ 4-2, "What's active matrix?"

PC

FAQ 4-53

PC, for *Personal Computer*, is a troublesome term. Technically speaking, a Macintosh is actually a PC.

In actual conversation, in most writing, and in this book, however, *PC* generally means the *opposite* of a Mac — it refers to IBM-compatible machines.

PCI

FAQ 4-54

After years of making Macs with NuBus connectors inside, the 1995 crop of Power Mac models introduced *PCI* connectors to the Macintosh world. (It stands for *Peripheral Component Interconnect*.) Why, after selling 12 million Macs with NuBus slots, would Apple switch to a new style of internal slot?

PCI cards and slots are common in the PC world. Therefore, PCI cards will be more plentiful, offer more variety, and (it's hoped) cost less than NuBus, which is for Macintosh only. Furthermore, PCI connections can handle more information, and handle it faster, than NuBus — which is great for people who work with digital audio and video. Mainly, though, Apple is gradually shifting Macs toward having more PC-type equipment, in an effort to approach a universal computer that can run both Mac and PC software.

See also FAQ 4-48, "What's NuBus?"

See also FAQ 14-15, "Should I sell my old Power Mac and get one of the ones with PCI slots?"

PCMCIA

A PCMCIA card is about the size of a credit card. It's designed to add some feature to a laptop or handheld computer — both recent PowerBook models as well as Apple's Newton handheld computer can take these cards. A PCMCIA card might serve as a modem, or a miniature hard drive, or as a pager.

PCMCIA may stand for *Personal Compuer Memory Card International Association*, but people can't even remember the *abbreviation*. Fortunately, people have started calling these cards simply *PC cards*, making that ridiculous acronym obsolete.

PDS

PDS stands for *Processor-Direct Slot*; it's the kind of connector and expansion card found inside many of the lower-cost Mac models, such as the LC series. A PDS card may add the same kind of features as NuBus cards. (Usually referred to in the phrase *PDS slot*, even though that's redundant, if you think about it.)

See also FAQ 4-48, "What's NuBus?"

port (v.)

To *port* a program means to rewrite it so that it works on a different kind of computer. For example, Microsoft created Word version 6 for the Mac by *porting it* — adapting it — from its Windows version. Programs ported to the Mac usually aren't as fast or as good as programs written from scratch.

PostScript

Technically, *PostScript* is a computer language. This term may be applied to laser printers, which create the image on a page by translating PostScript instructions; to drawing programs like FreeHand and Illustrator, which translate your onscreen drawings into PostScript instructions for the printer; and to a type of font.

PostScript fonts are noteworthy because they require *two* files in your System Folder for *each* typeface: one file for the screen and another for the printer. Contrast with TrueType, which requires only one font file.

See also FAQ 4-77, "What's TrueType?"

See also FAQ 10-3, "What's the difference between PostScript and TrueType fonts?"

See also Chapter 11, "Printers."

PowerPC

The PowerPC is a *chip*, not a computer. This very fast processor type forms the basis not only of the Power Macintosh line, but also of several IBM computers; game computers like the Pippin; and Mac clones from non-Apple companies.

See also FAQ 4-1, "What's 680x0?"

See also FAQ 4-47, "What's native?"

See also Chapter 14, "Power Macintosh."

PowerTalk

PowerTalk, an optional System 7.5 feature, is a great *concept* for anyone who uses a modem, a network, or both. It puts an In Box icon on your desktop. All your e-mail, faxes, and voice-mail — from *all* of your mail accounts, online services, and so on — gather in this single folder. See Figure 4-6.

Figure 4-6: The promise of PowerTalk: all your electronic messages in one desktop folder.

Unfortunately, getting PowerTalk to work requires serious sacrifice — of time (to set it up and figure it out); of money (you have to buy an add-on *gateway* program for each service you use); and of memory and disk space.

See also FAQ 25-2, "How do I set up e-mail in our office?"

PRAM

▼

Your Mac has a tiny piece of memory dedicated to storing your favorite settings: the desktop pattern you've chosen, your speaker-volume setting, and so on. This is called the *PRAM (parameter RAM),* and is pronounced *pea*-ram.

 See also FAQ 19-1, "This Mac keeps crashing. Is it a lemon?"

 See also Appendix C, "Troubleshooting Cheat Sheet."

QuickDraw GX

▼

QuickDraw GX is a powerful new font, printing, and typography feature of System 7.5 and later. If you have more than one printer, you can use one of its features right away — the ability to create an icon on your desktop for each printer you use. Just drag a document icon to the appropriate printer when you want to print.

However, software companies must rewrite their programs before you can access most of GX's other features, such as automatic creation of typographically correct fractions, swashes, ligatures, small capitals, and so on. Not many companies have done so. Furthermore, GX requires 1.5 megs of RAM all to itself — so for most people, QuickDraw GX is scarcely worth installing.

See also FAQ 11-17, "I installed QuickDraw GX, and now my HP DeskWriter doesn't work."

QuickTime

▼

Dropping the QuickTime icon — an extension — into your System Folder doesn't make your Mac do anything new right away. But it's like a master On switch for QuickTime-savvy *programs*. Suddenly those programs can play digital movies.

 See also Chapter 13, "Speech, Multimedia, and CD-ROM."

QuickTime VR

▼

This remarkable Apple technology lets a programmer electronically stitch together various photographs that were taken from all angles of a room or object. When you buy a game created with QuickTime VR, you can use your mouse to walk around a three-dimensional space in any direction; in a window on your screen, you see the corresponding sights.

See also FAQ 13-18, "Where do I get QuickTime VR?"

RAM

▽ RAM is memory. (It stands for *Random Access Memory*.)

See FAQ 1-11, "What's the difference between RAM and hard disk?"

4-65

RAM cache

▽ The proper term is *disk cache*.

See FAQ 4-22, "What's a disk cache?"

4-66

ResEdit

▽ You can download ResEdit from America Online and similar services. It's a program that lets you modify your software. Sometimes the modifications can be useful — you can, for example, change what the menu commands say, or give a keyboard equivalent to a command. Sometimes the modifications can be destructive — if you change things by experimentation alone, you can easily corrupt your own System file. (Reinstall your System if that happens.)

4-67

reset switch

▽ Every Mac ever made has this switch. It should be called the Restart switch, because that's what it does. Use this switch whenever your Mac freezes completely.

Many Macs — such as models 610, 650, 6100, 7100, and Quadras — have an actual switch or button that you push, somewhere on the case of the computer. It's usually marked by a tiny left-pointing triangle. The original PowerBooks have a pin-sized *hole* on the back panel with this marking.

Most other Macs (like most LCs, the IIsi, and recent PowerBooks) lack a physical switch. To restart *these* models, press the Control, ⌘, and the Power keys (on the keyboard) all at once.

See also FAQ 19-2, "My screen is frozen! What should I do?"

4-68

RISC

 See FAQ 4-15, "What's CISC?"

ROM

This special chip stores much of the information that makes a Mac a Mac. The Chicago 12-point font is stored there permanently, along with instructions to the Mac's own self for reading disks, managing memory, displaying windows, and so on.

ROM stands for *read-only memory,* meaning that it's memory *you* can't use; it's permanently stored on a chip. (Contrast with PCs, which use DOS — a *disk operating system* — an operating system that can be stored entirely on a disk. Actually, future Mac operating systems will be disk-based, too, to make life easier for Macintosh clone makers.)

SCSI

This acronym stands for *Small Computer System Interface.* It refers to the big wide jack on the back panel of your Mac — and to any gadget, such as a scanner, CD-ROM drive, or hard drive, that can be plugged in there. SCSI is a troublesome and complex technology; read Appendix C for details.

 See also Appendix C, "Troubleshooting Cheat Sheet."

SIMM

If you want to give your Mac more memory, you buy *SIMMs.* They're *Single In-line Memory Modules* — a series of memory chips carefully soldered onto a tiny circuit board the size of a stick of Wrigley's. (Power Macs introduced after mid-1995 require DIMMs — *dual in-line memory modules*— instead.)

 See also FAQ 24-2, "I need more RAM. What do I do?"

See also Chapter 6, "Memory."

terminator

A *terminator* is a plug that goes at the end of a chain of equipment. If you've set up a LocalTalk network, you need a tiny plastic terminator in the empty connector socket at each end of the Mac chain.

Chains of SCSI equipment — CD-ROM drives, scanners, and such — also require terminators. For instructions in using a terminator, see Appendix C.

See FAQ 4-41, "What's LocalTalk?"

See also FAQ 25-1, "How can I connect two Macs?"

third party

Apple is the first party. You are the second party. Therefore, if you buy a Mac product from anybody *else,* they're the third party. Typical usage: "My printer doesn't work!"

Apple help line: "Is it an Apple printer?"

You: "Yes, but I'm using a third-party cartridge in it."

Apple: "Sorry, pal; we can't help you."

TIFF

If you own a scanner, the graphic images you create with it are generally stored in *Tagged-Image File Format* — universally known as TIFF files. (Commonly used double redundancy: "I scanned in my logo. It's on this disk in TIFF file format.")

TLA

After reading this chapter, you may have discovered that the computer industry is crazy about inventing three-letter acronyms. The latest being, of course, *TLA,* which stands for *Three-Letter Acronym.*

TrueType

Beginning with System 7, Apple equipped every Mac with typefaces in a new, very convenient format: *TrueType*. A TrueType font never prints (or appears on the screen) with jagged edges, no matter what size you used in your document. (TrueType can also be used in System 6.0.7.)

See also FAQ 4-58, "What's PostScript?"

See also FAQ 10-3, "What's the difference between PostScript and TrueType fonts?"

virtual memory

When you use a program or a document, the Mac copies it from the hard drive into RAM (memory). Reason: RAM delivers info to the Mac's circuitry hundreds of times faster than the hard drive can.

If you're so tight on RAM that you can't even open a program you need, however, you can use this slow alternative scheme: *virtual memory,* in which pieces of the program you're trying to use are kept on the *hard drive*. Result: things run slower, but at least you can proceed.

See also FAQ 6-8, "What's virtual memory? Should I turn it on?"

See also FAQ 14-4, "Why do Power Mac programs require so much more memory?"

VRAM

The amount of *video RAM*, or VRAM, your Mac has determines how large a monitor you can use with it and how realistic the colors will be. For example, the Quadra 630 comes with 1 megabyte of VRAM (pronounced *VEE*-ram). That's enough to show very realistic color (thousands of colors on the screen at once) on a 13-inch screen — or limited color (256 colors) on a 15-inch screen. With only 1MB of VRAM, however, a Quadra 630 can't use a 17-inch screen (or larger) at all.

See also FAQ 9-7, "How do I get my Mac to show 'Millions of colors?'"

4-80

Windows 95

Windows 95 is the latest operating system from Microsoft that attempts to make a PC look and feel like a Macintosh. Wonder what it'll be like to use? This bumper sticker says it all: "Windows '95 is Macintosh '89."

4-81

Wintel

There are two kinds of people in the world: Mac people and *Wintel* people. Wintel is short for "*Windows/Intel*," referring to the operating system that imitates the Mac (Windows) and the manufacturer of the chip inside most IBM clones (Intel).

PART 2

About This
Macintosh

O K — now you're up and running. Great. But there's much more to Macintosh than turning it and off. You still have important productivity issues to address: fine-tuning your equipment, managing memory, making your printouts print out — as well as fun stuff to think about: personalizing the way your Mac looks, feels, and behaves.

In the next nine chapters, you'll find answers to the questions you'd ask if you were going on a guided tour inside your Mac and whatever's plugged into it.

CHAPTER

5

Look and Feel

*I*n *1989, an MIT study showed that people were actually* less *productive with computers than they were without them. By the time we're finished experimenting with fonts, selecting clip art, and troubleshooting our printouts, we've taken more time than we would have just typing the darned thing up.*

Of course, that study was of PCs, not Macs. Even so, you can see how that would happen, particularly if you get into customizing the way your Mac looks and feels. Here's how to indulge the interior decorator in all of us.

How can I put a picture on my desktop?

 You need After Dark or Decor.

After Dark (version 3 or later) is best known as a screen saver. But its WallZapper feature lets you turn any PICT (graphics) file into a backdrop (Figure 5-1). For the first time, After Dark does something *while* you're using your Mac.

Here's how you do it.

1. Open the After Dark control panel.

2. Click the Setup button at the top of the window. A Preferences window opens. See Figure 5-2.

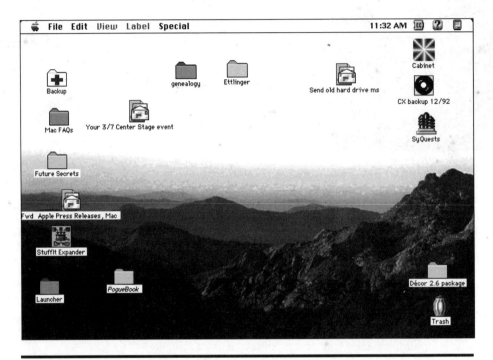

Figure 5-1: Banish that boring desktop pattern forever! All you give up is about a meg of memory (for a full-screen photo).

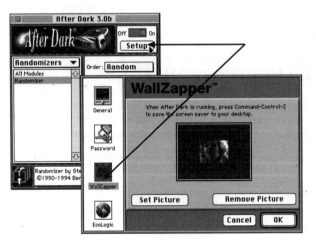

Figure 5-2: After Dark's Setup button provides access to the miraculous WallZapper feature.

3. From the list of icons on the left side, click WallZapper, then click Set Picture. An Open File dialog box appears.

4. Select the PICT graphics file you want. Click OK.

5. Close the After Dark window. Behold: Your graphic now appears on your desktop.

Connectix Desktop Utilities has a similar feature, by the way.

If you're not into spending much money, sign onto America Online and get Decor, a neat little shareware program. It lets you choose any graphics file and slap it across your entire screen. It can even change the photo throughout the day.

 See also FAQ 23-17, "Where should I buy stuff?"

See also FAQ 28-3, "How do I find a file I want to download?"

See also FAQ 28-23, "What are freeware, shareware, and so on?"

How can I change the pattern on my desktop?

▽ **Depends — do you want cheap, or do you want good?**

Apple changes the routine for editing your background pattern with every new version of the system. Maybe one of these days, they'll find a method they like.

Systems 6 through 7.1

Open your control panel(s) from the menu; open the one called General.

Use the little pencil to draw a new pattern in the *left-hand* square, as shown in Figure 5-3. When you're done, click the *right-hand* square to see the effect on your desktop. (Note to the artistic: To preserve your new pattern for future use, you must *double-click* the right-hand square.)

Performa (before System 7.5)

If your Performa isn't yet running System 7.5, you, too, should open your General Controls control panel. Depending on how old your Mac is, you'll either see a popup menu or a palette of pattern choices. Unfortunately, you can't make your own patterns; you have to choose from among the thrilling assortment Apple provided for you.

Click here to apply this pattern to your entire desktop.

Click the individual dots in this
enlarged view to change the pattern.

This is your color palette. Click a
square to change your "pencil's"
color.

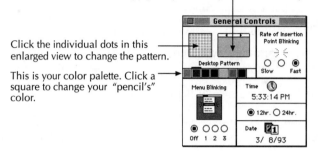

Figure 5-3: Create your own
desktop wallpaper by editing
the tiny easel at left.

System 7.5

Open the control panel called Desktop Patterns. Use the scroll bar to choose a pattern
you like, and then click the Set Desktop Pattern button to apply it to your backdrop. You
can also paste any graphic directly into Desktop Patterns to make your own designs.

 See also FAQ 1-13, "Do I have System 7.5? What system *do* I have?"

How do I get a cool sound to play when I turn on the Mac?

▽ **Drop it into your System Folder's Startup Items folder.**

Any sound file you put there gets played when you turn on the Mac. If you put several
files there, they'll play in alphabetical order.

This only works, by the way, with standard double-clickable System 7 sound files (see
Figure 5-4).

Figure 5-4: Sounds come in several different formats. Only
System 7 files, whose icons look like the one shown, play
automatically at startup — and only if they're in the Startup
Items folder, which is inside your System Folder.

Where do I get new sounds?

  Buy 'em, download 'em, or make 'em yourself.

Sooner or later, you, like millions of Mac owners before you, will get sick of Quack, Indigo, and the Wild Eep. Whether it's for a new error sound, for use as a startup sound, or just for general double-clicking sonic hilarity, adding new sound files for your collection is always a refreshing change.

An obvious source of sounds is your mouth, your friends, and your workplace. Few Mac models come with a microphone anymore, but all models sold since about 1990 have a microphone jack on the back panel. On all recent models, this jack accommodates Apple's own PlainTalk mike ($20 from mail-order catalogs or Apple dealers). You can plug some other mikes in there too, such as a few cheapo Radio Shack models — as long as the mike's cable ends in a "male miniplug."

When your Mac is wired for sound in this way, open your Sound control panel. Click the Add button, click Record, and start making noise. When you're done, click Stop, click Save, give your new sound a name, then click OK again. Your audio masterpiece shows up in the list of other sounds, ready for use as an alert sound.

Of course, recording sounds isn't much fun if all you can make is error beeps. See Figure 5-5 for instructions on turning an error beep into a real, bona fide, double-clickable sound file.

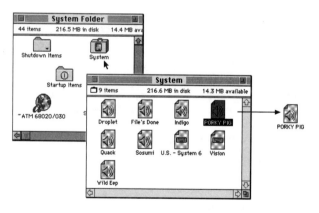

Figure 5-5: Open your System Folder; open your System file. Drag your sound icon to the desktop.

You can also buy collections of high-quality, prerecorded sound files. For example, you can get Star Trek sounds from Audio Source or fun, general-purpose sound effects in a collection called Kaboom.

If neither a microphone nor further stressing your credit card is in your future, log onto America Online or a similar service. Search the software libraries there; you'll find *thousands* of ready-to-download sound files. Their quality varies, but you can search for specific sounds by name, and the price (usually $0.00) is certainly right.

See also FAQ 13-10, "How can I record from an audio CD onto my Mac?"

See also FAQ 13-15, "How do I edit sounds?"

See also FAQ 28-3, "How do I find a file I want to download?"

Can I change my Mac's startup chime sound?

▽   **No.**

That sound is permanently burned into your Mac's ROM chips. You can, of course, designate a sound to play *later* in the startup process. But the sound you hear at the moment you switch on the power is yours forever.

See also FAQ 5-3, "How do I get a cool sound to play when I turn on the Mac?"

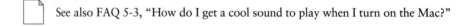

How do I make a new icon for something?

▽   Paste it into the Get Info box.

It's easy to create an entirely new icon for anything on your desktop except the trash can — or just make a good, healthy mess of one you've already got.

1. Highlight the icon you want to deface or improve.

2. From the File menu, choose Get Info. The Get Info window appears.

3. Click the icon picture as shown in Figure 5-6.

4. From the Edit menu, choose Copy.

5. Launch a graphics ("painting") program. ClarisWorks, Color It, SuperPaint, Canvas, Photoshop, or even HyperCard will do. Paste the icon you've copied.

6. Go to town: Dress up or demolish your pasted icon, as in Figure 5-7. Just be sure you don't make your replacement icon much bigger than the one you started with (32 screen dots square).

Figure 5-6: The Get Info window is the keeper of the icon. Click the icon to select it — or, if you're a power user, press Tab.

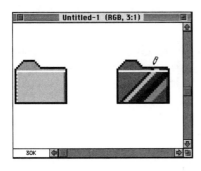

Figure 5-7: This illustration shows the icon before (left) and after (right) you've done your deed in the painting program.

7. Carefully copy the revised icon. Return to the Finder, click once again on the original icon on the Get Info window, and choose Paste from the Edit menu. The deed is done.

If you ever want to get rid of the new icon you've given something, repeat steps 1–3 and then choose Clear from the Edit menu.

Can I change my hard drive's icon?

 Sure, why not?

The instructions in FAQ 5-6 work equally well for hard drives, cartridges ... everything but the Trash.

 See also FAQ 19-15, "Why can't I rename my hard drive?"

How do I change the Trash icon?

   You have to use ResEdit.

5-8

For some reason (probably having to do with protecting novices from themselves), Apple doesn't let you change the Trash icon using the technique in FAQ 5-6. Still, if you're determined, defacing your own trash is an enjoyable and entirely possible act.

You can get ResEdit for free from America Online and other services. ResEdit is kind of a beginning hacker's toolkit — it lets you wreak havoc, beneficial or otherwise, with your system software. If you stay close to the road map provided below, you should have no problems.

1. Open your System Folder. Highlight the icon called System. From the File menu, choose Duplicate. You're going to operate on a *copy* of your real System file, so you'll have an untouched original to go back to if something goes wrong.

2. You should now see an icon called *System copy*. Drag it onto your Desktop.

3. Launch ResEdit. It usually begins by showing you the standard Open File box; click the Desktop button. Now you should see your System copy in the list of files; open it.

4. Don't be alarmed by all the scary, programmery gibberish you're about to encounter. In the screen full of icons, locate the one called ICN#. Double-click it (see Figure 5-8).

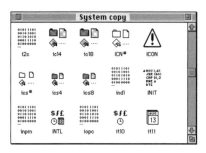

Figure 5-8: When you first open your System copy in ResEdit, you're confronted with a battalion of cryptic icons. Stay cool and open ICN#.

5. In the world of icons now arrayed before you, locate the bulging Trash — number -3984. Double-click it. As you can see from Figure 5-9, the Trash icon is now your personal easel. Use the painting tools to erase, embellish, or otherwise fancify your bulging bucket. Be sure to edit all four of the little full-size Trashes, as shown in the figure; as a handy shortcut, remember that you can drag one of those little icons on top of another to copy it into that slot.

6. When you're done editing, close the window.

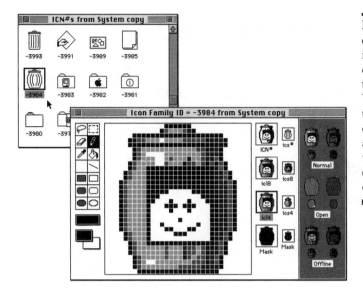

Figure 5-9: Double-click the bulging-trash icon to open. Use the drawing tools to touch up your Trash. When you've finished the colored version, drag it onto the others at the right side of the window, saving the effort of drawing each one manually.

7. Locate the nonbulging Trash icon — icon number -3993 — and double-click it. Paint away.

8. When it's all over, choose Save from the File menu and quit ResEdit. For safety's sake, create a new folder on your Desktop called Original System File. Open your System Folder, locate the System icon, and drag it into that new folder.

9. Remember the lonely *System copy* out there on your Desktop? Rename it System, and drag it into your System Folder. Open and close the System Folder to teach the Mac that its heart has been replaced.

10. Restart the computer. When it comes to, you should see your new Trashes in action.

ResEdit bushwhacking always carries with it a certain degree of risk; that's why you went to the effort of preserving an untouched, fully operational System file. If, when you start your Mac, its faculties aren't fully intact, restart the machine using your Disk Tools floppy as the startup disk. Replace your doctored System file with the one you put in the Original System Folder. Restart yet again, and your Mac will be back to normal.

See also FAQ 28-3, "How do I find a file I want to download?"

Can I print a list of what's on a disk?

   You sure can.

Double-click the disk's icon. Turn the printer on. Choose Print Window from the File menu. That's it.

Where do I get cool custom icons?

▽   **Online, of course.**

You'll find scads of gorgeous, funny, or symbolic ready-to-use icons on America Online and other services, all available for free downloading. Just use the file-search feature to search for the word *icon*. Then use the instructions in FAQ 5-6 to copy your favorite icons onto your favorite files and folders.

   See also FAQ 28-3, "How do I find a file I want to download?"

What's an alias for?

▽   **It lets an icon be in two places at once.**

Before the invention of aliases, launching Microsoft Word was a real pain. You'd have to open your hard drive window, open your Programs folder, open the Word folder, and finally double-click the Microsoft Word icon. You couldn't get clever by putting the Word icon on the desktop, because then — with Word separated from its original folder — your spelling checker wouldn't work.

Today, of course, life is much simpler: You make an *alias* of the Word icon — an alias being a duplicate of something's icon — and leave *that* on the desktop for easy access. You double-click the alias, and the original file opens. Because an alias is only a copy of the *icon* and not of the actual file, you can make as many aliases as you want without filling up your disk. Here are some examples of what aliases are for:

✦   Put aliases for all your favorite programs together in a single neat window for quick-n-easy launching.

✦   Put aliases for frequently used documents, folders, and programs into your menu.

✦ Put aliases of your favorite things into the Launcher (System 7.5 and Performa people only).

✦ Make aliases of the Trash and strew them in whatever folders you like. Whenever a file begs to be junked, drop it onto the nearest Trash alias.

✦ Massive time-saver: If you connect Macs together into a network, create aliases of the other Macs you log on to. Thereafter, you can bring another Mac online simply by double-clicking its icon, neatly bypassing all the usual rigmarole of Chooser, password, dialog boxes, and so on.

Oh, yeah: Here's how you make an alias. Highlight an icon (or a bunch of them). From the File menu, choose Make Alias. You'll see the aliases you've spawned, complete with the usual italicized names.

See also FAQ 2-5, "How do I put stuff in the menu?"

See also FAQ 17-6, "How do I add an item to the Launcher?"

See also FAQ 25-1, "How can I connect two Macs?"

Can I replace the "Welcome to Macintosh" screen?

 Yes — but to make your own, you'll need ResEdit.

The simplest way to replace that dullsville "Welcome to Macintosh" screen with a more lively image is to search the well-stocked libraries of America Online or CompuServe for the words *Startup screen*. You'll find hundreds of appropriately sized, ready-made images; download a likely prospect, make sure it's entitled *Startupscreen* (no spaces), and plop it into your System Folder. Next time you turn on the Mac, the dazzling new image greets you.

You can also draw or paint you *own* startup image, but the process is more technical. You need ResEdit. As mentioned earlier in this chapter, you can get ResEdit for free from America Online and various other sources.

Once again, ResEdit mucking isn't what you'd call novice-friendly. But if you follow these steps carefully, you won't get into trouble. Incidentally: Apple, the big party-pooper, introduced a bug in System 7.5 that makes this feature not work for some people. Apple promises to fix it.

1. Draw yourself a great graphic. If you're handy with Photoshop and have the artistic skills to design your own screen, off you go.

2. Copy the graphic to the Clipboard. Launch ResEdit. (If an Open File dialog box appears, click Cancel.)

3. From the File menu, choose New. The program asks for a title; call it *Startupscreen* (no spaces), and save it into your System Folder.

4. From the Resource menu, choose Create New Resource. In the next window, scroll down until you see PICT. Double-click the word *PICT*. (See Figure 5-10.)

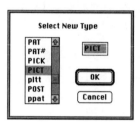

Figure 5-10: It takes a steady hand, but you, too, can create customized startup screens.

5. From the Edit menu, choose Paste. The graphic you copied appears, if only partly, in the window.

6. From the Resource menu, choose Get Resource Info. Change the ID number, initially 128, to 0. (See Figure 5-11.)

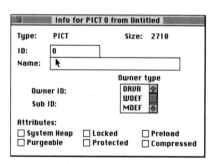

Figure 5-11: The final step in creating a ResEdit-born startup screen is changing the ID to 0.

7. From the File menu, choose Save, then Quit. When you next start your Mac, your new, improved onscreen welcome mat appears.

How do I view my icons in alphabetical order?

▽ **Use the Option key with the Clean Up command.**

Naturally, we're *not* talking about files in a list view, as shown in the middle of Figure 5-12. We're talking about alphabetizing your icons in *full-sized icon* view.

Here's what to do:

1. Open the window whose icons you want to organize. From the View menu, choose "by Name." Yes, I know, now you're in a list view. Hang on — this is all leading somewhere.

2. Go right *back* to the View menu, and this time choose "by Icon."

3. While pressing the Option key, choose Clean Up By Name from the Special menu.

As if by magic, your icons snap neatly into an alphabetical, space-saving lineup (see Figure 5-12).

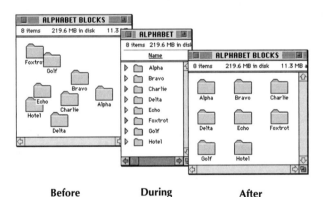

Before   **During**   **After**

Figure 5-12: Got the messy, out-of-order icon blues (left)? Switch to a list for a moment (middle) and then back to the icon view. Then use the Option key and the Special menu to see the stunning result (right).

So what on earth was the purpose of switching to the list view and back? Easy: Your icons will be sorted according to *the last list view they were in.* For example, if you had selected "by Size" in step 1, then your icons would have wound up sorted biggest-files-first in step 3.

In other words, you generally can skip steps 1 and 2 if an *alphabetical* list is what you're after.

Why is my Apple menu logo black instead of striped?

▷   See FAQ 19-25, "Why is my Apple menu black instead of striped colors?"

How come my cursor sometimes turns into a big minus sign?

▼ **Because you have After Dark.**

As the programmers are fond of saying: It's a feature, not a bug. When your cursor wanders into a certain corner of your screen — usually the lower-right — After Dark, America's best-selling screen saver, refuses to kick in and darken your screen. You would use this "never-sleep" mode, for example, when giving a presentation where the sudden appearance of flying toasters would be somewhat disruptive.

Anyway, to clue you in that you've stuck your mouse into the proper corner, After Dark turns the cursor into a big, fat minus sign. Sometimes the cursor even *remains* minus-shaped, even when you move it away from that corner.

To adjust which corner is the "never-sleep" corner, or to turn off this feature entirely, open the After Dark control panel and click the Settings button. All should become clear.

Every time I turn on my Mac, it seems to have forgotten my Views preferences.

▼ **Trash your Finder Prefs file.**

All those changes you can make in the Views control panel — such as the font and size used for your icons, icon-grid settings, and so on — are stored in a little file called *Finder Prefs*. You'll find it inside your System Folder, inside the Preferences folder. This file has a way of getting corrupted. Fortunately, if you toss it and then restart the computer, the Mac generates a fresh, healthy version.

See also Appendix C, "Troubleshooting Cheat Sheet."

Memory

F or something that's invisible, your Mac's memory sure gets a disproportionate amount of attention. Then again, it demands a lot of attention, seeming to use itself up, announcing that you've run out of it, suddenly becoming insufficient with each new system version, and so on.

Here's hoping that this chapter will make memory less mysterious.

What should I do about these "not enough memory" messages?

 Well, which of the two "not enough memory" problems are you having?

When you see an "out of memory" message, it's important to understand who's reporting it — the Macintosh or the program you're using. Let's take them one at a time.

When the Mac complains

Figure 6-1 shows what the messages look like when the Mac itself is running low on free memory.

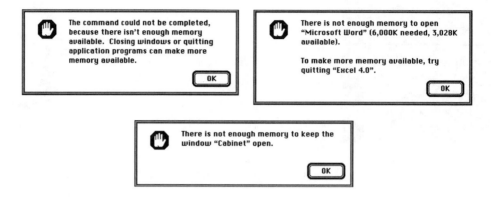

Figure 6-1: You see these messages when the computer itself is running low on free memory. The solution is to quit some of the programs you're running.

Novices, in particular, get zapped by these messages. What happens is that, all day long, they go about their business, launching programs. Microsoft Word here. ClarisWorks there. The calculator. Pretty soon, up pops the "out of memory" message — *because they never quit any of those programs!*

Each time you launch a program (by double-clicking its icon), the program uses a chunk of your Mac's RAM. The program gives back that RAM only when you quit the program (by choosing Quit from the File menu). You may *think* you've dismissed a program — you may distinctly remember closing the window you were working in. But that *isn't* the same as quitting the program. Check your application menu, as shown in Figure 6-2. If a program's name appears there, it's still running — and using memory.

Figure 6-2: Even if you can't see its window, a program may still be running. The application menu, at the far right side of your menu bar, is the only sure way to know what programs are actually still open.

If this — running programs with no windows visible — is the situation at the moment you try to launch *another* program, the Mac shows some intelligence. It displays the rightmost message shown in Figure 6-1, in which it tells you to quit one of those needlessly open programs.

In all other cases, however, figuring out how to solve the memory shortage is up to you. Go to that application menu, choose a program's name, and then choose Quit from the File menu. Suddenly, a fresh pool of memory is available.

When the application complains

When the memory message looks more like the ones shown in Figure 6-3, you have an entirely different problem. Your Mac may have plenty of RAM installed. It probably even has tons of *free* (available) memory. It's just that the *program* you're using doesn't know it!

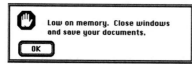

Figure 6-3: These messages are nature's way of telling you that the program you're using is gasping for breath, memory-wise.

Remember reading, a moment ago, that every program you launch grabs a chunk of your Mac's memory to itself? Well, obviously Photoshop grabs more memory than the Note Pad. Who decides how much memory each program takes?

You do. In the Finder, highlight the icon of a program whose memory situation you'd like to investigate. From the File menu, choose Get Info. The program's memory appetite is in the lower-right corner of the window that appears. See Figure 6-4.

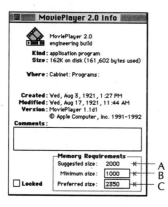

Figure 6-4: Box A shows how much RAM this application's programmers had in mind for typical use. Box B shows the *minimum* amount of RAM this program needs to run. If your Mac doesn't have this much RAM when you launch the program, you see the "out of memory" message. Box C shows the *maximum* amount of RAM this program claims when you launch it, if that much is available at the time. If not, the program launches just fine; it comes as close to that number as possible, free RAM permitting.

You can *look* at these numbers whenever you want. You can *change* them, however, only when the program isn't running. Therefore, to eliminate the out-of-memory messages, first quit the program in question. Then do the Get Info business; increase the number in the Preferred box by, say, 150, and close the Get Info window. The program is now much less likely to interrupt your important work with those niggling memory messages.

Giving a program a little more RAM to play with is a great way to grease its gears — it will run faster, work more smoothly, and even decrease the appearance of Type 1 errors. (Then again, don't forget that any additional memory you give Program A leaves less free RAM in your Mac for Program B.)

See also FAQ 6-8, "What's virtual memory? Should I turn it on?"

See also Appendix C, "Troubleshooting Cheat Sheet"

What's the right setting for my Disk Cache?

▽   **32K per megabyte of memory, unless you have System 7.5.**

The Disk Cache is a special feature of your Memory control panel (see Figure 6-5). It accelerates your Mac by keeping track of the little tasks you do most often — menu commands, folders you open, and so on — and storing them in this special portion of memory that it sets aside.

Figure 6-5: The famous Disk Cache setting is at the top of the Memory control panel.

Trouble is, the more of your Mac's memory you reserve for the Disk Cache, the less memory is available for your programs. So finding the correct setting is a balancing act, made no easier by the somewhat silly rules you're about to read.

As you read above, the first rule of thumb is to dedicate 32K of memory per megabyte installed in your Mac. If your Mac has 4 megs of RAM, set the cache to 128K and forget it.

The second rule, however, is that there is a bug in the Disk Cache (in Systems before 7.5). If you set the cache higher than 512, you'll actually *slow down* your Mac! Therefore, if you run any System earlier than 7.5, no matter how much RAM your Mac has, don't set the cache higher than 512K.

Fortunately, in System 7.5, Apple created a whole new cache feature that doesn't include that bug. If you have this (or a later) operating system, there is no 512K limit. Set the Disk Cache as high as you can afford, keeping in mind that doing so eats RAM that your programs could use.

See also FAQ 6-3, "Where'd all my memory go?"

Where'd all my memory go?

▽   **Every little feature wolfs down a little more.**

Consider these amazing statistics:

Software feature	RAM appetite
After Dark	350K
AppleTalk	107K
File Sharing	264K
Disk Cache (typical)	256K
QuickDraw GX	1,500K
GeoPort adapter	500K

Keep in mind that even a plain-vanilla, stripped-down System Folder, by itself, guzzles down nearly three megabytes of RAM just to turn the computer on!

To see exactly how much RAM your System Folder is sucking away, choose About This Macintosh from the menu. To make it take up less memory, turn off some of those extra features. (See Appendix C for instructions on extension management.)

See also FAQ 6-1, "What should I do about these 'not enough memory' messages?"

Why does my Power Mac need so much more memory?

 See FAQ 14-4, "Why do Power Mac programs require so much more memory?"

6-4

I checked my About This Macintosh box, and it shows that my memory disappears during the day!

 You're being zapped by memory fragmentation. Quit your programs.

6-5

When you launch a program, it won't open unless your Mac has enough available memory available. Actually, the circumstances are even more particular — your Mac must have enough available memory *in one piece*. See Figure 6-6 for an example.

When you choose About This Macintosh from the menu, you're shown how big the *largest unused* block of RAM is — not the total free amount, which is probably much larger. If you arbitrarily launch and quit programs during the day, you leave behind little pockets of free RAM, none large enough to accommodate the launching of another program.

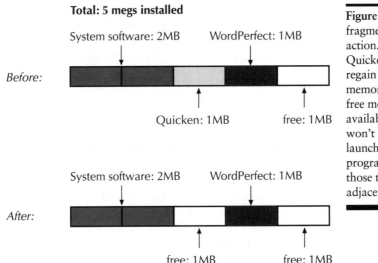

Total: 5 megs installed

System software: 2MB   WordPerfect: 1MB

Before:

Quicken: 1MB   free: 1MB

System software: 2MB   WordPerfect: 1MB

After:

free: 1MB   free: 1MB

Figure 6-6: Memory fragmentation in action. If you quit Quicken (top), you regain a megabyte of memory, leaving two free megabytes available. But you won't be able to launch a two-meg program, because those two megs aren't adjacent.

If you're a certain kind of person, you could actually avoid memory fragmentation. You would take pains to quit the most recently opened programs first, in reverse order.

In real life, however, it may be simpler to defragment your RAM all at once by quitting every program — or restarting the Mac. Now you have nothing but free, defragmented memory into which to launch your programs.

I read FAQ 6-5, but my Power Mac is still losing RAM, even when I quit all programs. Help!

▽   Shared libraries are the culprit.

As you'll learn in FAQ 14-4, a Power Mac doesn't use memory the same way non-Power Mac models do. Instead of loading one piece of your program at a time into RAM, it must load the entire program at once. As a result, Power Mac programs take longer to load and require more memory to run than their non-Power Mac counterparts.

As a partial solution, Apple created *shared libraries.* If you examine your Power Mac's Extensions folder, you may see them there: icons that represent program code (computer instructions) that can be shared among several running programs. For example, several Microsoft programs might all use the same central information for printing or graphing. Yes, Microsoft programs are enormous and RAM-hungry — but they would be much more so if it weren't for shared libraries.

If this shared-library information were loaded into the RAM chunk of any one program, it wouldn't be available to any *other* programs. Instead, therefore, shared libraries get loaded into the *system heap* (the chunk of RAM used by your operating system). If you choose About This Macintosh from your menu, you'll see a memory bar that represents your system heap. And if you have a Power Mac, you'll see that bar get longer as you launch Power Mac programs — and as that shared-library information joins the system RAM.

This long, techie narrative explains why your system software's memory usage may seem to increase during the day — and won't shrink down again even if you quit your programs.

Incidentally, if you turn Power Mac virtual memory on, as recommended in FAQ 14-4, you'll be less subject to this shrinking-RAM scenario. Those shared libraries will be loaded into RAM only as needed, exactly like Power Mac program data.

See also FAQ 14-4, "Why do Power Mac programs require so much more memory?"

Why is my system taking up 10MB of memory?

 **You need to turn on 32-bit addressing.**

Back in the 80s, the Mac was designed with a preposterously enormous amount of room for future memory expansion — *eight megabytes!*

As you probably know, it didn't take long before Macs with 8, 16, or even 256 megabytes of RAM were common. Therefore, with the creation of System 7, Apple lifted the memory ceiling. It rewrote the Mac's memory software so that it could accommodate those larger RAM amounts. The new memory feature, in typically friendly programmerese, was called *32-bit addressing*.

However, because not every software program would be instantly ready with a memory-savvy update, Apple provided an on/off switch for its new memory system in the Memory control panel. (More-recent Mac models don't offer this on/off switch; for those machines, 32-bit addressing is *always* on.)

Suppose, then, that you upgrade your LC from 4 megabytes to 10. Unfortunately, the Mac still believes that 8 megs is its maximum. If you choose About This Macintosh from the menu, you'll see something like Figure 6-7 — even though the Mac knows that it has more memory now, it's helpless. It can't make that extra memory available for your programs; it's still laboring under the delusion that 8 megs is its maximum.

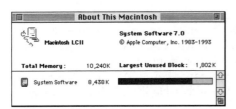

Figure 6-7: A sure sign that you need to turn on 32-bit addressing.

The solution: Open your Memory control panel and turn on 32-bit addressing, and then restart the Mac. Your system software will at last give up all the extra RAM it had been hogging.

 See also FAQ 6-13, "Can I install my own memory?"

What's virtual memory? Should I turn it on?

▽ **It's a mechanism for getting emergency memory. Use it in an emergency.**

The on/off switch for this feature is in your Memory control panel. It's available in System 7 or later, and it doesn't work on the Mac Plus, SE, Classic, original Mac II, or the LC.

Virtual memory tricks the Mac into using *hard-drive space* as extra memory. As you know from FAQ 1-11, disk space and memory are completely different. Disk space is a slow, mechanical storage mechanism; memory is fast, electronic storage. But when you're up against the wall and you absolutely must open Word, America Online, ClarisWorks, and Tetris *simultaneously*, then slow and mechanical is better than nothing at all.

To make virtual memory work, open your Memory control panel. See Figure 6-8 for further instructions. When you use the arrow buttons to specify how much phony memory you'd like, the Mac sets aside a big chunk of your hard disk to use for temporary extra-RAM storage. The size of this off-limits portion isn't the amount of *extra* RAM you'll be getting; it's that extra amount *plus* the amount of real RAM in your machine. So if your Macintosh has 8 megabytes of memory, and you would like to have 12, you will lose 12 megs of hard-disk space, not 4.

(Power Macs are a different story; see FAQ 14-4.)

So what can you expect from virtual memory? You'll be able to keep more programs open and running at one time, saving you the time and trouble of constantly quitting and relaunching. You'll notice a slight delay when you switch from one to another. Furthermore, anything you're doing in the background will take a lot longer than usual.

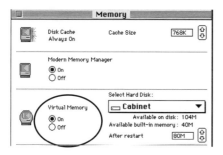

Figure 6-8: Click the On button, as shown; select the hard drive with the most free space; and indicate how much total RAM you want your machine to pretend to have. But don't give your Mac more than twice as much memory as it has actual RAM, unless you like things to move slowly.

In general, though, virtual memory's reputation for slowing down your computer has been greatly exaggerated. Whatever program is in front should run at its normal speed. The huge exception is when you try to run a program that you *couldn't* run before because you don't have real RAM. For example, if you try to run Photoshop, which requires 5MB to run, on a 4MB Mac, you'll be in agony. Sure, virtual memory will let you *open* Photoshop when you couldn't have before. But Photoshop will run so slowly — because it has to swap information frantically between the hard drive and RAM — that you'll want to give up and join the Peace Corps.

What about RAM Doubler? Does it work?

 Yes, as long as you obey the guidelines for virtual memory.

RAM Doubler, an extension from Connectix, appears to do something amazing: It doubles the amount of RAM installed in your Mac.

Of course, you can't actually create something from nothing — but RAM Doubler comes pretty darned close. Using a combination of complex behind-the-scenes compression schemes, it really does make your actual memory go a lot farther.

The main thing to remember about RAM Doubler is, like virtual memory, that it won't help you run one *large* program that you couldn't run before. It only helps you keep more *small* programs open at one time — and without the speed penalty associated with virtual memory.

When I start Photoshop, it warns me that I should turn off virtual memory. But virtual memory is off!

 Turn off RAM Doubler.

Photoshop, in its never-ending efforts to process your enormous, multi-megabyte graphics files, comes with its own built-in virtual memory system. If virtual memory — the one built into System 7 — is turned on, Photoshop complains, correctly pointing out that its own system is more efficient for its particular image-processing purposes.

If your System 7 virtual memory feature is already off, then there's only one possible solution: Turn off RAM Doubler, too. RAM Doubler is, at its heart, a vastly improved descendant of virtual memory. In fact, Photoshop thinks it *is* virtual memory; that's why you get that message even when your virtual memory feature is turned off.

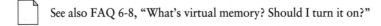 See also FAQ 6-8, "What's virtual memory? Should I turn it on?"

How come I can't use RAM Doubler and virtual memory at the same time?

▼ **Because they're essentially the same thing.**

RAM Doubler may do it faster and more smoothly. But under the skin, virtual memory and RAM Doubler both attempt to dedicate your actual RAM to whatever program is in front, while compressing or setting aside the background programs to make room. If they were working at the same time, chaos would result. Therefore, RAM Doubler won't even load at startup time if virtual memory is on.

See also FAQ 6-8, "What's virtual memory? Should I turn it on?"

I want to get more memory for my Mac . . . but I'm confused!

▼ **And no wonder. Get the Macintosh Memory Guide.**

Apple has made over 100 Mac models, and it seems as though every single one has a different requirement for memory chips, sizes, and speeds. When it comes time to increase your Mac's memory, this information becomes somewhat critical — you have to know ahead of time what kind of memory chips (*SIMMs* or *DIMMs*, as the tiny upgrade boards are called) to order, and how many.

I considered reprinting the complete table here but realized that it would consume 50 pages and become obsolete almost instantly.

Instead, I highly recommend that you get yourself onto America Online. There you will find the Macintosh Memory Guide or GURU, complete and up-to date programs that give you every possible statistic about every possible model.

See also FAQ 24-2, "I need more RAM. What do I do?"

See also FAQ 28-3, "How do I find a file I want to download?"

Can I install my own memory?

▽ **I don't know. Can you set the clock on your VCR?**

Technically speaking, installing SIMMs or DIMMs (memory upgrade cards) is a piece of cake. First, you figure out what *kind* of SIMMs or DIMMs your Mac requires (see the previous FAQ). You order them from a mail-order place like Mac Connection. Then, after turning off the Mac, you place the metal-edged, long side of the card into one of the similarly sized parallel sockets on the main circuit board inside your Mac. Once it's in position, you push its top edge, tilting the board toward 45 degrees, until it snaps into the little spring clips.

That's just supposed to be a quick overview. For actual instructions, order your SIMMs or DIMMs from a company that provides a how-to video or instruction booklet, such as Mac Connection.

Technically — and comically — installing memory yourself violates your one-year warranty. Frankly, however, *millions* of people do it regularly, and I've never heard of a warranty actually being invalidated as a result. (That's probably because it's impossible to tell by looking who installed a memory board.) And if your Mac is *older* than one year, there's absolutely no reason not to do the installation yourself, unless, of course, you're not a do-it-yourselfer. In that case, hire the local Apple dealer to do it.

See also FAQ 6-12, "I want to get more memory for my Mac . . . but I'm confused!"

See also FAQ 24-2, "I need more RAM. What do I do?"

FAQ 6-13

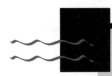

SAQ: Stupidly Asked Question

What's the CPU?

A true story from a true Apple technician:

Well, this lady came in and told us that she was having problems with her monitor. We suggested that she bring her monitor in, and we promised to check it out.

She brought in the monitor. We plugged it in. It worked without a flaw. We told her that the monitor wasn't the problem, and we asked her to bring in her CPU.

She stared at us blankly. "What's the CPU?", she asked. I explained, "You know, it's the central piece of equipment that all your devices plug into."

I guess I shouldn't have been surprised. She returned an hour later, carrying the piece of equipment she plugged everything into.

Her surge supressor.

And to make this all the more interesting, she was a grade-school computer class instructor.

6-14

I installed a Level 2 cache SIMM into my Power Mac. Is there any way to check if it's working properly?

▽   Other than experiencing generally faster computing, no.

What is the Modern Memory Manager?

   It's the new, native-mode memory-manager software for the Power Mac.

It came as a disappointment to many early Power Mac owners that the operating system itself hadn't been totally rewritten into *native code* — the faster programming format that takes advantage of the high-speed PowerPC chip. Fortunately, one critical aspect of the system software *was* rewritten: the Memory control panel. The native-mode memory routines have been given the name Modern Memory Manager.

When you're troubleshooting mysterious Power Mac glitches, remember this new feature — some programs simply don't work properly with it. That's why, in your Memory control panel, you can turn off the Modern Memory Manager. You'll be back to the older memory software, although Apple indicates that your software will run 20 to 30 percent slower — or even 50 percent slower in some programs.

See also FAQ 4-47, "What's native?"

See also FAQ 14-4, "Why do Power Mac programs require so much more memory?"

CHAPTER

7

Floppy Disks

I f you ask me, the humble floppy disk is ready to be put to pasture. Sure, it's dirt cheap, and it's easy to mail or stick in your pocket. But it doesn't hold nearly enough, and it can be flakier than a pie crust.

Here are some suggestions for surviving this ancient technology's final years.

How do I copy this too-big file onto a floppy?

▼ **Compress it, or break it up.**

Either way, you're going to need more software. Various programs, called things like StuffIt, DiskDoubler, and Now Utilities, let you either encode a file into a compressed format, or break it up into smaller chunks. Either technique lets you fit a big file onto floppies. Bear in mind, however, that *restoring* that file back onto a hard drive requires that same program.

Frankly, if I had to process a big file this way and didn't have much time or money, I'd get myself onto America Online and download Compact Pro. It's shareware, meaning you're free to use it immediately; you pay the author $25 by mail if you continue to use it. Compact Pro can handle both file compression and file-splitting.

7-1

(Of course, I'm assuming that you've already checked the *kind* of disk you're using. The high-density type, marked with a big upside-down HD logo beside the sliding shutter, holds nearly twice as much information as the more common double-density type.)

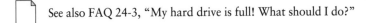 See also FAQ 24-3, "My hard drive is full! What should I do?"

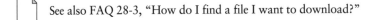 See also FAQ 28-3, "How do I find a file I want to download?"

How do I duplicate a floppy if I only have one drive?

▽   ### Use the hard drive as a temporary holding tank.

Here are the details. Figure 7-1 shows the steps, too.

1. Drag the original floppy disk's icon to your hard drive window.

2. When it's done copying, you'll find a new folder on the hard drive with the same name as the floppy. Double-click that new folder. Eject the original disk by dragging it to the Trash, and insert the one you want to copy onto.

3. Select all the icons inside the window, and drag any one icon onto the new disk's icon. You've now successfully made a copy.

1.

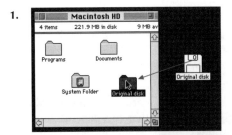

Figure 7-1: Duplicating a floppy: Drag the floppy's icon onto your hard drive icon. Drag the floppy's icon to the Trash. Insert a blank floppy. Drag the first disk's contents onto it from the hard drive.

2.

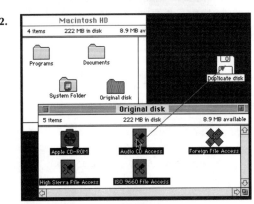

How come the floppy says "0 items," but I can't copy a 45K file onto it?

▼ **There's stuff in the Trash (or on the Desktop).**

You may see only one Trash can on your screen. But believe it or not, every disk holds an invisible Trash folder. Even when no icons appear in a disk's window, the disk may actually be full — of stuff in its invisible Trash folder.

To see what's in there, open your Trash can icon. To get rid of the trashed items, of course, empty the Trash. Now you *really* have 0 items on that floppy.

If that doesn't solve the problem, some files may be sitting on the desktop — outside the floppy-disk window

I've erased this 800K disk twice. It still only has 764K available. What's up with that?

▼ **You're forgetting about its invisible database.**

No 800K disk ever holds 800K, and no 1.4MB disk ever holds 1.4MB. Every disk, even when completely empty, sets aside a few K for its invisible *desktop files*. These files form a database that keeps track of what files are on the disk, where they're located on the disk's surface, and what their icons look like.

And besides, it's really not such a gyp — if you had a PC instead of a Macintosh, your 800K disks would only hold *720K* apiece.

◻ See also FAQ 4-20, "What's the Desktop file?"

◻ See also Appendix C, "Troubleshooting Cheat Sheet."

I keep getting a message: "This disk is unreadable."

▼ **It could be anything, but one of these tricks may help.**

At some time in its life, *every* floppy disk will go flaky on you, giving you the message in Figure 7-2. After all, a disk is just a flimsy piece of magnetized plastic inside a mechanical shutter. Anything from proximity to a magnet, to being around cigarette smoke, to particles from space (no joke), have been known to make a floppy un-readable. Hey, what do you want for fifty cents?

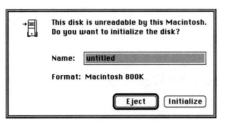

Figure 7-2: If you see this, your floppy is either brand new, formatted for a PC instead of a Mac, or just messed up.

But I suppose what you're really asking is how to read an unreadable disk. First of all, whatever you do, *do not click the Initialize button!* If you're inserting a brand new unused disk, then OK — you must initialize it before you can use it. But if there's good stuff on that disk, click the tempting Initialize button only if you thrive on disaster. You'll wind up with a completely blank disk.

✦ Try the disk in another drive. If it works there, maybe your floppy drive is misaligned, dirty, or broken. The drive that is misaligned or broken may not be the only drive that can't read the disk; try the disk in three or four drives to identify the drive with the problem.

✦ If you use a Quadra AV or Power Mac, maybe the newer, more precise floppy-drive mechanics are causing your problem. Such drives have particular trouble with disks manufactured by a mass-duplication process. Try the disk in another Mac, or ask the software company for a replacement disk.

✦ Make sure you aren't trying to use a high-density disk in a drive that can read only double-density disks (Mac Plus, original Mac, some SE models).

✦ If the disk is a high-density disk that was formatted as an 800K disk, you'll get a message like, "This disk is improperly formatted for this drive. Do you want to initialize it?"

   If so, put a piece of tape over the hole in the upper-left corner of the disk (as you look at the front) — cover both sides of the hole and make sure that the tape won't come off inside the Mac. Copy the files you need from the disk onto your hard drive, eject the disk, remove the tape, and reformat the disk as a high-density one.

✦ Let the disk return to room temperature, if it wasn't already.

If the disk still doesn't work, it may just be damaged. Make a copy of the disk, using Disk Copy (see FAQ 28-5); then try to fix the disk with a repair program like Disk First Aid, which came with your Mac. Try running Disk First Aid several times.

If you're still striking out, buy Norton Utilities or MacTools Deluxe, and see if they have better luck.

See also FAQ 23-17, "Where can I buy stuff?"

Can I reformat this floppy disk to make it hold more?

▼ **Sometimes, as long as it's not used for important files.**

You can generally get away with formatting one of those Jurassic-era 400K disks as a double-sided (800K) disk. Especially in System 7 and later, this practice is fairly safe.

Definitely do *not* attempt to format an 800K disk as a high-density (1.4 MB) disk. Not only would this require you to drill an extra hole in the disk's corner (which is how the Mac identifies high-density disks), but the resulting disk would be highly unreliable.

Can I reformat this floppy to make it hold less?

▼ **Yes, as long as you'll only be using it in *your* Mac.**

It's really not such a stupid question. You might do this, for example, when you're desperate and can only find a high-density disk to use as a blank.

Anyway, it's fine to format an 800K disk as a single-sided one, even though only older Macs still offer this option (when you use the Erase Disk command). Formatting a 1.4MB floppy as an 800K one is also possible — if you cover the hole in the upper-left with a piece of Scotch tape before inserting the disk. However, the resulting disk may give you problems, especially if you use it in somebody else's Mac.

For the longest, happiest life, then, format floppies to the capacities they're designed for.

I copied a 2K file onto my hard drive, and it ballooned to 64K!

▼ **The answer is technical, but mind-blowingly interesting.**

Ready?

Every disk, behind the scenes, is divided up into thousands of little parking places for information called blo*cks*. Every hard drive has exactly the same *number* of these blocks, no matter what its capacity. You can see, then, that a 500MB hard drive's little blocks are proportionately larger than a 200MB hard drive's.

With me so far?

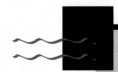

MAQ: Mistakenly Asked Question

Why isn't it working yet?

Another true tale of Mac troubleshooting:

Over the phone, we were trying to help our customer figure out how to operate a program. Because this was a Canadian customer, the call was long-distance, and the stress was high. Over and over again, we'd instruct our Canadian friend to press Command-A. But somehow, our communications were getting garbled; our customer was getting nowhere.

At last, trying to maintain our cool, we said: "OK. Just press Command-A, and tell us what happens."

Our customer, exasperated himself, replied, "OK. I've pressed Command, eh? And nothing happened, eh?"

It so happens, furthermore, that no file on your disk can take up less space than *one block*. A teeny-tiny text file that, in reality, is only 1K in size, nonetheless requires a full block's worth of space on your hard drive — which, since a typical hard-drive block is 4K or even 8K, means that several K are wasted.

Now suppose that tiny text file is on a floppy disk whose blocks are 1K apiece. Naturally, if you copy that file onto a 4,000MB hard drive whose blocks are 64K apiece, you'll see that tiny text file bloat to 64 times its actual size. Fortunately, you can still sleep well, secure in the knowledge that, when copied back onto a floppy, that text file will shrink back to its original 1K size.

See also FAQ 8-2, "Someone told me to *partition* by drive. What's that about?"

How should I back up my files?

See FAQ 3-2, "How should I back up my files?"

CHAPTER

8

Hard Disks

I don't know whether or not you have a modem, or a scanner, or a Zip drive. I do know, however, that you have a hard drive. I know that it has a fan, that it's probably filling up faster than you'd like, and that someday, it will have problems. Every drive does, if it runs long enough.

And if you're like most people, you have a few questions about that precious container for your life and work. Here are some answers.

Do I need a hard-disk optimizer, whatever that is?

 Not unless your hard drive has been 90% full for weeks.

8-1

Over time, as you create, edit, and delete files on your drive, things get a little messy behind the scenes. The Mac may split a file into several pieces if one big hunk of space isn't available on the hard drive. (Your drive, to use the geek term, becomes *fragmented*.)

Of course, that means that your files take longer and longer to open, because the hard drive must look farther and wider to find the pieces. Eventually, if the slowness gets bad enough, some people buy a program called a *disk optimizer*; its purpose is to restack every file on your drive, moving them around and rejoining their pieces. An optimized drive is faster than one with a lot of split-up files.

You'll notice the most dramatic speed difference if your drive has been nearly full for a long time — in other words, if *most* of your files are split into pieces.

The best-known optimizers are Speed Disk (part of Norton Utilities), CP Optimizer (part of Mac Tools), and DiskExpress.

See also FAQ 23-17, "Where can I buy stuff?"

Someone told me to partition my drive. What's that about?

▽ Partitioning a drive means dividing it into two or more smaller disks, each with its own icon.

As with optimizing, this techie procedure requires special software. The best known partitioning programs are SilverLining (LaCie), HD Toolkit (FWB Software), and Drive7 (Casa Blanca).

So why would you ever want your hard drive to have multiple icons on the desktop, each representing only a fraction of the whole thing? There are several reasons, none of which is very compelling for the average Mac fan.

✦ You might keep all your programs on one partition — and lock it to prevent accidental trashing or virus attacks.

✦ You can keep all your old junky documents on one partition and leave it off your desktop. That way, you won't waste time with the Find File command when you're looking for current stuff (with less stuff to search through, the search goes faster).

✦ Each partition can have a different System (such as System 7 on one, System 7.5 on another).

✦ As explained in FAQ 7-8, small files waste space on a hard drive. Since partitioning makes, in effect, several smaller disks, the little blocks are also smaller, so less space gets wasted overall.

Despite what the old wives say, partitioning doesn't generally speed up your Mac, unless you have a large-capacity drive. Partitioning may even slow down your drive — for example, if your Quark document and the QuarkXpress program are on different partitions. Keep in mind that partitioning your hard drive involves *erasing the whole thing,* and, of course, also requires buying one of those programs. Frankly, for most people, partitioning doesn't make much sense.

See also FAQ 7-8, "I copied a 2K file onto my hard drive, and it ballooned to 64K!"

I'm running out of hard-drive space! What should I do?

8-3

▽ (1) Prune. (2) Disk-double. (3) Do cartridges.

Begin by throwing away old, unidentified, and unnecessary stuff — after first, of course, backing up whatever you might need again. Classic examples: Do you really still need the tutorial files that came with the program you've been using for a year now? If you know your Mac pretty well, do you still need the gargantuan Apple Guide and Finder Shortcuts files in your System Folder? See FAQ 1-14 for a list of immediately trashable items.

If there's stuff you're not ready to part with, but you'd still like to keep around, consider *compressing* it. A program like DiskDoubler, StuffIt, Compact Pro, or Now Utilities can shrink files so that they take up less space — and expand the files when you need them.

Sooner or later, though, especially if you have a small drive, you're going to have to bite the bullet and buy more storage. It's true that hard drives are unbelievably inexpensive today (well, compared to only two years ago). Still, I encourage you *not* to buy a second hard drive. After all, that's just going to fill up, too. It makes more economic sense to get a removable-cartridge drive. Each cartridge holds as much as a hard drive — but when one gets full, just stick in an inexpensive blank one.

The most popular cartridge systems are made by SyQuest and Iomega, and they come in all different MB capacities. For example, the Zip Drive (Iomega) costs $200, and each $15 disk holds 100 MB.

See also FAQ 3-2, "How should I back up my files?"

See also FAQ 23-17, "Where can I buy stuff?"

How can I keep track of my disks and cartridges?

8-4

▽ It's tough — but VirtualDisk can help.

It's an age-old problem: If you use removable cartridges and they're in a desk drawer, how do you remember which cartridge holds which files? And wouldn't it be nice if the Find File command would magically search all those cartridges in your drawer, too?

A little $50 program called VirtualDisk does all that. It puts a new icon on your desktop that represents your entire cartridge and disk collection. You can search it, open individual "cartridge folders" within it — and when you double-click a file listed there, the Mac asks you by name for the correct cartridge or disk. (I'm not paid anything by these guys — I just find this program handy.)

See also FAQ 23-17, "Where can I buy stuff?"

Which should I get: Norton Utilities or MacTools?

▽   Flip a coin.

They're both made by the same company. They both do pretty much the same things — optimize your hard drive, back up your hard drive, rescue files when something goes wrong. They both cost about the same. Each can salvage sick hard drives that the other can't (the pros keep both programs around).

Symantec (the company) seems to aim Norton at the more experienced user, and MacTools at the less experienced one. Someday the two programs will probably merge anyway — but today, get whichever is on sale.

See also Chapter 7, "Floppy Disks."

If I upgrade to a bigger internal hard drive, can I turn the old one into an external drive?

▽   Yes, if you're technically inclined.

You'll have to buy a housing (case) for it, and you'll have to install it into that case yourself. APS, (800) 874-1428, sells a kit called the SR-2000, which includes the case and a video that shows you the way.

I have a 630-series Mac. Can any IDE drive be used for my computer?

▷   See FAQ 17-7, "I have a 630-series Mac. Can any IDE drive be used for my computer?"

How come my folders sizes don't add up to the "MB in disk" amount in my hard drive?

▽ You're forgetting a few files — some invisible and some not.

Here's the situation. You go into the Views control panel and turn on "Calculate folder sizes." You look at the list of folders in your hard drive. You add up their sizes. And the sum doesn't match the Mac's own calculations. See Figure 8-1.

Figure 8-1: It's a computer. You'd think it could add. But if you total the numbers in the vertical column, you'll discover that they don't equal the "MB in disk" number in the window header (circled).

When you see the "157MB in disk, 90MB available" at the top of a window in the Finder, it's not taking into account only the folders actually *inside the hard drive window*. It's also including everything waiting in the Trash . . . and everything sitting out on the desktop . . . and, if you're using virtual memory, even that colossal invisible "swap file" required by the virtual memory feature.

In fact, even when you add all *that* together, it *still* falls short of the Mac's "MB in disk" measurement. That's because there are numerous tiny, but also invisible, files. For example, every custom icon you've ever added to your folders and files takes up a little more disk space.

Incidentally, when you're finished with this little experiment, turn the "Calculate folder sizes" feature off again. It can slow your Mac down in the weirdest ways.

See also FAQ 5-6, "How do I make a new icon for something?"

See also FAQ 6-8, "What's virtual memory? Should I turn it on?"

HD SC Setup doesn't see my hard drive. What's wrong?

 It's not an Apple drive.

Every hard drive comes with a program responsible for formatting it, setting it up, and so on. The most common one is called Apple HD SC Setup. (For some low-cost models, such as the 630 series, the Performa 580, LC 5200, and so on, the program is called Internal HD Format.) You may not even realize it, but you have this program. It came with your Mac.

Lucky for you, somebody at the factory set up your hard drive before it ever reached the computer store, which is why you've probably never dealt with HD SC Setup. But if something ever goes catastrophically wrong with your hard drive, you'll need that program.

Anyway, to answer the question: HD SC Setup only works on hard drives sold by Apple, such as the one built into your Mac. If you buy another brand of hard drive, such as one from APS or LaCie, it comes with its own formatting program. HD SC Setup won't work on those brands, just as their formatters probably won't work on your Apple drive.

 See also FAQ 17-7, "I have a 630-series Mac. Can any IDE drive be used for my computer?"

How come I can't rename my hard drive?

 Probably because you have File Sharing turned on.

File Sharing, as you'll learn in FAQ 25-1, is the miraculous technology that lets somebody seated at one Mac see what's on another Mac in the same office. You can probably imagine how confused your Mac would get, therefore, if that person renamed his hard drive *while* you were working with it.

The Mac, therefore, doesn't allow changing disk names while File Sharing is turned on. (To turn File Sharing off, open your Sharing Setup control panel and click the Stop button.)

If File Sharing isn't the problem, your hard drive may be a victim of the system-software-won't-let-you-rename-disks bug. Fortunately, you can run the latest version of Apple's Disk First Aid program on your hard drive, and the bug will be eradicated. (Disk First Aid is available on America Online and similar services.)

See also FAQ 1-32, "Where do I get Apple software updates?"

See also FAQ 25-1, "How can I connect two Macs?"

See also FAQ 28-3, "How do I find a file I want to download?"

When I try to give my hard drive a new icon, I get this message: "This command cannot be completed because it cannot be found."

▼ Although this is a technical problem, the solution is easy: Use Disk Rejuvenator.

Behind the scenes, your Mac does two things when you paste a new icon onto a folder or a disk. First, it stores the picture itself in an invisible file called ICON (and there's a space after the word). Second, it reminds itself to use that icon by *setting a bit* (flipping an internal reminder switch). If the ICON file gets lost, but the "custom icon" bit is still on, that bizarre message results. (Actually, it isn't so bizarre — the "it" referred to is the missing ICON file.)

The simplest way to fix the problem is to use the free program called Disk Rejuvenator, which is available on America Online or similar services.

What's the buzz? Tell me what's happening.

▼ It's your hard drive extending its own life.

After ten minutes of sitting idle, a Macintosh 350, 500, or 700 MB hard drive may make a one- or two-second buzzing sound.

The sound is produced when the drive electronics instruct the read/write heads (the "needle" that plays the drive, so to speak) to perform some arbitrary searching. The point is to prevent the heads from remaining on one particular track (ring) of the hard drive for a long time. By preventing the heads from sitting in one place while you're not using your Mac, the drive extends its own lifespan.

Apple stresses that even if you start using your Mac hard drive at the moment one of these head movements happens, there's no measurable change in your drive's speed.

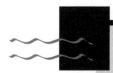

SAQ: Stupidly Asked Question

Why won't my Mac start?

Yet another true tale:

I work as the Macintosh support for a state agency. One day, a user called for help. She had moved her Mac to a new desk, and now it wouldn't power up.

I asked her the standard questions: Is it plugged in? Is the power strip on? Are all the cables connected? She answered yes to all them. I told her I would come take a look at it.

As I walked to her office, I was thinking maybe it was a bad keyboard or power supply, so I brought the appropriate equipment. Sure enough, the Mac would not power up from either the keyboard or the power button. Therefore, I proceeded to double-check all the cables. I followed the power cord through a jumble of cables to the power strip. The power strip's power switch was in the On position (although it had no power indicator light). So I followed *its* power cord to see where it led.

Much to my amusement, this woman had plugged the power strip's cord into one of its own outlets.

Monitors and Screens

F ortunately, Mac monitors don't go bad very often. Lucky thing — these 60-pound cinder blocks aren't much fun to carry to the repair shop.

But just in case, here are a few things for you to worry about.

There are faint horizontal lines across my monitor! What's up with that?

 It's not just yours — it's every Apple 13-, 14-, 16-, 17-, and 20-inch monitor.

And there's not a darned thing you can do about it. The faint line is a shadow cast by a hair-thin stabilizing wire. Apple says that *Sony* says that the wires support a special internal grid that gives these Trinitron tubes extra clarity and sharpness. (The severity varies from monitor to monitor.)

The picture on my screen isn't centered! Can I fix it?

Depends on the monitor model.

On a Performa Plus monitor, open the hinged front panel and adjust the knobs. On Apple's "multiple scan" models, those controls along the bottom front can adjust the picture position (but you need the manual).

On all other Apple monitors, you're out of luck in the self-monitor-adjustment department.

How can I get rid of the half-inch black border on my monitor?

▷   ☐   See FAQ 1-17, "How can I get rid of the half-inch black border on my monitor?"

9-3

Will I get cancer from my monitor?

▷   ☐   See FAQ 1-18, "Will I get cancer from my monitor?"

9-4

How do I clean the screen?

▽   **With glass cleaner, what else?**

9-5

The electricity in your monitor turns the glass into one giant dust magnet. You've probably read over and over not to spray glass cleaner directly onto the screen — spray it onto the *cloth* (or paper towel, if you're gentle), and wipe the screen with it. You've also probably read not to use ordinary glass cleaner on your screen. That's just hype — it's glass, and glass cleaner is just fine for it.

One caveat, however. It's by far the exception to the rule, but a few monitors have a special coating on the glass that doesn't like glass cleaner. The Apple 21-inch color monitor is one of these. Check your monitor's manual carefully for mention of this hitch before you spray.

My Mac keeps starting up in black-and-white. What gives?

▷   ☐   See FAQ 19-26, "My Mac keeps starting in black and white."

9-6

How do I get my Mac to show "Millions of colors"?

 Upgrade your video memory.

9-7

If you've ever inspected your Monitors control panel, you've seen how you can switch your color monitor to various "color depths" — 4 colors, 16, and so on. Every color Mac made today can show at least 256 colors on the screen at a time. For solid colors and computer-generated graphics, that's plenty. But look at a photograph in 256 colors, and it looks grainy. Look at that same photo in the "thousands" setting, and it starts to look like a photo. (See Figure 9-1.)

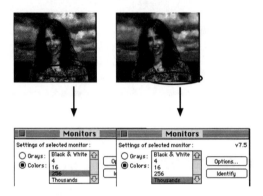

Figure 9-1: Two views of the same photo — only the monitor setting is different.

Even in the "thousands" setting, however, photos still aren't completely realistic. For photos to have the high quality of actual Kodak prints, your Mac must offer a "millions" setting in the Monitors control panel. Which brings us to the original question.

Your Mac's ability to display thousands or millions of colors has nothing to do with your particular monitor. It's strictly a function of how much *video memory* (VRAM) your Mac has and how big the monitor is. For example, a typical Power Macintosh 7100 can show millions of colors only on the smallest monitor (14-inch). You can connect a 21-inch monitor to it, but then you're back to grainy 256 colors.

This scenario is easily understood if you have a so-called multisync monitor — one that you can switch among different *resolutions* (image sizes). For example, suppose your 17-inch multisync monitor doesn't offer a "millions of colors" setting when you're seeing a full two-page image. Try clicking the Options button in your Monitors control panel to set a lower resolution (smaller amount of desktop shown on the screen) — the "millions of colors" choice might suddenly be available.

To find out how much it will cost to upgrade your Mac's VRAM — and if it's even possible — call a computer dealer.

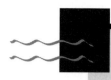

RAQ: Rarely Asked Question

My external monitor is all gray! How do I fix it?

When you first connect an extra monitor to a Mac, it's treated as an *extension* of the main screen — an extension off to the *right*. Well, beyond the Trash can, what do you suppose is out there? Correct: nothing. Or, actually, just more blank desktop, whether plain gray or patterned. You won't be able to make use of all that extra screen space until you drag a window onto it. That's right, drag a window that's on your main screen clear off the right side; it will appear on the external screen.

How do I hook a big monitor to my PowerBook?

See FAQ 15-17, "How do I hook up a large screen to this PowerBook?"

Can I use a TV as a monitor?

Yes, if you're willing to spend $250.

As much as a TV may resemble a computer screen, they're only distant cousins, technologically speaking. For example, a TV creates a picture by showing rapidly alternating interlocking lines of the screen. A Mac, on the other hand, paints its screen in one sweep from top to bottom.

This is all a long way of saying that you have to buy an adapter box if you want to see the Mac's image on a TV or record it on a VCR. There are dozens of these things on the market; don't buy one that costs more than $250, especially since all the different brands are essentially the same inside.

If you have a Mac with the letters AV in the model name, you don't need a converter. You can plug a TV right into your Mac. Ditto if you have a 630, 5200, or similar model equipped with the optional Apple Presentation System converter card.

See also FAQ 9-11, "My graphics look terrible on TV!"

See also FAQ 13-6, "How do I watch TV on a Mac?"

How come the picture's chopped off on the TV?

See FAQ 15-19, "I'm using an external monitor, and the picture is way too short."

9-10

My graphics look terrible on TV!

▽ No wonder — it's a 50-year-old technology.

9-11

It's true. A TV simply does not have the clarity or brilliance of a Macintosh monitor. However, you can fight back with the following tips from Apple's multimedia gurus.

✦ Don't even think about using fonts smaller than 18 point when you're creating graphics that will be displayed on a TV.

✦ If possible, have the TV connected *while* you create the presentation, so you'll spot problems as they arise.

✦ Assume that the outer half inch of screen area will get chopped off all the way around the edge of the TV. Keep your text and graphics well within that boundary.

✦ To avoid a flickering effect, use solid colors. Avoid areas of tiny repeating patterns, such as most typical desktop patterns.

Even with all these precautions, the picture will never look as good on a TV as it does on your Mac. Use the TV as a last resort or as a cheap means of magnifying your Mac's display for all to see.

See also FAQ 9-9, "Can I use a TV as a monitor?"

How do I set up multiple monitors?

▽ Use the Monitors control panel as your headquarters.

9-12

When you use more than one screen per Mac — for example, when you add a normal monitor to your PowerBook's built-in screen — you have several decisions to make.

Which monitor is on the right?

When you first attach an extra monitor, the Mac assumes that it's to the right of the main monitor. If, for some reason, you decide to put the extra monitor on the left, you must open the Monitors control panel and drag the Monitor 2 icon to the left of the Monitor 1 icon accordingly. See Figure 9-2.

Figure 9-2: When a Mac has two monitors, they show up in the Monitors control panel with separate icons. You can drag these icons to teach the Mac where these monitors are relative to each other. For example, you might decide to put the external monitor to the *left* of the PowerBook instead of to the right, as shown here.

Which is the startup monitor?

In other words, which of your two monitors will display the smiling Mac and the "Welcome to Macintosh" message? You decide. Open the Monitors control panel. You'll see icons representing both monitors, as shown in Figure 9-3.

Figure 9-3: Press the Option key. You'll see a microscopic happy-Mac icon. Keep the Option key down and drag the tiny Mac face onto whichever monitor you prefer. You've just changed the startup monitor. Isn't life great?

Which monitor has the menu bar?

You might decide, for example, that the menu bar looks better on your big external monitor instead of your dinky PowerBook screen. This one's easy: Just drag the tiny menu bar in the Monitors control panel, as shown in Figure 9-4.

Figure 9-4: Drag the microscopic menu bar from one itty-bitty monitor icon to the top of the other.

I tried to record the Mac screen with my camcorder, but the picture rolls.

 It's a problem for *anyone* who tries to film a computer screen with a TV camera.

Watching the evening news in this country, you'd think we had a nation of broken computers — because whenever they show a computer screen, it *always* has lines rolling up its screen.

What's especially weird is that, of course, the rolling doesn't exist when you look with your naked eye — only when you look through a camera's viewfinder. The problem results from the different ways TV and Mac monitors create video. There's really nothing you can do about it, except:

✦ Film a PowerBook screen instead. It uses a different technology than the big glass screens and doesn't produce the phantom rolling.

✦ Consider recording the Mac's video image directly, instead of shooting the screen, as described in FAQ 9-9.

✦ If you work in professional TV, there are new cameras and gadgets designed to eliminate the rolling phenomenon. Ask around.

See also FAQ 9-9, "Can I use a TV as a monitor?"

Why does my monitor's picture shake?

 It's electrical interference.

There are two typical causes of the shimmying-monitor syndrome. Either something large and electrical is sitting too close to your screen, or something large and electrical is plugged into the same *circuit* as your monitor. Either way, experimenting with your monitor's location usually leads you to a solution.

If the picture still shakes after you've tried a different room, then maybe there is truly something wrong with the monitor, and it's time for the repair shop.

The picture has shrunk. What should I do?

▽ **You can adjust the picture, if you have the tool and the guts.**

I assume that you're using a compact Mac like an SE or Classic. These black-and-white Macs' screens have a chronic shrinking-picture problem. Fortunately, you can fix it yourself, if you have the special bizarro screwdriver needed to open the computer's case. (You can get this tool for about $8 from those Mac mail-order places.)

After you've removed the Mac's shell, turn the two screws shown in Figure 9-5 until the picture is back to its full size. (Of course, you have to make this adjustment while the Mac is on, so you can see your progress. Don't touch any of the internal components.)

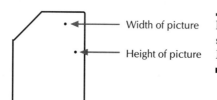

Width of picture

Height of picture

Figure 9-5: Monitor repair for the technologically stalwart. Turn the little screws of your compact Mac to expand the picture.

"Rearrange on close" and "512x384" are selected in the Monitors control panel on my AV-model Mac. But the TV resolution doesn't change when I close the control panel. What do I do?

▽ Restart the Mac.

The AudioVision icon has an X through it at startup. How come?

▽ Because your keyboard isn't plugged into your AudioVision monitor.

No harm is done, except for that X appearing through the AudioVision extension's icon. If it bothers you, plug your keyboard into the monitor, and plug the monitor into the Mac's keyboard jack.

The "Flicker free" option is greyed out in the Monitors control panel. What do I do?

9-18

▽ Change the Monitors control panel setting to 256 colors or less.

If you have an AV-model Mac and you're attaching it to a TV, the flicker-free feature is great. But it won't work if your Monitors control panel is set to more than 256 colors.

I have only one monitor connected to my Power Mac AV. Why do two icons appear in the Monitors control panel?

9-19

▽ Because the Power Mac assumes that a TV is hooked up, too.

A Macintosh can always tell how many monitors are attached to it. But an AV model can't tell whether or not a TV is actually connected to its S-video jack. So, when your regular monitor is plugged into the HDI45 built-in video port, the Power Mac shrugs its shoulder and assumes that you're using the TV jack too.

If this behavior bugs you, connect your regular monitor to the standard monitor port instead of the smaller, built-in, HDI45 port.

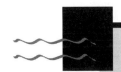

IAQ: Interestingly Asked Question

What can I plug in without shutting off the Mac?

Feel free to plug or unplug your printer or modem without turning off the Mac.

If you mess with mouse, keyboard, or SCSI connections without powering down, however, you risk damage to whatever you're unplugging (and, in the case of SCSI connections, to your Mac as well).

It's also OK to connect or disconnect your monitor, although you'll soon find out there's not much point — you generally have to restart the Mac to make it notice the change in monitor setup anyway.

10

Fonts

Fortunately, fonts aren't such a big deal anymore. Three years ago, you'd spend hours trying to figure out why your printouts had jagged type. Today, especially with the invention of TrueType, fonts are a low-maintenance technology.

That doesn't mean they're question-free, however.

Where do I get new fonts?

▼ **Buy 'em or get 'em free. You get what you pay for.**

Your Mac comes with ten delightful fonts. To expand your typographical horizons, hie thee to a user group or to America Online, where you'll find hundreds of free or very cheap fonts ready for dumping into your System Folder. These fonts may not have quite the high quality of fonts you *pay* for. Best case: A few insignificant symbols are missing from the font (¥ and ¬, say). Worst case: You get only capital letters.

For more spit, polish, and completeness, you can always buy fonts. I'm particularly fond of the Apple Font Pack, 35 really neat TrueType fonts. For the highest quality, get typefaces by companies like Adobe and Bitstream. (Of course, those fonts are also the most expensive.)

See also FAQ 28-3, "How do I find a file I want to download?"

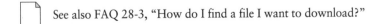

How do I install a font?

▽ **Drag its icon onto your System Folder icon.**

10-2

Even if it's a two-part font like a PostScript font, the Mac automatically places the font files into the correct locations in the System Folder. It will ask you to confirm, as shown in Figure 10-1.

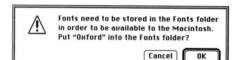

Figure 10-1: Drag a font icon onto the System Folder icon to install it (top). When the Mac suggests a location for the font, click OK (bottom).

Click OK. Your new fonts appear in the Font menus of any programs you launch *after* the installation. (If you're still using System 6, installing fonts requires the abominable Font/DA Mover.)

Behind the scenes, if you have System 7.1 or later, your Mac has placed the font icons into the Fonts folder. That's handy if you're the kind of person who needs to see things in order to believe that they exist. If you have an earlier version of the System software, there's no Fonts folder. Screen-font files become part of the System file, and printer-font files drop into the Extensions folder.

📄 See also FAQ 10-3, "What's the difference between PostScript and TrueType fonts?"

📄 See also FAQ 11-13, "My fonts are coming out all wrong!"

What's the difference between PostScript and TrueType fonts?

▽ **Only their history, icons, file locations, and technological underpinnings.**

10-3

Both PostScript and TrueType fonts serve the same purpose: eliminating jagged-looking fonts, both on the screen and in printouts. Both are known by the techno-weenies as *scalable* fonts, meaning that they'll look smooth no matter what size you make them.

PostScript fonts, however, are the older technology. They're clunkier to handle. They come in several pieces, as shown in Figure 10-2, and all pieces must be present if you want consistent, smooth lettering. There's a font "suitcase" full of fonts for screen display, plus a set of printer fonts (one each for italic, bold, and so on). A TrueType font, on the other hand, is self-contained in one suitcase file. (If you're using QuickDraw GX, as described in FAQ 4-62, life is sweeter: A Post Script font's pieces are contained in a single suitcase file.)

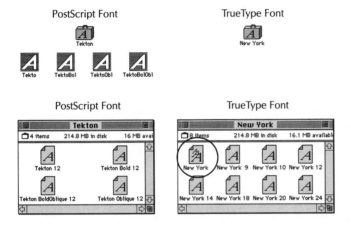

Figure 10-2: Above: PostScript fonts require a font suitcase plus printer fonts. A TrueType font needs only its master suitcase file. Below: Double-click a suitcase to see what kind of font it is. If the suitcase contains an icon with multiple letter A's (lower right), it's TrueType.

If you double-click a suitcase icon, you can find out what kind of font you're dealing with. A PostScript suitcase is full of icons for individual point sizes. A TrueType suitcase always contains the special icon circled in Figure 10-2. That's the actual mother-ship font; while there may be several individual-point-size icons, too, they're not necessary for the font to work. They're only on hand to make fonts appear faster on the screen.

There's one more difference between TrueType and PostScript. A TrueType font always looks smooth, whether printed or displayed on screen. A PostScript font, even when all of its little printer-font pieces are installed, still looks jagged on the screen (and when printed on a StyleWriter) unless you also install America's favorite control panel, Adobe Type Manager.

Despite the relative mess of PostScript font files, the world of professional graphics still prefers PostScript fonts — mainly because so many fonts are available in that format. On the other hand, everybody else in America uses TrueType fonts, because they come preinstalled on every Mac.

See also FAQ 11-13, "My fonts are coming out all wrong!"

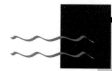

RAQ: Rarely Asked Question

How come there are no spaces in software titles — like PageMaker and ReadySetGo?

In the early days of computers, you *couldn't* use spaces when you were programming. For example, if you wanted a software program to treat the term Mickey Mouse as one word, you'd have to write it either *MickeyMouse* or *Mickey_Mouse*. To this day, you'll see that limitation in, say, macro names in Microsoft products and in Internet addresses.

Apparently, that strange typographic convention became more than just a machine-language necessity; it came to symbolize computers and programmers and brainy chic. So here we are, years later, and you see that "InterCaps" style used in everything from software titles, to company names, to e-mail addresses.

As the saying goes: When life hands you lemons, make LemonAde.

Will TrueType fonts print on my PostScript printer?

▽ Yes. Forget all about the difference.

When people say *PostScript printer*, of course, they're talking about laser printers. Since there's no such thing as a TrueType laser printer, and since most Macs today primarily use TrueType fonts, this is a question worth asking.

If you type a memo in the TrueType Times font, the laser printer will actually use its built-in *PostScript* version of Times. You won't know the difference.

If you've used a TrueType font and the printer doesn't *have* its PostScript equivalent, the Mac takes an extra moment to transmit (download) the TrueType font to the printer. In this case, TrueType is what prints.

Either way, it's automatic. You never need to know what's going on behind the scenes.

See also FAQ 11-12, "Printing takes forever. Can I speed things up?"

How do I word process in other languages, like Japanese?

 Get WorldScript, the appropriate language kit, and Nisus.

You also need System 7.1 or later. Add the WorldScript extension and a language kit, which you buy from an Apple dealer, and you've got yourself a Mac that can actually word process right-to-left, bottom-to-top, or whatever. Furthermore, you need to own a word processor that can handle non-English languages, such as Nisus Writer or WordPerfect.

Unfortunately, you may have trouble finding this stuff; it's not exactly sitting on your neighborhood dealer's shelves. Good luck in your quest.

Can I convert a PostScript font into TrueType?

 Yes, with FontMonger or Metamorphosis.

Each of these programs costs about $90 and can convert any kind of font to any kind of font.

 See also FAQ 10-3, "What's the difference between PostScript and TrueType fonts?"

How do I make my own fonts?

 With Fontographer.

This program isn't cheap, and it's not simple, but it's definitely the program you want for creating fonts. You can draw them from scratch, you can base them on stuff you scan in, and you can create both TrueType or PostScript fonts — even PC fonts — complete with symbols, fractions, and whatever else you dream up.

How do I make a ¹/₂ or ¹/₄ symbol?

▽   **(1) Type it. (2) Use subscript and superscript. (3) Add the symbol to your font.**

If you're in a hurry, type the fraction as number-slash-number, like this: 1/2.

For a little added class, give each number a slightly smaller point size. Then make the first number superscript (raised slightly) and the second number subscript (lowered slightly). Every word processor offers subscript and superscript commands. (They're called inferior and superior in ClarisWorks 4.0.) See Figure 10-3.

Before   # He had only 1/2 a brain.

After   # He had only ¹/₂ a brain.

Figure 10-3: Type your fraction (top). Go wild with the point size and superscript/subscript commands to make a realistic-looking fraction (bottom).

If fractions crop up often in your work, consider adding them to the fonts you use; you'll need a font-editing program like Fontographer. Alternatively, you can buy fonts filled with ready-made fractions. Consult, for example, the nearest Adobe font catalog.

See also FAQ 10-1, "Where do I get new fonts?"

Everything's printing in Courier. Help!

▷   See FAQ 11-13, "My fonts are coming out all wrong!"

CHAPTER

11

Printers

There are two dominant kinds of printers in the Mac world: inkjet, like the StyleWriter; and laser, like the LaserWriter.

Depending on your luck, you might categorize printers differently: those you feel like throwing out the window of a tall building, and those you don't. If that's your attitude, this chapter is for you.

How do I turn off that stupid start-up test page?

▽   **The on/off switch is in the LaserWriter Utility program.**

Lord knows why laser printer manufacturers design their products to spit out an irrelevant test page every time they're switched on. I just wish everyone knew how easy it is to stop this problem. On the disks that came with your Mac, you'll find a little program called LaserWriter Utility. (With System 6, it was called LaserWriter *Font* Utility.) Anyway, find this program. Launch it. From the Options menu, choose Set Startup Page — and click the Off button.

11-1

Why isn't the printer showing up in the Chooser?

▽ **The driver is missing, the printer is turned off, or the wiring is messed up.**

In other words, one of two different things might be missing when you say "the printer doesn't show up." You might mean the printer's *icon* (on the left side of the Chooser) — and you might mean the printer's *name* (on the right side).

The icon is missing

When you open the Chooser, you're supposed to see an icon on the left side of the window that represents your printer, as in Figure 11-1. If that icon is missing, then your *printer driver* is missing from your Extensions folder, where driver icons usually hang out.

If using the Find File command fails to turn up your driver (called StyleWriter, Laser-Writer, or whatever), get your system disks and reinstall it.

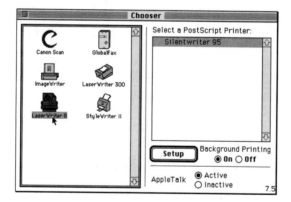

Figure 11-1: When all is well, your printer's icon appears on the left. When you click LaserWriter, you should see your actual printer's name on the right.

The printer's name is missing

If you have a laser printer, such as a LaserWriter, then clicking the icon on the left is supposed to make your printer's name appear on the right. (See Figure 11-1 again.) If it doesn't, one of two things is wrong:

✦ The laser printer is turned off.

✦ Something's wrong with the wiring.

I trust you know how to solve the first problem. As for wiring, the rules are fairly simple. The cables must be firmly plugged into the Mac and the printer. Check to make sure that no bent pins are inside the connector — a frequent culprit in printer-not-responding situations. The telephone wire that connects these connectors can't be crimped or loose. And finally, especially in multi-Mac networks, be sure that the empty socket in the connector at each end of your network chain is filled by a little terminator plug, as Figure 11-2 shows.

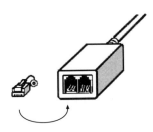

Figure 11-2: Having network troubles? Be sure that the empty socket in every network connector is filled.

If all else fails, check your Network control panel. Make sure that the correct network format is selected (LocalTalk vs. Ethernet, for example).

 See also FAQ 25-1, "How can I connect two Macs?"

Every time I open the Chooser, it has forgotten the printer choice I made last time.

11-3

▽ **Just because the correct icon is never highlighted doesn't mean that the Chooser forgot.**

The Chooser is actually used to choose more than just printers. All kinds of icons might show up there: for file sharing, for your fax/modem, for your scanner, and so on. Because of this arrangement, the Chooser actually remembers several selections at once. That's why no one icon is ever highlighted when you open the Chooser.

In the Chooser, what's the difference between LaserWriter and LaserWriter 8?

11-4

▽ **LaserWriter 8 offers some neat new features — and some neat new incompatibilities.**

Both of these icons — LaserWriter and LaserWriter 8 — are *drivers*. They represent the software that lets your Mac converse with the laser printer. The newer driver, LaserWriter 8, offers several interesting advantages:

✦ faster printing, especially of graphics

✦ better looking gray shades in photos

✦ onscreen controls for accessing your printer's special paper-handling features: multiple paper trays, unusual page sizes, double-sided printing, and so on

✦ dozens of little behind-the-scenes tweaks for better printing of complex, color, or patterned documents

You get that faster-and-better stuff no matter what laser printer you own. But you only get the printer-specific features (paper handling and so on) if your laser printer is "PostScript level 2 compatible" (check the manual or the shipping box).

As with any worthwhile technological development, embracing LaserWriter 8 may mean a few bumpy software moments — you may have problems printing from programs that predate the new driver. Get a newer version of that application, and all should be well.

See also FAQ 1-32, "Where do I get Apple software updates?"

Which cheap color printer should I get?

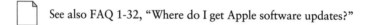 **This market changes twice a week, but you can't go wrong with the Epson Stylus or the Apple Color StyleWriter.**

The Epson is the first inkjet printer to print color so realistically it looks like a photograph. The printer costs about $500; to get that breathtaking photorealistic output, you also have to use special paper that costs 10 cents per sheet. Of course, you can use regular paper for most projects — but those printouts will look just like any other color inkjet printer's.

If you'd rather have more speed and a slightly lower price, consider the Apple Color StyleWriter. It costs around $500. Its printouts won't convince anybody that you've got a Kodak lab in your spare room, but it's great for lending some colorized zest to the headline on your résumé.

Because these recommendations will probably become out-of-date during this book's life on your bookshelf, check the reviews in *Macworld* magazine to keep current. (You can read the reviews on America Online, if you're modem-equipped.)

What's the difference between the Color StyleWriter and the StyleWriter Pro?

 Price, speed, and cartridge format.

The earlier printer is called the Color StyleWriter 2400. It takes three minutes to print one color page, it costs $500, and you must replace the entire four-color cartridge when any one of the ink colors is used up.

The Color StyleWriter Pro, on the other hand, costs $100 more. It's faster, printing just over one page per minute. It's also handier — the cartridges may be replaced individually, and they're transparent, so you can anticipate their running dry.

Otherwise, these two Apple inkjet color printers are similar: Both print best on clay-coated paper; both have 360-dpi resolution; and both will be replaced soon by better and faster models.

How do I share my StyleWriter between several Macs?

 Use the Chooser and your modem port.

Strange as it may sound, you must connect your StyleWriter to your Mac's *modem* jack, not its printer port. (If you have a modem attached to your modem jack, you'll have to buy a switch box and click between the printer and the modem as needed.) Then open the Chooser, click the StyleWriter II icon, and click the Setup button on the right side of the window that appears. As Figure 11-3 shows, you can now name your StyleWriter or even give it a password. The important thing is that you turn on the "Share this printer" checkbox.

Everything is now ready. Any Mac on your network can now print on the StyleWriter attached to your Macintosh; all your coworkers have to do is open their Choosers and select your StyleWriter.

Figure 11-3: Turn on the "Share this printer" checkbox, and presto! — other people can use your StyleWriter over the network.

There are only two drawbacks to this economical and convenient setup. First, when somebody else is printing on your StyleWriter, your Mac will slow down to process that printing task. Second, your Mac must have installed all the fonts used in the printouts.

 See also FAQ 25-1, "How can I connect two Macs?"

This darned StyleWriter keeps jamming!

▽ **Check the likely suspects.**

You won't find this in the StyleWriter manual, but I've found this otherwise wonderful printer to be somewhat crotchety when it comes to the *amount* of paper you stick into it. The StyleWriter often has trouble printing just a single sheet laid into its feed slot; likewise, you're asking for paper jams when you insert a stack thicker than half an inch.

If your stack thickness isn't a problem, then try each of the following:

✦ Check the sliding paper guide on the paper feed slot — that plastic sculpted piece that's supposed to nestle against the left side of the paper (as you look from the front). Too loose or too tight, and you'll make it tough for the StyleWriter to pull the paper in straight.

✦ Years of muggy summers in New York City have taught me about Sticky StyleWriter Paper Syndrome. That's where the humidity contributes to paper jams. Solution: Take the stack of paper out, fan it or riffle it, re-square it, and insert it again. That should solve it.

✦ Sometimes, especially if the paper stack was pushed in too far or was too thick, a catch deep inside the printer gets tripped. That catch is supposed to keep the paper feeder in the correct position; when it's been tripped, it's Paper Jam City. To solve this snafu, take out the paper, turn the printer off and on again, and finally re-insert a stack of paper less than half an inch thick — gently.

Can I print a whole bunch of things without doing them one by one?

▼ Yes. Highlight their icons on the desktop and choose the Print command from the File menu.

Amazingly enough, the Mac briefly opens each document, prints it, moves to the next one, and so on, until all the highlighted icons have been printed. This even works, memory permitting, when the documents were created by different programs. The only work you have to do is to click the OK button in the Print dialog box that appears at the very beginning.

I'm getting streaks in my laser printouts. How come?

▼ There's probably some crud on a critical interior component.

The culprit is that sooty black powder — toner. Toner is great, of course, because it's what makes your printouts. But when it escapes into your printer's innards, the results are streaks and smudges.

Turn off your laser printer. If it's been on a while, let it cool. Open it. Remove the cartridge and set it somewhere darkish, like in a drawer. Get some Q-tips.

If you look closely, you'll usually see some thin, taut, diagonal metal wires; clean them *very* carefully with the Q-tips. While you're at it, clean any other rollers or surfaces the page passes as it's being printed. When you replace the cartridge and close the printer, all should be well.

How long will my cartridge last?

▼ Let this table be your guide.

Table 11-1 lists cartridge prices for some typical printers. The numbers of pages per cartridge are, of course, averages.

Table 11-1

Printer cartridge list prices

Printer	Price	Number of pages
LaserWriter Select 300/310	$108	4,000
LaserWriter Select 360	$108	4,000
Personal LaserWriter SC, LS, NT, & NTR	$80	3,500
Personal LaserWriter 300/320	$75	3,000
LaserWriter Pro 810	$300	12,000
LaserWriter Pro 600/630	$125	6,000
LaserWriter II-SC,NT,NTX, F, and G	$100	4,000
Original LaserWriter and LaserWriter Plus	$110	3,000
StyleWriter I, II, Portable	$25	500
Color StyleWriter 2400 color-and-black cartridge	$50	900
Color StyleWriter 2400 color-only ink tank	$21	2,000
Color StyleWriter 2400 black-only ink tank	$8	900
Color StyleWriter 2400 high-performance black	$33	600
Apple Color Printer (SCSI) each color cartridge	$35	100
Apple Color Printer (SCSI) black ink cartridge	$25	350

Here's a wise word of advice for StyleWriter (and other inkjet) owners: Keep an extra cartridge on hand. Laser printer cartridges give you some warning before they croak. StyleWriter cartridges, on the other hand, look good all the way until the moment they die — which is generally right in the middle of some important project.

Printing takes forever. Can I speed things up?

▽   **Yes, especially if you're willing to spend some money on it.**

If not, you have only two options for speeding up printing.

◆ **Turn off background printing.** Do this by opening the Chooser and clicking the Background Printing Off button.

Background printing is one of God's greatest creations; it lets you continue to work with your Mac while the printing goes on. (Compare with the dark days of old, when you had to wait for your Mac until the printing was finished.) But this feature does slow down the works — both your Mac and your printer take longer.

✦ **Make your document less fancy.** In particular, using fonts that aren't built into your laser printer makes printouts take longer, because your Mac must transmit that font information before the printout can begin. The fonts that are built into most laser printers are Times, Helvetica, Helvetica Narrow, Avant Garde, New Century Schoolbook, Courier, Bookman, Palatino, Zapf Chancery, Symbol, and Zapf Dingbats.

I know plenty of people who have chosen, say, Futura to be their official "company font." There's nothing wrong with that — the world is already too full of documents printed in the Times font. All I'm saying is that, every single day, those people are waiting an extra moment for the first printout.

If slow printing has annoyed you to the point of opening your checkbook, the rules are simple: The Macintosh and the printer are equally at fault. Upgrading either one — or both — to a faster model will take care of your slow printing headaches.

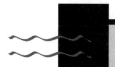

RAQ: Rarely Asked Question

My Color StyleWriter is so slow! What's up with that?

The software that controls your printer is particularly sensitive to how much memory is available in your Mac — that is, how much isn't being used at the moment by open programs.

Therefore, for greater speed, quit as many open programs as possible before printing. Even reclaiming one megabyte of free memory can cut the printing time nearly in half.

My fonts are coming out all wrong!

 Your fonts aren't installed properly.

As you know from the previous chapter, there are essentially two Macintosh font formats: TrueType and PostScript. Every Macintosh sold since 1990 comes with TrueType fonts, which are incapable of printing jaggedly, no matter which printer you own.

If your printer is churning out funny-looking or incorrect fonts, I'll bet you have a laser printer, and I'll bet you used a PostScript font in your document. As you know from FAQ 10-3, a PostScript font doesn't work right unless all of its pieces — screen fonts and printer font files — are present and in the right places.

The simplest solution is to reinstall the font from its original disk. If that's not possible, the next best solution is to burrow into your Fonts folder and try to determine which pieces are missing.

 See also FAQ 10-3, "What's the difference between PostScript and TrueType fonts?"

How can I make my printer stop spewing out copies?

 Have a stern talk with PrintMonitor.

The scenario goes like this: Having completed a 20-page opus, you choose Print from the File menu. When nothing happens immediately, you assume that the Mac didn't hear you, and you choose Print again. Then maybe you give up in disgust and turn off the computer.

You may think that you're done for the day, but behind the scenes, our friend the PrintMonitor program quietly took note of everything you tried to print. Its purpose in life is to make sure that your work gets printed, come hell or high water. Therefore, the next time your Mac is on, even if it's months or years later, PrintMonitor will immediately start to print those still unprinted documents.

The solution, therefore, is to make PrintMonitor go back to sleep. Choose PrintMonitor from the Application menu. If the trouble is what I think it is, you'll see something like Figure 11-4.

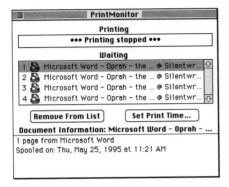

Figure 11-4: PrintMonitor thinks it's doing you a favor by remembering every Print command you've issued and dutifully chugging through them the next time you turn on the computer.

One after another, click on something in the list of waiting-to-be-printed documents, and then click the Remove button. Clicking the Cancel button a few times should eventually take care of whatever is currently being printed, and calm will once again reign.

 See also FAQ 4-5, "What's the application menu?"

OK, I'll bite: What exactly is PrintMonitor?

▽ **It's a secret program that handles background printing.**

This thing really is a program. Even though few people ever see its icon, let alone double-click it, it's there. Open your System Folder, open your Extensions folder, and there it is.

In real life, of course, the only interaction you usually have with PrintMonitor is to swear at it. That's because PrintMonitor generally makes its only appearances when it has bad news to report, such as a paper jam or that your laser printer is out of toner. It makes such announcements in a way that flusters many beginners: by blinking a printer icon on your Application menu icon, as shown in Figure 11-5, or sometimes by showing the none-too-friendly message also shown in the figure.

The flashing printer and the error message are PrintMonitor's subtle persuasive techniques. PrintMonitor really wants you to look in your application menu, where you'll see a similar diamond beside PrintMonitor's name. If you choose PrintMonitor at this point, its window springs forward with a message explaining in more detail what the current printing problem is.

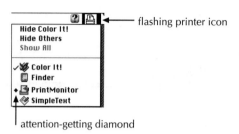 — flashing printer icon

attention-getting diamond

Figure 11-5: Above, the flashing printer icon that's supposed to signal you to look in the application menu, where a diamond appears beside PrintMonitor's name. Below, the message that sometimes appears, telling you to look there.

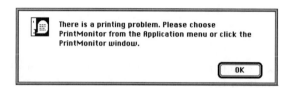

There is, of course, a simple way to eliminate PrintMonitor, flashing diamonds and all: Open the Chooser and turn off background printing. You won't be able to use your Mac for anything while you print, but at least you won't be frustrated by PrintMonitor's peculiar behaviors.

See also FAQ 4-5, "What's the application menu?"

Can I refill my laser printer cartridges?

11-16

▽ You can, but don't. Use *remanufactured* cartridges instead.

Plenty of companies will be happy to dump new toner into your old cartridge. Unfortunately, there's no guarantee on the toner quality, and if some of the cartridge components are worn, they don't get replaced. I've heard horror stories about black powder leaking out of poorly refilled cartridges into the innards of expensive printers.

Apple and others, on the other hand, sell *rebuilt* cartridges at a great discount. These have had any necessary parts replaced, and the toner is the same stuff the cartridge had originally.

I installed QuickDraw GX, and now my HP DeskWriter doesn't work.

▼ Serves you right for buying a non-Apple printer. Just kidding. Get the upgrade.

When Apple's system software gets updated, lots of other stuff has to be upgraded, too. In this case, QuickDraw GX is a new set of printing software. Therefore, you may have to get a new version of whatever software controls your printer (and probably your fax modem, too).

And where do you get this upgraded software (a new "driver")? The manufacturer is one source, but drivers are usually also available from online services. (The HP DeskWriter driver, for example, is posted on America Online.)

In the meantime, you can always turn off QuickDraw GX. To do so, open Extensions Manager (in your Control Panels folder), click off QuickDraw GX, and restart the Mac. (If your fonts print out funny after doing this, drag the font files from the •Archived Type 1 Fonts• folder back into the Fonts folder. Both of those folders are in your System Folder.)

 See also FAQ 21-1, "I heard that System 7.5 requires 8 megs of RAM and 20 megs of disk space. Is it worth getting?"

How come my EPS graphics print out jaggy?

▼ Because of the unique dual-personality nature of EPS files.

EPS stands for Encapsulated PostScript — PostScript, of course, being a complex behind-the-scenes language Macs speak to laser printers. To create an EPS graphic, your printer requires a string of PostScript instructions amounting to: "Start here, draw a skinny line diagonally to here," and so on.

Those instructions produce, say, a handsome tetrahedron on the printed page. But when you look at this drawing in PageMaker or QuarkXpress, you'd probably appreciate seeing something other than 50 lines of computerese. Therefore, for the benefit of us ordinary humans, the typical EPS file also includes a standard PICT file — a low-resolution onscreen graphic image. Thus everybody's happy: The printer gets its special codes, and you get to see something resembling a visual onscreen image.

The problem arises when you work in a program like PageMaker or QuarkXpress. You place some elegant EPS diagram into your document; the PICT portion appears normally. As you may know, those page-layout programs don't actually import graphics — they just remember where the graphics file was on your hard drive. So what happens when that EPS file gets moved, or renamed, or deleted before your document gets printed? The PICT onscreen portion of your EPS file remains in the page-layout document, but it gets separated from the printer instructions on the hard disk. You print, and sure enough, all you get is a low-resolution PICT representation of what the EPS file was supposed to be.

Solution: Put the EPS file back in its original folder, with its original name (and restore the folder's original name). PageMaker and QuarkXpress both offer a command, by the way, for checking the status of any graphics you've imported.

How come my boldface words print so far apart?

▽ **Because the printer is trying to duplicate the spacing on the screen.**

The symptom: Your laser printer puts extra-wide spacing between words, especially in boldface — it looks like several spaces separate each word. And yet everything looks OK on the screen.

The solution: Somewhere in your word processor, you'll find a checkbox called *Fractional Widths* or *Fractional Character Widths*. When you turn on this feature, your printouts don't have that *funny spacing*. (If you have Word 5, WordPerfect, or WriteNow, this control is in the Page Setup window. In ClarisWorks or MacWrite, it's in the Preferences dialog box. In Word 6, choose Options from the Tools menu, then click the Print tab.)

So why isn't this feature on all the time? Because when you turn on Fractional Widths, the text looks squashed and funny on the *screen*. The problem is that the screen is composed of a relatively coarse 72 dots per inch. But your printer has much sharper resolution, probably 300 or 600 dots per inch. Without Fractional Widths, the printer tries to match the word spacing of the screen; with Fractional Widths, the screen tries to match the spacing of the printout.

The compromise: type your document with the Fractional Widths feature off — then print it with Fractional Widths on.

12

Scanning and OCR

*E*verybody knows how to get a document from the Macintosh onto paper — by using *a printer. Going the opposite direction — from paper into the Mac — gets easier and less expensive every year. All you need is a scanner.*

Scanning is a blast: scanning in photos to repair or transform them, scanning in typewritten pages to avoid having to retype them, scanning in articles to preserve them forever . . . you've got to try it to believe it.

What dpi setting should I use when I scan?

 The answer is complicated — and surprising.

In scanning, as in printing, *dots per inch* is everything. The reason faxes look terrible is that they are printed at 200 dpi; the reason magazines look great is that they are printed at 2400 dpi. In printing, the higher the dpi, the better looking the printout.

In scanning, however, more dots per inch *doesn't* necessarily make better scans. High-dpi scans take up more space on your hard disk, take longer to process when you edit, and take longer to print. See Figure 12-1. Think about it: What sense does it make to scan a drawing at 1200 dpi if you're going to print it on a 300 dpi printer?

FA Q

12-1

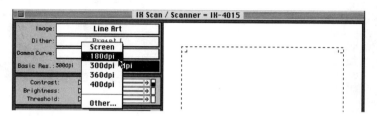

Figure 12-1:
Before you scan,
you must choose
a dpi setting.
The wrong
choice could
make your life
miserable.

In other words, the ideal resolution of your scanning really depends on the printer it's destined for. That's the first golden rule of scanning:

Find out the dpi of the printer you'll eventually be using before you scan.

Your assumption, then, might be to scan at the *same* dpi as the printer. Actually, that's not quite right, either. Suppose you have a beautiful grayscale photo on the screen (grayscale = composed of dots of various shades of gray). But you own a standard laser printer. How is it supposed to print different shades of gray, when it can only print black dots? Answer: with great difficulty. It tries to create the *illusion* of gray shades by varying the sizes of the solid black dots it puts on the paper. There is, of course, a good fat computer term for this, both a noun and a verb: *halftone*. See Figure 12-2.

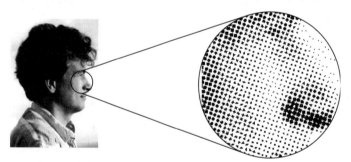

Figure 12-2: To create grayscale images, a laser printer puts several of its tiny dots together into larger clumps. This is called halftoning.

Obviously, it takes *several* of a laser printer's smallest dots to create *one* of these larger, variable-size halftone dots. That's why it doesn't make sense to scan something at the same resolution as the printer: It takes at least *two* printer dots to represent each gray dot on the scan as a halftone. Which brings us to rule number two:

When the printout will be a halftone, your scan is just wasting time and disk space if it's more than half the dpi of the printer.

That is, if you have a typical 300 dpi laser printer, your grayscale image should be composed of no more than 150 dpi!

Whether or not you were able to follow that techie discussion, Table 12-1 should guide you in setting up your scanner software.

Table 12-1

Scanner dpi guidelines

Printer and image	Maximum useful dpi
Professional color images	300
Color slides	300
Color laser printer	180
Onscreen display (multimedia)	72
Laser-printed grayscale	150
StyleWriter-printed grayscale	180

Believe it or not, this is going to get even more complicated before it gets better. You may have noticed that, in the previous verbiage, I never really said that those were the dpi settings you should *use* when you scan. Those should be the *final* dpi of your images at the time you print.

If you have a scanner, you probably also have a scan-editing program such as Photoshop or Color It; indeed, it's a rare scanner today that doesn't come with one of these programs. You definitely need such a program, if only to fix the funny coloration that often results from scanned photographs.

For the very best results, then, follow these steps when you scan:

1. Set the scanning software to its *highest* dpi setting! This may seem to fly in the face of everything you've just read, but you'll see why in a moment.

2. Bring this enormous, high-dpi file into Photoshop (or equivalent) if it isn't there already. Use the Image Size command (or equivalent) to change the image's dpi to the correct setting, according to Table 12-1.

For example, suppose you have a 300 dpi laser printer and a 800 dpi grayscale scanner. Set the software to scan at 800 dpi. Then, in Photoshop, change the resolution to 150 dpi, the ideal setting for a 300 dpi printer.

The purpose of that little exercise was to let *Photoshop* create the lower-dpi image *from* the original high-dpi scan. This process — converting a graphic to a lower-resolution edition — is known as *downsampling*. The result, especially when Photoshop does it, is a better-looking image than you'd have received by scanning at 150 to begin with.

This all seems crazy, I know — every instinct in your body probably tells you to create 300 dpi images for a 300 dpi printer. Over time, however, you'll come to appreciate the time and disk-space savings gained by using the correct dpi values — and the fact that the printout quality won't suffer!

But what if I want to enlarge the original?

▼ **That's a special case; keep as many dots as you can.**

12-2

If you're scanning a small photo, but you want it to be as large as possible on the screen, scan at a high dpi setting. Remember that enlarging involves making the individual dots larger; therefore, the smaller and more plentiful they are to begin with, the clearer your final enlargement will be.

I plan to print on a fancy color printer at a local output shop. What dpi should I use?

▼ **If it's a dye-sublimation printer, none of the usual rules apply.**

12-3

I assume you plan to take your finished Photoshop (or equivalent) file to a local print shop, where you hope to have them print it on one of those $10,000 photographic-quality color printers. (For instant respect, toss around the shorthand *dye-sub printer*.)

A dye-sublimation printer does *not* create images using the halftone process described in the previous FAQ; it doesn't have to. It can print any dot in any color. In this case, then, don't consult Table 12-1 to calculate the final resolution of your image file. Instead, just call up the print shop. Say, "What's the maximum dpi of your dye-sub printer?"

The answer is usually something like 220 or 300, depending on the machine. The rules for scanning successfully still apply — start by scanning at the highest possible setting, then downsample it in Photoshop. The difference is that this time, you want the finished dpi of your image file to *match* the resolution of the dye-sub printer.

(Incidentally, I highly recommend this pursuit! How else can ordinary people like us take a photo, edit out somebody's head, and get it printed again as what looks like an original photo?)

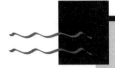

RAQ: Rarely Asked Question

I think there's a ghost in the machine...

A true report from an Apple technician:

A very disturbed woman called and explained that her mother had died a few months ago. Lately, she had been noticing that all of her files, when viewed in a list view, were displaying the date Jan. 1, 1904. She said her mother had been *born* on Jan. 1, 1904. The caller thought that perhaps her mom was trying to talk to her from the spirit world — through the Mac.

I tried to explain that this was not related to her mother, that this date-change syndrome often happens when a battery is dead in a computer, and that replacing the battery would make the correct dates show up.

She wouldn't believe me.

My scanner makes me choose: line art, grayscale, or color. Which should I use?

 Depends on the original artwork — and what you want it for.

It would help, I guess, to first understand those three terms.

Line art is black-and-white only, with no shades of gray. Use the line-art setting for newspaper or magazine text, because both are pure black on pure white. Other kinds of art that use this setting include typewritten letters, line drawings like the Clorox bottles in newspaper advertising supplements, and so on. Line art scans are especially likable because they don't contain any color information; as a result, the files are compact on your hard disk and easy to edit in Photoshop.

Grayscale, of course, is an image with shades of gray, but no colors. Think of "black-and-white" photographs, "black-and-white" television sets, and so on. Figure 12-3 shows you the difference between line art and grayscale.

Figure 12-3: At top: a line art scan. At bottom: grayscale. I suppose now you'd like an example of a color scan, right? Sorry — you would have had to pay $10 extra for this book.

And *color*, of course, is color. Actually, your scanner software may even offer you a *choice* of color settings: 8-bit, 16-bit, or 24-bit. These numbers indicate how much information is stored for every dot in the scan. Higher numbers are good because they look more realistic and photo-like — but they're also bad because they create much larger scan files on your disk. In general, 16-bit scans are the best trade-off. They look like photos, but aren't such space gluttons.

Of course, there's no law saying that you must scan to match the artwork. For example, if you don't have a color printer, there may not be much point in scanning color photos in color; you could scan them in grayscale instead. They'll look great, and the files will only be one-third as big.

Don't scan *upward* from the artwork, though — there's no artistic point whatsoever to scanning a line drawing as a color scan, for example. You'll just wind up with a pointlessly enormous file that's slow to manipulate.

I have all these old manuscripts. Do I have to type them all into the Mac again?

▽ **Nope. You can scan then in and use OCR to turn them into word processing documents.**

When you scan a typewritten page, the Mac doesn't see words. It sees the same thing it always sees when you scan something: a collection of tiny dots. That piece of paper is stored as a graphic image. You can't spellcheck it or edit it — unless you call wiping out chunks of it with an eraser tool "editing."

OCR stands for *Optical Character Recognition*. That's software the Mac uses to analyze each little clump of scanned black dots and guess what typed letter it's supposed to be. It then types that letter into a text file. When the OCR process is finished, you have yourself a typed Microsoft Word (or whatever) document that you can edit and format. See Figure 12-4.

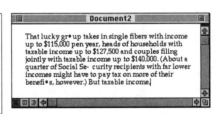

Figure 12-4: At left: the original scan. As far as the Mac is concerned, this could be a Picasso, a photograph, or any other group of random scanned dots. At right: the WordPerfect document produced after an OCR program analyzed the scan.

As you can imagine, the Mac's accuracy in reading the scan depends a lot on the quality of the original; old, crumbly originals don't do well, and neither do faxes, or things typed with a dirty, muddy typewriter ribbon. When everything works well, you'll find only one typo per paragraph or so; some OCR programs do automatic spellchecking to prevent even those from appearing.

The most accurate OCR program is OmniPage Pro; it's also among the most expensive. Other popular OCR programs are Read It, Word Scan, and so on. Be warned that OCR programs require lots of memory; you won't get far in OCR if your Mac only has four megs of RAM.

12-6

What's the difference between optical and interpolated resolution?

▽ **One is real; the other is marketing.**

The *resolution* of a scanner is a measurement of how many dots per inch it can "see" — 600 or 1200, for example. Some scanners are advertised to have an impressively high *interpolated* resolution, especially considering their price.

These scanners actually have, as you'll find out when you read the small print, a lower *actual* resolution. The software that comes with it, however, examines every two real dots that the scanner sees, averages their colors, and produces a third dot in between. Adding the actual scanned dots and these artificially generated in-between dots produces the interpolated dpi figure. In short, interpolation is an advertising trick to make a scanner sound more capable than it really is.

12-7

Can I scan slides?

▽ **Yes. But unless you scan lots of them, a PhotoCD makes more sense.**

There are two kinds of slide scanners. First, you can buy a slide-scanning attachment for some regular flatbed scanners. Unfortunately, the quality will probably disappoint you; a slide is just too tiny to get a good scan from a machine designed for entire pages.

You can also buy a machine intended solely for scanning slides. Unfortunately, these dedicated slide scanners cost around $2,000.

I have an ingenious alternative for you. Take those same slides to any neighborhood Kodak film developing outfit. Tell them you want a PhotoCD made of the slides. A few days later, at a cost of about $1 per slide, you'll be given a CD-ROM. The disc contains each slide, represented as a scanned graphics file, in five different sizes (resolutions). Not only is this a less expensive route (for small numbers of slides, anyway), but you also save the time and hassle of having to do the scanning yourself. And, of course, you don't have to use up any hard-disk space; those enormous files are safely, and permanently, stowed away on that CD-ROM.

Can I scan negatives?

 Yes, but once again, the equipment is expensive. Consider PhotoCD.

To scan a negative, you need a special scanner, such as one Nikon makes. It costs $2,000. As mentioned in the previous FAQ, however, you may save time and money by having your negatives transferred to a PhotoCD.

I scanned a newspaper photo. How do I get rid of all those annoying ripple patterns?

They're called Moiré patterns. Photoshop or Color It can get rid of them for you.

Moiré patterns occur when you try to scan (represent as dots) a photo that has been *halftoned* (already represented as dots). The result is something like the rippling pattern you'd see if you put one piece of screen mesh on top of another, at an angle, and tried to look through them.

To solve the problem, bring the scanned image into Photoshop (or whatever image-processing program you use), if it's not already there. First, choose Gaussian Blur from the Filters menu, type in 1 or 2, and click OK. You've just succeeded in slightly fuzzing those dots. See Figure 12-5.

Figure 12-5: At left: the original Moiré pattern. Middle: after applying the blur command in Photoshop. Right: after using the sharpen command.

Now compensate for the added blurriness by choosing the Sharpen command from the Filters menu. Type the same number you used a moment ago. Presto: Your image should now have the same degree of detail, but the patterns are gone.

 See also FAQ 12-2, "What dpi setting should I use when I scan?"

13

Speech, Multimedia, and CD-ROM

I f there's one area where the Mac shines in its superiority over other kinds of computers, it's in multimedia. Inexpensive, high-quality sound, movies, pictures, and CD-ROM are the Mac's exclusive domain.

This chapter has it all — movies, sound, CD-ROM, speech recognition, talking Macs, and using your Mac to answer the phone. Forgive the lumping.

How do I play a QuickTime movie?

 Get a QuickTime-savvy program (and the QuickTime extension, of course).

You'd be surprised at how many programs can play QuickTime movies: SimpleText, Microsoft Word, WordPerfect, HyperCard, the Scrapbook, any of several free or shareware programs, and so on. As with Mac graphics files, however, you generally can't double-click a QuickTime movie file and expect it to play; you must launch your movie-playing program *first* and use the Open command in the File menu to locate the movie you want to play.

Actually, there's an even simpler way to play a movie — one that doesn't involve any playback program at all. Name the QuickTime movie *startup movie* and drop it into your System Folder. It will play automatically every time you turn on the Mac.

Of course, you also need the QuickTime extension to play a movie, regardless of the program you use. Older versions of this extension are available for free from America Online and similar services; the latest version is slightly harder to get (see the next FAQ).

See also FAQ 4-63, "What's QuickTime?"

Where do I get QuickTime 2.0?

▽ **It comes with System 7.5, with Christmas Lights, or for free from America Online.**

QuickTime 2.0 is a dramatically improved version of Apple's movie technology. It's an extension. As with previous versions, adding QuickTime to your system doesn't do anything by itself — but it acts as the master switch that permits QuickTime-savvy *programs* to work. Version 2.0 is especially significant because it can double either the smoothness or the "screen size" of the movies you play on your Mac.

Apple doesn't make QuickTime 2.0 available to the public, except as part of System 7.5. If you don't want to make that leap, there are two ways to get your hands on QuickTime 2 inexpensively.

✦ Get it as part of a book or software bundle. The least expensive is Christmas Lights, a merry little $19.95 program from Atticus, (203) 324-1142.

✦ This method costs less, but requires more effort. On America Online, use keyword *Raster Ops*. Double-click the Software Library icon. Download the file called Video Installer 3.0. It takes 30 minutes at 14.4 Kbps (about $1.50 in connection time).

What you get is a file that ends with the letters *.sea*, indicating that it is a self-expanding archive (a compressed file). Double-click it and save it onto your desktop. You wind up with three files known as *disk images*. To turn these files into actual floppy disks, you need yet another program — a disk image utility, such as DiskCopy, MountImage, or MungeImage. All three are also on America Online.

Once you've finally converted those images into actual floppy disks, you'll find the three QuickTime 2.0 components — QuickTime, Musical Instruments, and Power Plug (for Power Macs) in folders called Apple extensions. Install them by dropping them onto your System Folder (and clicking OK).

See also FAQ 21-1, "I heard that System 7.5 requires eight megs of RAM and 20 megs of disk space. Is it worth getting?"

See also FAQ 28-2, "What's a keyword?"

See also FAQ 28-5, "What am I supposed to do with these '.image' files I downloaded?"

Ever since I installed QuickTime 2.0, my CD-ROMs freeze.

▽ **Install the Apple Multimedia Tuner.**

The Multimedia Tuner is a free extension from Apple that improves the smoothness of QuickTime-movie playback and CD-ROMs in general. It also solves various freezing and sticking problems with those multimedia programs.

See also FAQ 1-32, "Where do I get Apple software updates?"

When I start my Macintosh, it says that QuickTime could not be installed because it was already installed.

▽ **You have two copies of the QuickTime extension.**

Open your System Folder, open your Extensions folder, and remove one of the copies of QuickTime. (Use the Get Info command on each one to find out how old it is, so you'll be sure that you're throwing away the older one.)

See also FAQ 4-29, "What's an extension?"

How do I make QuickTime movies myself?

▽ **You only need two things: hardware and software.**

The software part is easy. You need a program that lets you cut, paste, and otherwise rearrange your little camera shots into one creative, cohesive, cinematic whole. Either Movie Player (usually comes with the QuickTime extension) or Movie Play (free; available on America Online and other online services) suffices for simple stuff. To get fancy, or serious, you need a commercial program like Adobe Premiere. It lets you make scrolling credits, smooth cross-fades, and so on.

The hardware part is harder. You need something that can convert a camera's (or a VCR's) signal into digital information for the Mac. And, of course, you need the camera (or VCR) itself. Here are your options:

✦ Buy a Mac with a built-in video digitizer. Some examples: any model with the letters AV in its name, a 630 or 5200 model with the Apple Video card option, and so on. Into this card, you plug a VCR, video camera, or camcorder.

✦ Buy a video-digitizing card and install it into your existing Mac model. These cards aren't cheap — the least expensive ones cost about $500. To find out what's available, call up Mac Connection at (800) 800-4444. But, once installed into a Mac's NuBus or PDS slot — and you *do* need a Mac with a slot — it actually does a better job of creating smooth movies than those Apple AV cards. Once again, you have to come up with a VCR or video camera to accompany your card.

✦ Buy a QuickCam. It's a $100, golf-ball sized camera *and* digitizer that plugs into the back of your Mac. The movies it makes are pretty jerky — only about 15 frames per second, tops — and they're grayscale, not color (at least in the first incarnation of the QuickCam). But this is the least expensive option, and the *only* option if you have a PowerBook.

How do I watch TV on a Mac?

▽ **You need an AV, 630, or Mac TV model.**

The Mac needs a special circuit board inside if it's to double as a TV set. Here are your options:

✦ a Quadra AV, Centris AV, or Power Mac AV model

✦ a Performa/Quadra/LC 630-something, or a 5200-something, with the optional Apple TV card installed

✦ a Mac TV (remember that model?)

You can probably buy a non-Apple TV card that goes into other Mac models; but for those prices, you'd probably save money buying a big, beautiful 25-inch actual color TV to put on your desk.

Anyway, once you have your Mac equipped, you also need to figure out some way to bring a TV signal to it. That means connecting it to your cable TV cable, or running a cord from your VCR to the Mac, or using an antenna with the right kind of adapter jack.

There's no sound coming from my Mac's speaker!

 Make sure that nothing is plugged into your Mac's speaker jack.

For example, it's quite easy to plug your *microphone* into the speaker jack by accident, since they look nearly alike. But when anything is plugged into the speaker jack, your Mac's built-in speaker is automatically disconnected.

How do I play music CDs on my CD-ROM's player?

 Use the AppleCD Audio Player desk accessory.

It's in your menu, and it looks exactly like the front panel of a real CD player. Click the Play button, and you're in business.

Well, probably. If you're using an external CD-ROM player, you must hook up headphones or external speakers — you can't listen through your Mac's built-in speaker. If you have an internal CD-ROM player, visit your Sound control panel. From the popup menu at the top, choose Sound In; then click the CD-ROM icon, and select the Playthrough checkbox (if you have one). Now open the AppleCD desk accessory, and boogie down.

 See also FAQ 13-9, "Why don't I get any sound when playing audio CDs?"

Why don't I get any sound when playing audio CDs?

 Maybe the Sound control panel needs attention. Maybe you don't have an internal CD-ROM.

Open your Sound control panel. Choose Volumes from the popup menu at the top; make sure that the volume slider is turned up. Then choose Sound In from that same popup menu, and make sure that your CD-ROM player is selected (as opposed to, say, your microphone). Finally, make sure that the Playthrough checkbox is selected (unless you have external speakers).

This brings up another point — you *can't* listen to audio CDs through your Mac's built-in speaker with an *external* CD-ROM drive. Only built-in CD-ROMs can use the internal speaker.

 See also FAQ 13-24, "When I'm listening to music on my AppleDesign speakers, it seems like the CD is skipping or cutting out."

How can I record from an audio CD onto my Mac?

▽ **Open the Sound control panel, and go wild.**

If you have an internal CD-ROM drive, go to your Sound control panel. Use the popup menu at the top; choose Sound In. Click the CD-ROM icon. Now, using the same popup menu, switch back to Alert Sounds. Click the Add button; record a new sound snippet from the CD exactly as you would record from the microphone.

Here's an alternate method that neither requires an internal CD-ROM drive nor limits you to 10-second sound clips:

Launch any QuickTime-savvy program, such as SimpleText. Choose Open from the File menu, navigate to the audio CD, and double-click a track file. Click the Options button to specify a sound quality level. (**Hint**: Set the controls to *16-bit* quality. The file will take up more disk space, but you'll avoid the audible playback hiss of 8-bit recordings.)

Once you've opened the track, save it onto your hard drive and give it a name. It's now a sound-only QuickTime movie, which you can play in any of the usual ways. (Use a shareware program like Movie2Snd, available from America Online and other services, if you want to convert that movie to a regular, double-clickable System 7 sound file.)

See also FAQ 13-1, "How do I play a QuickTime movie?"

See also FAQ 28-3, "How do I find a file I want to download?"

I can't seem to record sounds from a CD on my Quadra.

▽ **Unplug the microphone.**

When a microphone is plugged into a Quadra 800, a Mac IIvx, or a Centris 610 or 650, the internal CD-ROM is automatically disconnected, as far as recording is concerned.

See also FAQ 13-10, "How can I record from an audio CD onto my Mac?"

My old Mac microphone doesn't work with my new Power Mac!

 Correct. Apple now uses a new microphone style.

Most newer Mac models require the Apple PlainTalk microphone. If your Mac didn't come with one, you can buy it for $20. It differs from the previous Apple microphone in that its plug — the straight silver pin — is somewhat longer than standard miniplugs.

Can my Macintosh play CD-ROM discs for a PC?

 See FAQ 26-5, "Can my Macintosh play CD-ROM discs for a PC?"

How do I make my own CD-ROM disc?

 Assemble the contents on a great big hard drive. Then take it to a CD-ROM pressing company, or do it yourself.

Remember that a CD-ROM holds 600 megabytes of information. Of course, you don't actually have to fill the disc. But you do need a hard drive large enough to hold everything that will be on your custom-made CD.

Once you've assembled all the files you want on the CD, there are two ways to turn it into a CD-ROM. First, you can press it yourself by buying a CD-ROM recorder/player. These devices are becoming less expensive than they once were — about $2500 is the going rate. You wouldn't buy one if your idea is to market 50,000 copies of one disc. But if you work for some company where data backup is so important that it's cost-effective to regularly generate one-shot CDs, owning such a recorder makes sense.

Otherwise, you can take your file-filled hard drive to a service bureau — a company who, for $1000 or so, will press the CD-ROM for you (and usually give you several hundred copies for that price). Locating such a company is easy in large cities, harder in small ones. But check the ads in the back of Mac magazines, ask around, and inquire online.

How do I edit sounds?

 Get a microphone and an editing program, and get busy.

Several excellent commercial programs let you copy, paste, and otherwise mangle the sounds you record onto your Mac. For example, SoundEdit 16 (from Macromedia) lets you manipulate multiple tracks, add special effects and echo, and save your finished sounds in any of several useful file formats.

There are also, however, several shareware or free programs that do almost as well. For example, waiting for you on America Online and similar services is SoundEffects, which behaves almost exactly like SoundEdit.

The really amazing part about all of this is that, if you're using one of the recent Mac models, such as a Power Mac or a PowerBook 500 series, you can do your sound editing in CD-quality format. Hook up some speakers to your Mac's speaker jack, and you'll be amazed at how crisp and clear your creations sound.

See also FAQ 28-3, "How do I find a file I want to download?"

How do I play IBM .wav sound files?

Download a shareware program like SoundBuilder or Brian's Sound Tool.

See also FAQ 28-3, "How do I find a file I want to download?"

How do I view JPEG and GIF files?

Double-clicking won't work. You need Photoshop or Color It.

Lots of programs can open this kind of specialized graphics file: commercial programs like Photoshop and Color It, free programs like America Online, and shareware programs like GraphicConverter.

What they all have in common is that they won't open a JPEG or GIF picture when you double-click the picture's icon, as you would open any normal document. Instead, you must use one of these two techniques:

✦ Drag the graphics file's icon on top of the program's icon, as shown in Figure 13-1.

✦ Launch the graphic-capable program first. From its File menu, choose Open. Navigate to the location of the graphics file you're trying to open, and double-click it.

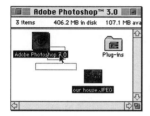 

Figure 13-1: To open a graphics file, drag its icon on top of a graphics program icon (left). The program launches, opening your graphics file in the process (right).

 See also FAQ 18-4, "It says, 'Application could not be found.' What gives?"

Where do I get QuickTime VR?

▽ **You don't, unless you're a software company.**

When you use a program that uses QuickTime VR, you view a photo on the screen. If you drag your mouse around inside the photo, your camera angle changes. You can actually turn completely around, viewing your environment from every angle; you can even look up or down, zoom in or out, and otherwise get a spooky feeling that you're really there.

Unfortunately, *you* can't make a QuickTime VR movie. All you can do is buy products that *incorporate* VR technology, such as Paramount's Star Trek: the Next Generation Interactive Technical Manual CD-ROM.

Actually, QuickTime VR *is* available for purchase, but only as a programming kit. Still interested? Contact APDA, (800) 282-2732.

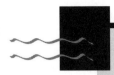

RAQ: Rarely Asked Question

Whatever happened to John Sculley?

In 1993, after several years at Apple, during which he built the company to ten times its original size, CEO John Sculley resigned. At the time, Apple's fortunes were in a downswing, and (rumor has it) the board of directors was unhappy with the direction Sculley had chosen.

Sculley's next job was as CEO of Manhasset, New York-based Spectrum Information Technology, which develops wireless data communications products, such as cellular modems. A bizarre corporate soap opera then played itself out in national headlines: Spectrum found itself under investigation for various financial and stock-reporting scams, whereupon Sculley resigned from Spectrum, claiming to have been misled. He also sued the Spectrum president, Peter Caserta, and Caserta sued Sculley.

Since that 1994 debacle, Sculley has devoted his time to consulting for Kodak, giving speeches, and writing.

And meeting with lawyers, of course.

How do I make my Mac talk?

▽ **Get System 7.5.**

System 7.5 comes with two special extensions called Macintalk Pro and Speech Manager. If these files are installed in your System Folder, a Sound menu appears when you launch SimpleText. Just type something or paste some text, and choose Speak Selected Text from the Sound menu. You'll hear the Mac read your text — in a nasal, Norwegian-sounding voice, but unmistakably clear.

If you have System 7.5 on a CD-ROM, you're in for a *real* treat. In that SimpleText Sound menu is a Voices submenu that lists 18 different voices. They range from standard male and female to bizarre, bubbly-sounding aliens. (For these options to work, you must install the PlainTalk software from your CD-ROM, which should put a Voices folder inside your Extensions folder.)

How do I make my Mac type what I say?

▽ **Get a fast, memory-maxed Mac, and buy PowerSecretary.**

PowerSecretary is a program from Articulate Systems that actually lets your Mac take dictation. You wear a headset microphone; you speak normally, except — you — separate — words — like — this; and, sure enough, the Mac types what you're saying.

That's the good news. Here's the bad: Speech recognition is still an infant technology. Getting PowerSecretary to work quickly and accurately requires the following:

✦ a Mac with at least 24 megs of RAM (40 for best results)

✦ at least 20 megs of disk space

✦ 16-bit sound capability (either a Power Mac or similar model, or an older model with a *16-bit sound card* installed)

✦ a word processor that isn't Microsoft Word version 5

✦ a lot of money ($2500 for the full version, or $1000 for a version that only works in WordPerfect)

Finally, PowerSecretary takes a lot of time to get good. It gradually learns your voice, but only because you constantly correct its errors during the first week or so. If you use the program all day, it will start to seem amazing after about two weeks.

All that is a lot of money and effort, true. On the other hand, it works — because I had terrible tendinitis in my wrists, I wrote this book by dictating it into Power-Secretary!

My Mac's built-in voice recognition is so lame!

▽ **Try letting it "adapt" — and try a Jabra microphone.**

In a way, Macintosh speech recognition *is* lame. It's available only on Power Macs (but not the 5200 series), Quadra AVs, and Centris AVs. It can be used only to control menus and to trigger certain canned responses ("what time is it?") — it doesn't do dictation. It wolfs down an enormous amount of RAM while it's turned on. And, as you may have noticed, it doesn't work very well for many people. These tips may help:

✦ Open your Sound control panel. From the popup menu at the top, choose Sound Out. In the window that appears, make sure the rate is set to **24.000 kHz** (for a Quadra 840AV or 660AV), or **22.050 kHz** (for a Power Mac).

Now choose Sound In from that same popup menu. In the Options section, make sure Playthrough is not selected.

◆ If the speech recognition doesn't recognize you very well, maybe you need to let it learn about your background — that is, your office's background sounds. Open the Speech Setup control panel. Speak into the microphone at a normal distance and volume for about 20 seconds (Power Mac) or several minutes (Quadra or Centris AV). You should have better luck thereafter.

◆ If you see a message that the SR Monitor is having trouble due to lack of memory, save all your open documents and quit the applications you have open. Then open the Speech Setup control panel; choose a voice that takes up less memory, or turn off voice feedback. (The voices named Agnes, Bruce, and Victoria take up the most memory.)

◆ If you still aren't getting accurate recognition, replace your Mac microphone with a Jabra EarPhone. This little gadget is a microphone that sits in your ear. This close, fixed position gives you much better voice recognition results.

See also FAQ 13-20, "How do I make my Mac type what I say?"

How do I use my Mac as an answering machine?

See FAQ 2-16,"Can I make my Mac into an answering machine?"

13-22

My Sound control panel is set to listen to CDs, and won't let me change it. What should I do?

▽ **Turn off PlainTalk.**

13-23

If your Mac is an AV, Power Mac, or another that works with voice command, your Mac can only "listen" to one sound source at a time. If it is set — in the Sound control panel — to use the CD-ROM as the sound source, then you can't use voice recognition, and vice versa. Solution in this case: Turn off speech recognition (in the Speech Setup control panel). You'll then be allowed to change the Sound In setting in the Sound control panel.

When I'm listening to music on my Apple Design speakers, it seems like the CD is skipping or cutting out.

13-24

 Connect your speakers to the RCA jacks of the Power Mac instead of the miniplug.

The AppleDesign speakers have a special feature you may not know about: *noise gate circuitry*. It automatically cuts out very soft sounds coming from the Mac, so that you don't go crazy hearing the Mac's internal electronic whirs and clanks amplified. Unfortunately, when you play soft passages of classical music, for example, the speakers cut out then, too.

Open your Sound control panel. Choose Volumes from the popup menu. Drag the CD-ROM volume slider all the way to the top — and use the volume knob on the speakers to control the speaker volume. This action may make the signal strong enough to overcome the noise-gate circuitry.

If that doesn't work — it might not on a Power Mac, whose sound circuitry provides a weaker signal — you can connect your Mac (or the CD-ROM) to the *RCA jacks* of the speakers instead of the usual miniplug input to bypass that noise-gate feature. Your music will never cut out, although you will now hear your Mac's internal noises. To perform this rewiring, you need a Y adapter cable (such as item 42-2481 from Radio Shack).

 See also FAQ 6-9, "What about RAM Doubler? Does it work?"

Hey! Weren't there more files on my CD-ROM?

13-25

 If you have System 7.5 and RAM Doubler, maybe.

An obscure conflict between System 7.5 and RAM Doubler makes icons appear to vanish from your CD-ROM discs. Upgrade to a RAM Doubler 1.5.2 or later to solve the problem.

Why don't CDs eject automatically at shutdown, like they did on my old Mac?

▽ Because Apple switched to a new CD-ROM type — the one with a built-in tray.

Actually, the tray-style drive is nicer for two reasons. First, you don't have to fumble with those flimsy CD caddies. Second, the fact that the trays don't eject when you turn off the Mac makes life much easier when you want to *start up* the Mac from the CD-ROM (when you're troubleshooting, for example).

When I start up my Mac, I get a message: "Some of the File Access Modules could not be loaded." What's wrong?

▽ You're missing some CD-ROM startup files, like ISO 9660 and High Sierra File Access.

Re-install your CD-ROM software from the original floppy disk.

I'm pressing the eject button on my Mac, but the CD won't eject!

▽ No wonder. You must drag the CD's icon to the trash (onscreen) first.

PART 3

Mac Models, Inc.

In 1984, you could have whatever Mac configuration you wanted — as long as it was beige, one-piece, and loaded with 128K of memory.

Today, of course, over 120 models, new and used, are kicking around — over 18 million computers. Differentiation was inevitable; knowing your way around one model doesn't mean that you know your way around another.

The next four chapters containing everything you've always wanted to know about several special classes of Macintosh: Power Macs, PowerBooks, Duos, and Performas.

14

Power Macintosh

*S*ure, we're all used to hearing about new Mac models that are faster than the one we already own. But eight times faster?

That was the news in 1994 when Apple introduced the Power Mac line. With appropriately rewritten software, these models were so fast that all kinds of new computer features were suddenly possible. The Power Mac would be capable of taking voice commands, acting as a telephone, and doing things not even imagined at the time.

What, exactly, is a Power Mac?

 It's a Mac whose main processor chip is a PowerPC chip.

Until 1994, every Mac model was based on a Motorola processor chip of the "sixty-eight thousand" series: the 68000, the 68030, the 68040, and so on. Apple, IBM, and Motorola, hoping to remain competitive in the 90s, collaborated to create the next-generation computer chip, which they called the PowerPC. Its speed stems from the fact that it's a RISC chip — Reduced Instruction Set Computing, meaning that it uses a smaller vocabulary of commands that it processes extremely quickly.

14-1

Apple's Power Mac line has completely replaced the non-Power Mac line; all future models will be built around a PowerPC chip. Power Macs are fast enough to offer special features like speech recognition (of menu commands) and telephone answering-machine simulation. But, in short, what actually makes a Power Mac a Power Mac is simply the presence of a PowerPC chip inside.

    See also FAQ 4-1, "What's 680x0?"

    See also FAQ 4-59, "What's PowerPC?"

If I get a Power Mac, do I need all new programs?

▽   No, unless you want to take full advantage of the Power Mac's speed.

Unfortunately, when it rolled off the drawing board, the PowerPC chip was so different from the 68000 series chips that it couldn't run Macintosh programs! It required a whole new type of software, called *native PowerPC* software. Fortunately, native programs seemed worth writing, since they run between two and eight times faster on the PowerPC chip than on a 68000 chip.

But what about all the thousands of *existing* Macintosh programs? Answer: Apple wrote an *emulator,* a program built into the Power Mac that automatically translates those older programs into a form the PowerPC chip can understand. Unfortunately, this extra conversion takes time; non-native (pre-PowerPC) programs run slower on a Power Mac than on, say, a Quadra. But at least they run! (Fortunately, this slowdown isn't as severe on the latest Power Mac models as it was on the original 6100, 7100, and 8100 series.)

In other words, you don't have to buy new, all-native software for your Power Mac. But if you don't, you won't be getting much benefit from owning one; you'll be running at slower-than-Quadra speeds. Furthermore, if you own a pre-PowerPC program, you don't have to buy that program all over again; most software companies offer the Power Mac version as an inexpensive upgrade.

    See also FAQ 4-25, "What's emulation mode?"

    See also FAQ 4-47, "What's native?"

Can my old Mac read the documents made by my Power Mac programs?

 Yes — only the programs are different, not the documents.

Why do Power Mac programs require so much more memory?

 The answer's pretty technical, but here it is.

To follow this discussion, you have to understand the basics of how a program runs. When you double-click a program's icon, the hard drive spins, and your Mac reads the program's *code* — the computer instructions that constitute a program — into memory.

Don't forget that the Power Mac processor chip is completely different from the chips in non-Power Mac models. As a result, it doesn't handle this hard-disk-to-memory process the same way. A non-Power Mac program may read pieces of its code from the hard disk — and get rid of that code — as necessary. For example, when you print, your program reads the printing code on the hard disk and loads it into RAM; when the printing is finished, those printing instructions are dumped out of memory.

Power Mac programs, on the other hand, don't have the luxury of being able to read and dump code fragments as necessary. Their code is stored on the disk as one giant chunk. Therefore, a native program requires much more memory than its non-native counterpart because it must load the entire program code into RAM when you launch it. As you can imagine, this also means that a native program takes longer to load.

Fortunately, there is a quick and easy solution to this problem — a simple mouse click that permits a Power Mac to handle a native program in code-fragments-as-necessary, just like non-native programs. Just open your Memory control panel and turn on Virtual Memory. Adjust the setting so that the amount is only about one or two megabytes more than your actual installed memory, as shown in Figure 14-1.

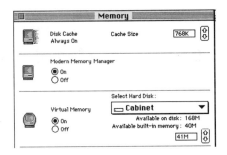

Figure 14-1: If you own a Power Mac, proceed this instant to your Memory control panel. Set virtual memory only slightly higher than your actual Mac's installed memory amount.

Because virtual memory, at heart, is simply a method of rapidly swapping information between the hard drive and RAM, it works beautifully on a Power Mac. Microsoft Excel, for example, requires 6500K less memory when virtual memory is turned on! FreeHand requires 7 megs of RAM on a Power Mac — but only 3 megs when virtual memory is turned on. In fact, it's easy to find out how much memory savings you'll get: Highlight a program's icon and choose Get Info from the File menu. As you can see in Figure 14-2, the savings are easy to spot.

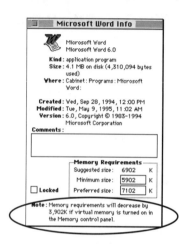

Figure 14-2: Every native Power Mac program has exaggerated memory requirements — until you turn on virtual memory.

In other words, when it comes to virtual memory on a Power Mac, forget everything you've heard. On a Power Mac, turning on virtual memory not only doesn't slow down your machine — it actually speeds you up.

See also FAQ 6-8, "What's virtual memory? Should I turn it on?"

Why does my system keep bloating memory?

See FAQ 6-6, "I read FAQ 6-5, but my Power Mac is still losing RAM, even when I quit all programs. Help!"

14-5

Can I upgrade my old Mac to be a Power Macintosh?

See FAQ 24-5, "Can I upgrade my old Mac to be a Power Macintosh?"

14-6

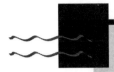

DAQ: Desperately Asked Question

I can't get my Power Macintosh Upgrade Card to come up in Power Macintosh mode!

The Power Mac Upgrade Card is the small circuit board that adds the PowerPC chip to a non-Power Mac computer, such as a Quadra or an LC. The beauty of it is that you can switch it on or off, using a control panel, depending on whether or not the software you want to use is Power Mac native.

You already know, of course, that you can't just switch the card on in the control panel; you also have to restart the computer. According to Apple, however, using Restart from the Special menu isn't enough. You actually have to shut down the Mac and then turn it on again.

Can I upgrade my Power Macintosh to a newer model?

▷ ☐ See FAQ 24-6, "Can I upgrade my Power Macintosh to a newer model?"

14-7

What is the Modern Memory Manager?

▷ ☐ See FAQ 6-15, "What is the Modern Memory Manager?"

14-8

Should I get a clock-chip accelerator for my Power Mac?

▷ ☐ See FAQ 24-7, "I've heard about these 'clock-chip accelerators' for the Power Mac. Do they work?"

14-9

14-10

Can I use my old memory SIMMs in a Power Mac?

▽ **Yes, if it's a pretty recent model.**

Memory upgrade boards (SIMMs) come in different speeds and different sizes. If your old Mac is one of the models listed below, the SIMM size is already right for the Power Mac — 72 pins per card. (Older Macs, such as the Mac II series, use a 30-pin memory card, which won't fit the Power Mac.)

You also have to worry about the SIMM's speed — how fast it delivers information to the Mac's brain. It's OK to have a SIMM that's faster than is called for, but installing a slower one is asking for trouble.

These are the models whose memory chips will work in the Power Mac 6100, 7100, and 8100 models.

- ✦ LC III
- ✦ Performa 450 through 467
- ✦ LC 475, LC 520 and higher
- ✦ Quadra 605 through 650, 800, and AV models
- ✦ Centris (all models)

All bets are off, however, if you're inquiring about the 1995 PCI-slot Power Mac line, such as the 9500. They require a new type of memory chip called DIMMs; your old memory won't work.

See also FAQ 4-72, "What's a SIMM?"

See also Chapter 24,"Upgrading the Thing."

14-11

I just bought a Power Mac, and my old monitor doesn't work!

▽ **Right — Apple changed the video signal.**

The Power Mac (and Quadra AV) monitor jack provides a signal different from that provided by all previous models. The jack lacks the so-called *sync on green* signal that most pre-Power Mac monitors require.

Call the company that made your screen; there may be a replacement cable or video card that will make your old monitor work with your new Mac. Unfortunately, in some cases, a new monitor is the only solution.

Why am I getting "No FPU" error messages? Doesn't my Power Mac have an FPU chip?

 See FAQ 18-6, "Why do I get 'No Coprocessor Installed' errors? My Mac *has* an FPU!"

I can't connect to America Online anymore!

▽ **It's a memory thing.**

AOL needs more memory on a Power Mac than on previous models. Allot more RAM to the America Online application, bringing the total to 2000K, as described in Appendix C.

If you don't have two megabytes of RAM to spare, you can use America Online at its regular memory setting. But first, open the Memory control panel, turn off the Modern Memory Manager, and restart the computer.

See also FAQ 6-1, "What should I do about these 'not enough memory messages?"

See also Appendix C, "Troubleshooting Cheat Sheet."

I read something about a bug that makes Power Macs slow. What's the story?

▽ **You're referring to the NuBus data-transfer bug, no doubt.**

Because of a design flaw, when the Mac tries to transfer huge amounts of information between its brain and an installed NuBus card, the speed is actually slightly slower than it would be on a Quadra. This problem is present in every Power Mac 6100, 7100, and 8100/80 (but not the faster 8100 models).

This problem only affects you if you bought a NuBus card for processing digital video, such as the Radius VideoVision Studio board. For all other purposes, it's unlikely that you'd ever even notice.

Should I sell my old Power Mac and get one of the ones with PCI slots?

 Maybe in three years.

The big news in the second generation of Power Macs is not just their faster chips; it's also that the time-honored NuBus slot (a kind of expansion slot that has been in every Macintosh since the Mac II) is dead. It has been replaced by a similar kind of slot known as PCI. Just by looking, you almost can't tell the difference between a PCI slot (or a PCI card that goes into it) and a NuBus slot (or a NuBus card).

So why would Apple bother? Money. PCI slots (and cards) are common in the IBM-compatible world. Therefore, a lot more of them are available, and for much less money. For example, a NuBus video card on the Mac (for making richer colors and faster display on your monitor) may cost $1000 or more. The first PCI video card for the Power Mac only costs about $200. There's also a technical advantage: PCI cards can transfer information faster than NuBus can.

However, at least for the next few years, the 18 million Macs that have NuBus cards will still greatly outnumber the newer models. NuBus cards will still be available in great numbers and variety; not only that, but you can buy an adapter that lets one kind of card fit the other kind of slot. It isn't, therefore, worth upgrading your Mac just to get PCI. (Digital video editors who need enormous transfer speeds may disagree.)

☐ See also Chapter 24, "Upgrading the Thing"

Why can't I switch my monitor to black and white?

▽ **It's a feature, not a bug.**

On the Power Mac, you might have noticed that there are actually *two* places you can plug a monitor: one, with a funny jack, in the row of other jacks on the back panel; and another, more standard jack, way up high on the back panel by itself.

You probably plugged your monitor into the standard jack, which is the only visible portion of the PDS video card that comes in every non-AV Power Mac. That's the problem: The regular jack can only be set to 256 colors or higher. No black and white, no 4- or 16-color mode. See Figure 14-3.

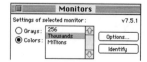

Figure 14-3: On a non-AV Power Mac, you may be shocked to discover that, for the first time in Macintosh history, you can't set your screen to black and white.

If you can't stand working in color, you have two choices:

◆   Get the adapter cable that lets you plug the monitor into the built-in video jack at the bottom of the case, which doesn't have that problem.

◆   Upgrade your Power Mac to the AV version, which also doesn't limit you to that more colorful existence.

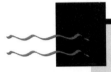

EAQ: Embarrassingly Asked Questions

Why won't this computer turn on?

(A true story from a Macintosh technician.)

I am a service tech.

I received a desperate call from a woman about 75 miles away. Symptom: The Mac was dead — no lights, no display, no ringie-dingie, nada. My first question to this lady was, "Have you verified that it is plugged in to a working power outlet?" She was so insulted, she just about ripped my lungs out over the phone.

I jumped into my van and drove the 75 miles to this customer's site. As I was getting out of the van, a little voice in my head said, "Leave your tools in the van." So I did.

When I walked in and saw the setup, I saw the problem immediately. The computer was plugged into one of those multi-adapters that lets you plug in half of your house into a single outlet. It was falling out of the wall, dangling at about a 45-degree angle!

The lady was standing there, breathing fire by this time. I laid my hands on top of the monitor and stated loudly, "If you believe in the Lord Jesus Christ, BE HEALED!," and at the same time, I kicked the plug into the wall while slapping the top of the monitor. Lo and behold, everything went beep, the monitor lit up, and everything was OK. I pulled out my service book, wrote on the ticket "I healed it," and left.

She never called again.

In the Sound Control Panel, my Sound In setting keeps reverting back to Microphone.

▽ It's a bug. Get and install System Update 3.0.

    See also FAQ 1-32, "Where do I get Apple software updates?"

    See also FAQ 28-3, "How do I find a file I want to download?"

Why does my Power Mac sometimes take so long to start up?

▽ Because it wasn't shut down normally last time.

AV and Power Macs perform a lengthy disk-integrity check if they start up after having been shut down improperly (for example, after crashing). You'll notice the extra delay between the appearance of the happy Mac icon and the "Welcome to Power Macintosh" message.

When I leave some of my SCSI devices off, I get crashes. This never happened on my old Mac.

▽ The Power Mac's SCSI circuitry is much more sensitive; keep all your SCSI devices on.

The new sensitivity makes possible new speed, too, so your switching to a Power Mac wasn't a total loss.

What is a type 11 error?

▷   See FAQ 18-5, "What's a Type 11 error?"

CHAPTER

15

PowerBooks

They're small, they're compact, they're the only Macs you can get that aren't pale corporate gray. They're the most desirable laptops in the world — and they inspire a disproportionate number of the world's frequently asked questions.

Hey! How come my battery only lasts an hour?

 Because there's no truth in advertising. But these tips may help.

Yeah, yeah, I know: The brochure said that you could use your PowerBook for "up to three hours" on one charge of its battery. In fact, you *can* get three hours per battery — if you don't touch your Mac all during that time. Trouble is, if you try to *use* the thing, you only get an hour or so.

In rough order of battery-sapping potential, here are the culprits, and what you can do about them.

✦ **AppleTalk.** This feature alone sucks away about 30 minutes per charge. AppleTalk, of course, is that amazing feature that lets Macs talk to each other, and to laser printers, over network wiring. But when you're on the airplane, all AppleTalk does is use up your juice by frantically looking for the network that isn't there.

Turning AppleTalk off is easy. Choose Chooser from the menu and then click the AppleTalk Inactive button. Turn AppleTalk back on, if you need it, when you're back at the office and plugged in.

✦ **The hard drive.** Making these platters spin at 3600 rpm takes a considerable amount of energy. Of course, trying to avoid using your hard drive is like trying to avoid breathing — you *need* your hard drive. Still, you can *minimize* your reliance on the thing, secure in the knowledge that your PowerBook will *stop* spinning the hard drive a few minutes after the last time you used it.

First of all, use any word processor *except* Microsoft Word, which makes the hard drive spin all the time. Second, if you have the Control Strip on your PowerBook (it comes with System 7.5, as well as all PowerBooks from the 500 series on), you can make the hard drive rest at your command; see Figure 15-1.

Figure 15-1: If you put your hard drive to sleep whenever it seems to be spinning needlessly, your battery will last much longer. Click the hard-drive icon on the Control Strip, as shown, and slide onto the little popup command.

Finally, if you're really serious about battery savings, you can run your PowerBook off a *RAM disk*. This technique is clearly in the advanced power-user category. It works only on PowerBooks with six or more megs of RAM. You create a tiny little stripped-down System Folder and copy it (along with whatever program you intend to use) onto a phony, memory-based floppy disk. If you're still interested, this multistep procedure is described in *More Macs For Dummies* and *Macworld Mac & Power Mac Secrets*.

✦ **The screen.** The PowerBook screen's backlighting is another big battery consumer. Turn it down as much as possible if you're trying to conserve juice.

✦ **Accessories.** The keyboard, mouse, modem, and external floppy drive all use battery power. Unplug them if possible. In fact, you should even quit any *program* that uses a modem — such as America Online — as soon as you're offline.

Using the PowerBook control panel (called Portable on older models), you can make several battery-saving adjustments; they're clearly labeled. My guess is, though, that all of them combined will only buy you another ten minutes per charge.

After putting yourself through all of those hoops, don't forget the easiest way of all to double your battery life: Buy a spare and carry it with you.

How long can my PowerBook sleep?

▽ Forever, although the battery will lose its charge after two months.

How do I charge the battery?

▽ It charges whenever the power cord is plugged in.

It doesn't matter whether the PowerBook is on, off, or asleep — it always charges when it's plugged in. It stops charging as soon as it's full.

What's that clicking noise?

▽ It's either the speaker or the hard-disk arm.

Both are designed to save you battery power: After playing the sound, the Mac turns off the speaker, causing a tiny pop sound. Likewise, if your hard drive has just been accessed, the "needle" (read/write head on a movable arm) locks itself off to the side of the disk platter, making a tiny click.

This PowerBook goes to sleep too often!

▽ Then adjust it!

The PowerBook goes to sleep automatically if you haven't actually used it for, say, ten minutes. It's trying to conserve battery power, assuming that you must have walked away to take a phone call or something.

Not only can you adjust the interval before it sleeps, but you can also tell it *never* to sleep when it's plugged into the wall. To do so, open the PowerBook control panel. There, as shown in Figure 15-2, you can modify your laptop's battery-saving behavior. (On older PowerBooks, this control panel is called Portable.)

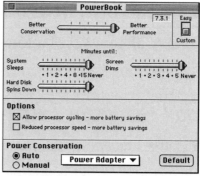

Figure 15-2: When you first open the PowerBook control panel, it may be in its collapsed condition, as at left. See the tiny "switch" between Easy and Custom, on the right side? Drag it downward to the Custom position to expand the window, as shown at right. Then drag the System Sleeps slider to the right to increase the interval before the PowerBook sleeps.

In fact, if you examine the bottom part of that control panel's window, you'll see a popup menu. (This feature is only available in PowerBook control panel version 7.2 or later.) It offers only two choices: Battery and Power Adapter. In other words, you can establish a sleep delay *independently* for those two situations — when your PowerBook is running from its battery and when it's plugged in. To prevent the PowerBook from sleeping when it's plugged in, choose Power Adapter from the popup menu, and move the System Sleeps slider all the way to the right (to the Never position).

The darned thing won't go to sleep by itself!

▽   **It's either doing something or it has been told not to sleep.**

The PowerBook won't go to sleep if it's busy — sending or receiving using the fax/modem, connected to a monitor, in a dock (Duos only), being used as a SCSI device (SCSI disk mode), minding the network (because AppleTalk is on), and so on.

If that doesn't explain your problem, then perhaps somebody has told it, using the PowerBook control panel, *not* to sleep. See FAQ 15-5 for details.

Can I move my PowerBook while it's on?

▼ **Yes, but preferably when the hard drive isn't spinning.**

If your PowerBook has the Control Strip installed, you can see when the drive is spinning (such as when you're opening or saving a document). Otherwise, you'll just have to listen for it. In any case, if you jostle the hard drive while it's in use, you run the risk of bumping the read/write head against the disk's platters, which could damage the drive or your data.

    See also FAQ 15-1, "Hey! How come my battery only lasts an hour?"

How come my new 500-series PowerBook battery won't charge?

▼ **Its "intelligent battery" isn't very smart. Try these steps.**

The PowerBook 520 and 540 models (and their color counterparts) use a special "intelligent battery" that's sometimes a little too smart for its own good. If the battery's charge is too low when you buy it, it may never charge. Do this:

1. Put the questionable battery into the right-side battery compartment; leave the left compartment empty. See if the right-side battery charges now (by looking for the lightning-bolt icon on the Control Strip).

2. The PowerBook gives up after about ten minutes. If the battery still won't charge after ten minutes, take it out and put it back in, which prompts the PowerBook to try charging again.

3. Still no luck? Repeat that in-and-out process four more times.

4. If nothing has worked so far, you need a replacement battery. Call (800) SOS-APPL.

Do I need a screen saver?

▼ **No; a PowerBook screen can't get permanent burn-in.**

If you leave the same image on the screen for days, it may appear to have formed a permanent ghost — but turn the PowerBook off for a few hours, and the screen will fix itself.

I can't get this PowerBook to work with SCSI.

▽ **Decide what you want to accomplish, then be sure you have the correct cable.**

A PowerBook can actually do two different things, SCSI-wise. It can accommodate a CD-ROM player or a scanner, just like any Macintosh. But it can also *be* a SCSI device, serving as an external hard drive for *another* Macintosh. This peculiar arrangement, where your expensive laptop is reduced to serving as a glorified hard disk, is known as *SCSI disk mode*. You can do SCSI disk mode with all recent PowerBook models, several older ones (100, 160, 165, 165c, 180, 180c, for example), and a Duo in a MiniDock.

The thing is, a PowerBook doesn't have the same kind of SCSI jack as a desktop Mac. Instead of the wide, low-slung connector with thumb screws on each side, you get a strange-looking little square doodad. To use it at all, you have to buy a special adapter cable. And, as you could probably have predicted, each of these two scenarios — where the PowerBook is a computer, and where the PowerBook is an accessory — requires a *different* special adapter cable.

When the PowerBook is the computer

When you want to connect a SCSI peripheral gadget *to* your PowerBook (a CD-ROM, scanner, external hard drive, and so on), you need an **Apple HDI-30 SCSI System Cable** — a fat, light-gray cable with 29 pins on the PowerBook end (and a very wide 50-pin connector at the other end).See Appendix C for more about SCSI chain rules.

For now, however, if you follow these rules, you should have no problem using the laptop with external SCSI gizmos:

✦ A PowerBook needs a terminator plug at the end of the SCSI adapter cable, where it attaches to the first SCSI appliance. If you're attaching a *chain* of SCSI devices, a *second* terminator plug is still supposed to be on the last device of the chain (for a total of two).

✦ The SCSI address of the PowerBook's internal hard drive is 0, exactly as with a desktop Mac.

✦ Turn on the PowerBook last.

When the PowerBook is the external device

To make the PowerBook a slave to a regular desktop Mac, you need the **Apple HDI-30 SCSI Disk Adapter**. This cable is *dark* gray, its connector has 30 pins instead of 29, and the far end is a 25-pin connector that mates with a standard desktop Mac SCSI jack.

Remember, your laptop is about to serve as an external SCSI hard drive. It must follow all the usual rules of SCSI gadgetry, including having a unique SCSI address number. And how do you change the SCSI ID of a computer? There's a control panel for just this purpose. It's called PowerBook Setup on most models. (On older PowerBooks, it's simply called PowerBook.) Figure 15-3 shows the idea.

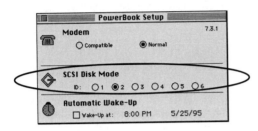

Figure 15-3: Make sure your PowerBook has a SCSI number between 1 and 6. Make sure that you don't duplicate the number of another SCSI gadget, such as your desktop Mac's internal CD-ROM (which is usually 3).

Finally, turn everything off. Connect the adapter cable to the PowerBook (or, if it's a Duo, to the MiniDock), and attach a terminator plug at the far end. Connect the terminated end to either the desktop Mac (via a standard SCSI cable) or the end of the SCSI chain. (Nobody said this was simple!)

When you turn on the PowerBook (which you must do first), a bizarre sight greets you: An enormous diamond-shaped SCSI logo bounces around the PowerBook screen like a screen saver. Inside the logo is a huge number that identifies the PowerBook's SCSI address. When you turn on your desktop Mac, the PowerBook's icon appears on your desktop, ready for accessing as the world's most expensive external hard drive.

When you have lots of stuff to copy between the PowerBook and another Mac, there's no faster or simpler method than SCSI Disk Mode. When you're finished, shut down the desktop Mac first; then turn off the PowerBook by pressing the power button for two full seconds.

I hate this trackball! It's all jerky and sticky.

 It must need cleaning.

All day long you rub your grubby fingers on the top of that ball, then promptly roll the grease and grime down into the PowerBook interior. You'd get a little jerky, too.

To solve the problem, turn the ring around the ball, pushing hard counterclockwise. When the ring comes out, remove and rinse the ball. More importantly, though, go after the caked-on crud and little dust bunnies that you'll see on the little rollers inside the cavity. Use a bright light and tweezers. When everything's clean, put the ball back in, put the ring back on, and enjoy your rejuvenated Macintosh.

15-11

Should I buy a battery conditioner?

▽ Nope; you can do it yourself.

If you always use your PowerBook plugged in, skip this one. If you always use your battery up completely and then charge it completely before using it again, skip this also.

If you deplete the battery part way, then charge it, however, you may be inadvertently shortening its life by creating the "memory effect." That's where the battery gets confused as to where its actual full and empty points are.

To avoid this problem, *condition* the battery every 15 chargings or so. Let it drain completely, ignoring the warning messages, until the PowerBook blinks to sleep — and then charge the battery completely before using the PowerBook again. (This applies to all models except the PowerBook 100; it has a different kind of battery.)

Uh-oh. Why isn't my PowerBook starting up?

▽ Either the battery or the Power Manager is dead.

Here's the usual thinking: "Oh — the battery probably died in its sleep. I'll just plug the power cord into the wall." But even when you plug it in, the PowerBook still won't start up. Little-known answer: *The battery must charge for at least ten minutes*, even when you're using the power cord, before the PowerBook can start up again.

If, even after charging the battery awhile, the PowerBook still won't start, then maybe the Power Manager is confused. Read the next FAQ.

And if *that* doesn't work, call (800) SOS-APPL and schedule a repair.

My PowerBook won't sleep/start/charge/track my trackpad right!

▽ It's time to reset the Power Manager.

Much as it may sound like a Saturday morning cartoon character, the Power Manager is actually some circuitry that handles the PowerBook's various sources of electricity. When the Power Manager is corrupted, all kinds of strange havoc may result: The laptop may run on battery but not AC power (or vice versa), the battery life may drop overnight, the PowerBook may shut off intermittently, and so on. Here's how you straighten it out.

PowerBook 150

Unplug the PowerBook and remove the battery. Hold down the Forced Shutdown switch on the back panel for about 20 seconds.

Reinstall the battery and power cord, then press and release the Forced Shutdown switch again to power on.

PowerBook 100 and 500 series

Remove the battery from the PowerBook *and* unplug the power cord. Leave the laptop in this energy-deprived state for five minutes. Then:

✦ If it's a PowerBook 160, 165, or 180-something, briefly press the power button about four times.

✦ If it's a PowerBook 140, 145, or 170, straighten two paper clips. Locate the tiny holes on the back panel, next to the power button. Insert the straightened paper clips into both holes simultaneously, pressing the recessed buttons (commonly known as the Reset and Interrupt buttons) for about ten seconds.

✦ If it's a PowerBook 500-something, simultaneously hold down the Control, Option, ⌘, and Power keys for about five seconds.

Reinstall the battery, plug the power cord into the wall, connect it to the PowerBook, and try turning it on again.

PowerBook Duo series

Locate the capsule-shaped power button on the *back* of the Duo; press it steadily for about a minute. Then try turning the thing on normally.

I can't see my cursor when I'm editing. Any suggestions?

 Yeah. Get FixCursor.

15-15

FixCursor is a little system extension, free, that you can download from a service like America Online. It fattens up the cursor whenever it's near text, as shown in Figure 15-4.

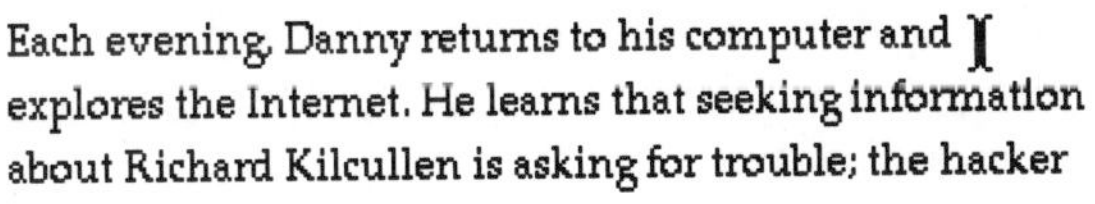

Each evening, Danny returns to his computer and ⌶ explores the Internet. He learns that seeking information about Richard Kilcullen is asking for trouble; the hacker

Figure 15-4: The FixCursor extension makes the PowerBook cursor easier to see.

And if you have trouble *finding* your cursor, consider this quick trick: Just slap the trackball or trackpad frantically toward the upper-left corner of the screen. Eventually, sure enough, your pointer will appear there.

My PowerBook's frozen!

▽ ### Here are the secret keystrokes.

First, try pressing ⌘-Option-Esc; if the gods are smiling, you'll be asked if you want to *force quit* whatever program is in front. If it was only that *program* that froze, and not the entire laptop, you'll arrive back at the Finder. This technique gives you the chance to save your work in whatever programs are still open.

If that doesn't work, then the PowerBook itself has probably frozen. While holding down the Control and ⌘ keys, press the power-on button to restart the machine.

How do I hook up a large screen to this PowerBook?

▽ ### It's pretty easy, actually. Use the included adapter cable to plug it right in.

Almost any PowerBook with model number 160 or higher has a video jack on the back — an inch-wide connector with 15 tiny holes. Into this jack you can plug in a regular desktop monitor and enjoy full-screen color, even if you only have a grayscale PowerBook. You can't connect as *big* a monitor as you would to a desktop Mac, and it can't show as many colors. Furthermore, the PowerBook can't run on battery power when an external screen is attached; it must be plugged in.

The low-cost PowerBook models (numbered 170 and 140 through 150) don't have that monitor jack. You can, in theory, connect a big monitor via those models' SCSI jack, but you won't like the result. It's expensive, clunky, and very slow. Financially speaking, you'd probably come out ahead selling your old model and buying one with a monitor jack.

Once you have the external screen connected, you have to make a couple of decisions. The first one has to do with your PowerBook's *built-in* screen. Do you want to see the *same thing* on the large screen as you see on the PowerBook screen? Although that's a handy arrangement when you're giving a speech to a room full of people, it's kind of a waste when you're home, because that "mirroring" arrangement means that a large part of your (usually larger) external screen is blank.

Open your PowerBook Display control panel, as shown in Figure 15-5, and choose which arrangement you want; video mirroring *on* is when the PowerBook and the external screen show the same thing.

When video mirroring is *off*, a strange thing happens: The external monitor acts as an extension of the PowerBook screen. If you roll the pointer off the right side of the PowerBook screen, it reappears at the left side of the external monitor!

See also FAQ 9-12, "How do I set up multiple monitors?"

See also FAQ 15-19, "I'm using an external monitor, and the picture is way too short."

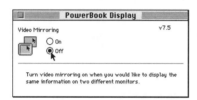

Figure 15-5: Use this control panel to specify what you want to see on the external monitor.

Video Mirroring off

Video Mirroring on

Isn't there any way to make an external monitor, not the PowerBook, be the "main" screen?

15-18

▽   Yes. Use the Monitors control panel.

In the Monitors control panel, if everything is properly connected, you'll see something like Figure 15-6. The tiny icons represent the two screens, PowerBook and external.

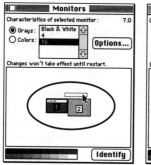 

Figure 15-6: Drag the tiny menu bar to make the external monitor the main screen (left). At right: You can also rearrange the monitor icons to reflect their actual positions on your desk.

See the tiny menu bar on the PowerBook screen? Carefully drag it onto the top of the external-monitor icon, also as shown in the figure. From now on, your programs will use the external screen as their home base, including putting their menus and primary windows there.

If that arrangement — having a lame-duck, essentially unused PowerBook screen sitting off to the left of your full-screen monitor — bothers you, consider putting the monitor to the *left* of your PowerBook. To inform the Mac about the change, drag the little icons into the appropriate new positions, as in Figure 15-6. From now on, the *PowerBook* screen is considered the extension, off to the right side of the big monitor.

See also FAQ 9-12, "How do I set up multiple monitors?"

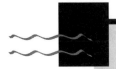

RAQ: Rarely Asked Question

I have a monitor attached to my PowerBook. Can I make the happy-Mac startup icon appear on the external monitor?

Yes. Open the Monitors control panel. If you press and hold the Option key, you'll see a really tiny happy-Mac logo show up on the tiny PowerBook-screen icon. Drag that microscopic smiling Mac icon over to the external-monitor icon. From now on, the startup process will appear on the external screen, not the PowerBook.

I'm using an external monitor, and the picture is way too short.

 Open the Monitors control panel and turn off Video Mirroring.

The purpose of video mirroring is to reproduce the image from the PowerBook screen on the external monitor. While you may not realize it, the dimensions of most PowerBooks with model numbers below 500 aren't the standard 640 by 480 screen dots (pixels); they're actually 640 by *400*, over an inch shorter. Therefore, when that image appears on a standard 14-inch external monitor, the missing inch is unusually obvious. The only solution is to turn off video mirroring, as explained in FAQ 15-17.

How do I transfer stuff between my PowerBook and my other Mac?

 See FAQ 25-1, "How can I connect two Macs?"

15-21

How can I set it up so an incoming fax wakes up the PowerBook?

▽   If it's a Duo or PowerBook 500-something, you can't. Otherwise, use the PowerBook Setup control panel.

In that control panel, you'll find a checkbox called Wake on Ring. If your PowerBook has a built-in fax/modem, that option lets you use your PowerBook as a fax machine — when the phone rings, the sleeping PowerBook wakes up to receive the fax. (Having received a fax, the PowerBook won't go back to sleep by itself, however.)

For some reason, this feature has been replaced in the Duo and 500 series. The new feature lets you specify a particular date and time that you want the PowerBook to wake up — not exactly the same thing.

15-22

How can I prevent my PowerBook from crashing when I wake it up?

▽   Nobody seems to know for sure, but here are some ideas.

This strange phenomenon — a freeze or crash when you wake up a sleeping PowerBook — only affects a small percentage of PowerBook owners. And nobody can ever seem to make it happen on cue, let alone devise a solution that works for everybody.

One Apple technician I spoke to indicated, believe it or not, that this freeze-on-wake syndrome is a result of having *Microsoft* programs on the hard drive. He indicated that the problem was a conflict with the Power Book's automatic backlight-dimming feature; turn it off (using the PowerBook control panel), and the problem is gone. This worked for me.

If that doesn't work, try this alternate solution, which has also solved the problem for many people.

1. Back up your entire PowerBook hard drive.

2. Get the latest version of the program called Apple HD SC Setup. It comes with every Mac, including your PowerBook; a more recent version may well be available on America Online or another service.

3. Use Apple HD SC Setup to *reformat* your hard drive. Reformatting, of course, involves *erasing your full disk,* so don't proceed until you have a backup.

4. Install System 7.5. (If your PowerBook didn't come with this version of the System Folder, you can buy System 7.5 from any Mac mail-order company or computer store.)

See also FAQ 1-32, "Where do I get Apple software updates?"

Can I put my machine through the scanning machine at the airport?

▽ **Yes. It's absolutely 100 percent safe.**

Don't put your floppy disks through the airport scanner, though.

Can I use my PowerBook overseas?

▽ **Yes, but you may need to buy an outlet adapter.**

PowerBooks automatically adjust to the voltage and frequency of non-American wall outlets. However, you may need to visit a Radio Shack to buy an adapter for the actual *shape* of foreign wall outlets. For example, the outlets in most of Europe have two *round* holes; you'll need a little plug adapter to accommodate your PowerBook's power cord.

Do I have to turn the PowerBook off to attach things?

▽ **Depends on what you mean by "things."**

You can freely plug and unplug the **printer cable, external modem, telephone line** (for the internal modem), and the **power cord,** even when the PowerBook is on. The **keyboard, mouse,** and (for the Duo) **floppy drive** or **MiniDock** should only be attached or removed when the computer is *asleep* (or off). You must *shut the PowerBook down* to add or remove **SCSI devices** or the **monitor.** You must shut down the Duo before inserting it into the full-sized **Duo Dock.**

The plastic door broke off the back of my PowerBook!

▽ **Call (800) SOS-APPL, and they'll send you a replacement.**

15-27

Why won't my PowerBook print on my StyleWriter?

▽ **Probably because your PowerBook has an internal modem.**

If so, open the PowerBook control panel and make sure that it's set to "external modem." If that doesn't solve your problem, see Chapter 11.

15-28

My PowerBook only has one printer/modem jack. How am I supposed to print?

▽ **Take a deep breath, and read this.**

Some PowerBooks, such as the Duo, the PowerBook 150, and the 500 series, only have a single jack on the back, whereas desktop Mac models have *two* (separate modem and printer jacks).

This jack shortage makes life considerably more interesting. For example, suppose you have a PostScript laser printer, which means that you can't print unless AppleTalk is turned on. (The on/off switch is in the Chooser.) Every time you want to use an external modem, you must go to the Chooser and turn AppleTalk off — and you must reverse the procedure when you want to print again. (It's times like those when the System 7.5 control strip, with its handy AppleTalk on/off button, seems especially valuable.)

Here's an even tougher problem. Suppose you have a built-in modem, and you want to print on a StyleWriter II. When you open the Chooser, you're supposed to select either the printer port or the modem port! Well, you only have one port, so which do you select? Here's the drill:

1. If your modem is an *Apple Express Modem:* Open the Express Modem control panel; select **Use External Modem.** (If you have a Duo 280 or 280c, your Express Modem control panel offers a different set of choices; yours should be set to External.) Then open the PowerBook Setup control panel; select **Normal.**

    If your modem is a *Global Village PowerPort:* Open the Global Village PowerPort 500 control panel (or PowerPort for Duo) control panel. Click the Configure Port button; in the following dialog box, choose **Normal.**

2. Open the Chooser. If you have a Duo, select the **AppleTalk Inactive** button. (You don't have to do that if it's a PowerBook 500-something.) Click the StyleWriter icon on the left side of the Chooser window. On the right side, click the **printer/modem** icon; if you must choose between the printer or modem-port icons, as you must for the StyleWriter II, click the **modem** icon.

16

Duos

A Duo, of course, is a smaller, lighter version of the PowerBook. It's so slim because it doesn't have a floppy disk drive like other PowerBooks, the premise being that you won't have much use for floppy disks when you're on the plane or in the meeting. Instead, you leave the floppy drive at home on your desk. In other words, this is a two-part PowerBook — a Duo.

If I want a Duo, I have to buy a Dock, right?

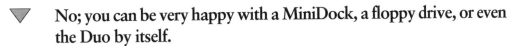

▽ No; you can be very happy with a MiniDock, a floppy drive, or even the Duo by itself.

The Duo has two jacks on its back panel: a modem/printer port and a wide 130-pin slot. This special connector can accommodate any of three attachments: a Duo Dock, a MiniDock, or a floppy drive adapter. To use a Duo successfully, you don't *need* a full dock; indeed, you may have a great time without *any* of those accessories.

The full-sized, full-priced *Duo Dock* is a hulking, two-tone desktop machine. You close your laptop and insert it into the dock's opening, whereupon it gets sucked in like a videocassette. At this point, your Duo has become the brain of a full-fledged desktop Macintosh system, complete with an external color monitor, a real keyboard and mouse, and whatever else you've attached to it.

A less expensive *MiniDock* provides almost all of the same features — in a compact gadget about the size of a hole punch. It has the same back-panel jacks as the full dock. The only advantages of the big dock are:

✦ It can accommodate NuBus cards.

✦ You can upgrade its video memory.

✦ It has a built-in floppy drive.

My guess is that very few people ever avail themselves of those first two features. And you can always attach a floppy drive to a MiniDock.

If you don't particularly care about attaching a large external monitor or SCSI devices, here's an even simpler idea: Just get a *floppy drive adapter* alone. It lets you attach a floppy drive as well as a keyboard/mouse ensemble.

In fact, if you already have another Macintosh, you may not need to buy *anything* to go with your Duo. You can connect it to your other Mac by network, and add or remove software from the Duo that way.

How do I back up my work if I don't have a floppy drive?

▽   **Over a network, via e-mail, or on paper.**

The easiest method, of course, is to connect your Duo to another Mac. You can connect them directly with a SCSI cable (see FAQ 15-20) or over a network (see FAQ 25-1). (The latter method doesn't even require any dock — the network cable goes into the Duo's built-in printer/modem port.)

If you're on the road or on a budget, and if your Duo has a modem, here's another tactic: Send your documents to yourself by e-mail! When you send a file as an attachment to an e-mail on America Online or a similar service, you are, in fact, sending that file to another computer somewhere. You've just made a backup. At any time, you can sign on, read your own e-mail, and click the Download button to retrieve your own file.

Finally, of course, you can always print something—or fax it, if your Duo has a modem. Hardcopy: the original backup system.

See also FAQ 25-1, "How do I connect two Macs?"

The Duo Dock won't accept my Duo.

▽ Shut the Duo down, and open its back panel, before inserting it into the dock.

Also make sure that the dock is plugged in and unlocked (using the little key that came with it). If, after checking those conditions, your dock still won't gracefully slurp up the Duo, try this:

1. Unplug the power cord from the dock.

2. Push the Duo gently into the dock. While maintaining pressure on the Duo, plug in the dock.

The latch mechanism should spring to life and pull the Duo in.

My Duo's space bar sometimes doesn't register, especially if I'm typing fast.

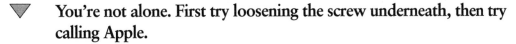

▽ You're not alone. First try loosening the screw underneath, then try calling Apple.

To loosen that center screw on the bottom of the Duo, you need a Torx screwdriver, which you can get from a hardware store. Use it to loosen the screw by a half turn.

If that doesn't fix the keyboard problem, call (800) SOS-APPL. The technician will arrange to put in one of the redesigned Duo keyboards that's less susceptible to flakiness.

What does the switch on my Duo battery do?

▽ Nothing. It's supposed to help you remember whether the battery is charged or not.

This mysterious sliding switch confused so many people that Apple took it off the Type II and Type III Duo batteries shipped with later models.

16-6

I lost the keys to my Duo Dock! Can I get replacements?

▽ **Yes, especially if you lost only one.**

The keys provided with your dock are a pretty good idea. If you work in an office, you don't want somebody to wander by, press the Eject button on the dock, and walk away with your PowerBook.

If you still have one of two keys that came with your dock, write to: Fort Lock Corporation, 3000 N. River Road, River Grove, IL 60171, (708) 456-1100. You'll need to provide the code number from the tag that came with the keys.

If, on the other hand, you have lost *both* keys (and the code number), you have to get a whole new lock-and-key mechanism. Call your Apple dealer.

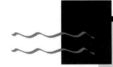

UAQ: Unbelievably Asked Question

What's that beeping?

Another incredible, but true, tale from a Mac consultant:

One customer kept reporting a problem to us. She repeatedly complained that her Mac was beeping at her. The beeping would happen at the strangest and most random times — sometimes even when nobody was at the computer. This random behavior, of course, made our trouble-shooting by phone much more difficult. There wasn't much we could do, other than to ask her to call us the next time the problem occurred.

She did. This time, we were ready. We had her close her windows, quit her programs, and even turn off the Mac. The beeping continued!

From that point, it didn't take long to discover the source of the beeping. Her coworker's pager had been dropped under her desk.

17

Performas and Other Special Macs

W hen the Performa was invented a few years ago, it was a ploy to introduce Macs to non-techie families who wouldn't be caught dead in a computer store. The concept was: Put everything — computer, keyword, monitor, software, even a modem — into one box and sell it for one discounted price.

Today, however, the Performa has shed its reputation as a dumbed-down Mac. It's now sold in computer stores; its specialized, easier system software is now found on the mainstream Mac lines; and even the Mac elite admits that buying a Performa saves money over assembling the components yourself.

At the end of this chapter, you'll also find a few frequently asked questions about other particular Mac models.

Hey! There are no system disks with this thing!

 That's right — you're supposed to create your own system disks using the Apple Backup program.

No wonder your Performa was so inexpensive. Omitting system disks was one way Apple saved itself (and you) money. Of course, if your Performa has a built-in CD-ROM drive, as most do today, then you received something better than a pile of floppies: A system *CD-ROM* disc. You're in good shape.

If your Performa doesn't have a CD-ROM drive, you're supposed to buy a big stack of blank floppy disks. You're supposed to run the program called Apple Backup, which came installed on your hard drive. You're supposed to choose a backup option — either to copy the System Folder alone or to copy the entire hard drive, which takes enough floppies to reach from your desk to the moon.

If you ask me, it's probably worth backing up only the System Folder using Apple Backup. Then copy the free programs (actually, only the ones you care about) onto whatever floppies you have left — manually (or using a real backup program, such as Redux Deluxe).

And by the way: If something should go wrong with your system software before you've had a chance to back it up, call (800) SOS-APPL. They'll send you a genuine set of system disks by overnight delivery.

See also FAQ 3-2, "How should I back up my files?"

What are all these free programs? Are they any good?

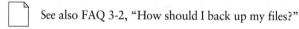 **Actually, they are pretty good.**

The free software that comes with a Performa varies according to which model you bought. (That's the difference between, say, the 6115, 6118, and so on.) You can generally count on finding ClarisWorks and Quicken on the hard drive — two outstanding programs — plus a bunch of educational and entertainment titles.

How come this fax modem won't receive faxes?

▽ **They want more money from you.**

The deal may be different by the time you read this. But for most of 1994 and 1995, at least, the Global Village fax/modem you get with your Performa can only *send* faxes, not receive them.

For an additional two-digit dollar amount, however, Global Village will send you a software upgrade that lets your fax/modem receive faxes (and gives you many more features). Instructions were included somewhere among all those boxes and manuals.

How do I get rid of At Ease?

▽ **I don't care, just as long as you turn it *off* first.**

To turn off version 1, open the At Ease Setup control panel and click the Off button. To turn off version 2, launch the At Ease program, and click *its* Off button.

The point is, *don't just throw pieces of At Ease into the trash*. You will completely confuse your hard drive, and you'll need a hard-drive utility program to resurrect it. Trash the pieces of At Ease — but only *after* turning At Ease off.

(Alternatively, you can run the Installer on the original master disks, if you have them. Option-click the Install button to remove At Ease, according to the manual's instructions.)

Can I remove the Launcher?

▽ **Yes. The procedure varies depending on how old your Performa is.**

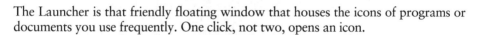

The Launcher is that friendly floating window that houses the icons of programs or documents you use frequently. One click, not two, opens an icon.

Turning this feature off is simple, but the protocol depends on the version of the Performa software you're using.

- ✦ Purchased since late 1994: You probably have System 7.5. Open your General Controls panel, and turn off the checkbox called "Show Launcher at system startup."

- ✦ Purchased in 1993 or 1994: You probably have a control panel called Performa. If so, open it. You'll find the on/off switch for the Launcher.

- ✦ Purchased before early 1993: Your Control Panels folder includes a control panel called Launcher. Drag it completely out of the System Folder and restart the Mac. You've just turned off *all* of the Performa's special features — the Launcher, the self-hiding Finder, and the Documents folder on the desktop.

How do I add an item to Launcher?

▽ **Once again, it depends on how recent your system software is.**

Open your System Folder. Inside it, you'll find a Launcher Items folder. Anything you put into this Launcher Items folder — an icon or an icon's alias — appears on the Launcher screen. See Figure 17-1 for further advice.

Figure 17-1: If you have one of the newer Launcher versions, you get an added bonus: different Launcher *pages* (left). Click a topic button, and the new page appears. To create a page/button, open the Launcher Items folder inside your System Folder (right). Make a new folder there, named whatever you want, as long as its name is preceded by a bullet symbol (•), which you produce by typing Option-8.

Of course, if your Performa came with System 7.5.1 — or if you had System 7.5 and then installed the System 7.5 Update #1, which *gives* you System 7.5.1 — life with the Launcher is even easier. Just drag any icon directly onto the Launcher window to install it there. (And Option-drag it away to remove it.)

I have a 630-series Mac. Can any IDE drive be used for my computer?

▽ **Yes, with only a few exceptions.**

Certain low-cost Mac models (630-somethings, PowerBook 150, and so on) have a different kind of hard drive inside. Instead of the usual SCSI-format drive, these models have a less expensive type known as IDE. Except that you paid a lower price for your Mac, you'd never know the difference.

IDE drives are very common on non-Macintosh computers. As a result, you might wonder if you can inexpensively upgrade to a larger one. The answer is yes. Just ask, before buying your new IDE drive, whether it meets the following technical qualifications (even if you have no clue what these mean):

✦ Does the IDE drive support the *identify* command?

✦ Does it work at least at *PIO mode 2* performance level?

✦ Is *write caching* on so that auto-reallocation of new spares is invoked?

Apple suggests that drives manufactured by IBM, Quantum, Conner, Seagate, or WD (Western Digital) will give you the best luck. All that remains is for you to figure out where to buy one, and how to install it.

See also Chapter 8, "Hard Disks."

My hard drive formatting program doesn't work on my Performa 630. How come?

▽ **Because the hard drive inside is an IDE drive.**

If you are using an existing copy of, say, Norton Utilities or MacTools, you're right — they won't know what to do with the IDE (not the usual Macintosh SCSI) hard drive inside a 630-something Mac model: LC, Quadra, or Performa. (And the PowerBook 150, too.) To avoid possible problems in formatting, be sure to use the Internal HD Format program that came with your Mac. If you want something more powerful, a few new hard-drive formatting programs (such as the latest Drive7 from Casa Blanca Works) are IDE-savvy; call Mac Connection and inquire.

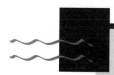

UAQ: Unfortunately Asked Question

How am I supposed to know what file this is?

True story:

An executive secretary, a first-time computer user, devised her own unique file management system. Instead of using descriptive words to name her files, she *numbered* the files (1, 2, 3, and so on) — and kept a notebook listing the file numbers and what the corresponding files were.

This system worked well enough for her; in time, her notebook listed files well over #5000. And it would have continued to work for her had disaster not struck — she lost the notebook! Every single file had to be opened — to find out what it was — and renamed.

Fortunately for her, she was the secretary of an executive who had been there forever, so her job was safe.

Is there any way to turn my LC on from the keyboard?

▽   **Yes. Buy a Power Key.**

A Power Key is a surge-protected, four outlet power strip that turns on when you press the power key on your keyboard (marked by the left-pointing triangle). If your Mac model must be turned on by a back panel switch, and you'd rather turn it on from the keyboard, the Power Key (made by Sophisticated Circuits) is the only option. As an added bonus, your Mac will shut down completely when you use the Shut Down command.

(P.S. — Actually, the Power Key works great on other Mac models, too, in that it turns *all* your appliances — printer, scanner, and all — on and off along with the Mac.)

Isn't there anything I can do to speed up my IIsi?

▽   **Yes — set your Disk Cache to 768 K.**

Open your Memory control panel. Click the arrow buttons until the Disk Cache is set to 768 K. Because of the unusual way the IIsi handles memory and video, the result is a noticeable speedup in onscreen activities like scrolling, opening and closing windows, appearance of graphics and dialog boxes, and so on. IIsi owners swear by this trick.

Will it hurt my Mac to be put on its side?

▷   See FAQ 3-5, "Is it OK to keep my Mac turned on its side?"

PART 4

How to
Fix It

There's plenty to know about how the computer works when everything's working *right.* If you're like most people, however, you're happy to let the inner workings work — and you only raise your hand when things go *wrong.*

Here are five chapters' worth of answers, designed for getting you out of panicked tight squeezes. They cover a broad spectrum of desperate situations: error messages, startup problems, System 7.5 snafus, and other miscellaneous weirdnesses.

18

The Error Message Hall of Fame

Here they come: the most frequently asked of the frequently asked questions. Before delving into these explanations, however, a disclaimer: What we'd all like is a message that says, "You shouldn't have clicked the title bar during printing; there's a bug in this program that makes it crash." What we get is, "Sorry, a system error occurred."

The point is that system crash-type error messages aren't for you. They may pop up in your face, seeming to scream with importance and significance — but they're not supposed to make sense to you. These messages are for the programmers who created your software. As a result, the explanations you're about to read are probably techier than you'd like.

With that disappointing caveat in mind, here we go.

What's a Type 1 error?

 It usually involves out-of-date software — especially extensions.

For example, if you use a 1990 version of, say, After Dark — or any other program — on a new Power Mac, you'll probably get Type 1 errors. The software is simply too old for the hardware. If you've copied programs from an older Mac — especially a System 6 Mac — onto a newer model, and you're getting Type 1 errors, contact the software company and order the latest version.

18-1

Similarly, if you install System 7.5 on a hard drive that has been running System 6 for years, you'll probably get these errors. In this case, it's because your invisible *hard-disk driver* software is too old. Run the program called Apple HD SC Setup that came with the new system software. (It may be called Internal HD Setup on some models.) Of course, you also use a commercial hard drive-formatting program such as HD Toolkit (FWB).

> See also FAQ 18-8, "Isn't there a table someplace that tells what all the error messages mean?"

> See also Appendix C, "Troubleshooting Cheat Sheet."

What's a "bad F-line instruction"?

▽　**It's a bad mistake some programmer made.**

As your software executes hundreds of computer instructions per second, it may enter an *F-line instruction*—a direction to consult the math chip, or *floating point unit* (FPU), attached to your main processor chip. Trouble is, some Mac models don't *have* an FPU chip (see FAQ 4-31). Up pops this message.

But you may as well ignore that explanation; most people encounter the "bad F-line instruction" message on Macs that *do* have an FPU. Or they get the message when running software that *doesn't* require an FPU.

In other words, this message appears most often in error — basically, the Mac lies. Your software may be trying to access a nonexistent memory location, or it may have encountered the letter F in the wrong place in the programmer's code!

If you're getting a lot of this message, try re-installing the program you're using. If that doesn't work, do a "clean install" of the system software, as described in Appendix C.

> See also FAQ 18-6, "Why do I get 'No Co-Processor Installed' errors? My Mac *has* a FPU!"

How come my "Application unexpectedly quit"?

▽　**It's either a memory problem or an extension conflict.**

If a program you were using — either in the foreground or the background — unexpectedly quits, it probably bumped its head against a memory ceiling. It had no choice except to bail out. Try giving it more memory, as described in Appendix C.

If that doesn't seem to be the problem, you probably have an extension conflict. Solving this, too, is explained in Appendix C.

It says, "Application could not be found." What gives?

 You're double-clicking a document of unknown origin.

Possibility # 1: You're trying to open a memo that was written in ClarisWorks, but you don't *have* ClarisWorks. The Mac is letting you know that the program you need to read the file isn't on hand.

Possibility #2: You *do* have the program that created the troublesome document, but the Macintosh has gotten muddled in its little head. It happens sometimes. You need to make it relearn the relationships between your programs and your documents. You do this by "rebuilding the desktop." (See Appendix C.)

Possibility # 3: You're double-clicking a text, graphics, or music file that's so generic that your Mac can't decide *which* of your programs to use. Some file formats, such as plain-text files (for typing) and PICT files (for graphics), can be opened by almost any Mac text or graphics program, respectively. These file formats are terrifically useful, because they let you exchange information among programs. In the case of plain text files (also called ASCII files), they even let you exchange information among different kinds of *computers,* such as Macs and IBM clones. But because the Mac doesn't associate such generic files with any particular program on your hard drive, you get the "application not found" message.

Fortunately, this third scenario is becoming a thing of the past. Starting with System 7.5, a new control panel called Macintosh Easy Open handles this generic-document problem. When you double-click a generic document, Easy Open shows you a *list* of every program you own that *can* open it. You choose which to use to open that mysterious document.

If you don't have Easy Open, you can still get around this generic-document problem manually. Instead of double-clicking the problem *document* icon, launch the program you want to open it with *first.* Then, from within that program, choose Open from the File menu, and select the mystery document *that* way. Figure 18-1 should make this clearer.

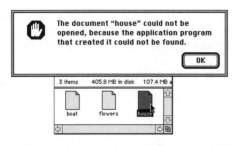

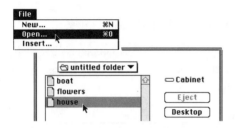

Figure 18-1: Top: When you double-click a standard TIFF graphics file, you'll probably get the "application busy or missing" message. Bottom: One solution is to launch a program that can open it, such as ClarisWorks, and use the Open command. The troublesome file shows up in the list of files.

What's a Type 11 error?

▽ It's a Power Mac-specific, generic error message of the type you can fix with Appendix C.

Technically, a Type 11 message is a *hardware exception* error. Realistically, you have yourself a troublesome extension, a corrupted font, or a Power Mac-hostile program.

To rid yourself of this nasty problem, follow the usual steps described in Appendix C — particularly the clean reinstall of your System Folder.

Why do I get "No Co-Processor Installed" errors? My Mac has an FPU!

▽ Your computer is mistaken; some other bug is at work.

The "No Co-Processor" message almost never appears truthfully. Yet it seems to crop up more than most messages. The reason would be funny, if it weren't so annoying: When some miscellaneous software problem erupts, the Mac rapidly runs through its internal list of error messages, trying to find an accurate description. If it doesn't find anything appropriate to report to you, it throws up its hands and shows you the *last error message* in its list of possibilities. You guessed it: The "No Co-Processor" error is last on the list.

As you can see, the "No Co-Processor" message has absolutely nothing to do with whether or not your Mac has an FPU — or whether or not your software needs one. Other than trying the techniques described in Appendix C, there's little you can learn from this message.

See also FAQ 4-31, "What's an FPU?"

"This is not a Macintosh disk: Do you want to initialize it?"

▷ See FAQ 7-5, "I keep getting a message: 'This disk is unreadable.'"

Isn't there a table someplace that tells what all the error messages mean?

▽ **There is now.**

Again, not much of this makes sense to the nonprogrammer. But so many people have requested this information that I'm printing it here as a public service. I've translated it into plain English to the best of my ability.

As you'll see, sometimes these descriptions provide a clue for action on your part (such as *disk is full*). In others, however, your software has a bug, and you can't do much about it. As you'll read below, all too many such bugs result from programmers failing to clean up after themselves before sending the program into the world — or being unable to anticipate their program's interactions with other software.

There are two categories of error messages. Those with positive numbers are the so-called DS errors (which stands for *deep doo-doo*). These are serious system crashes that require you to restart the machine. Errors with negative numbers aren't so severe; usually you just have to click an OK button to proceed.

ID=01: Bus Error

Think of your Mac's RAM as a wall of post-office boxes, numbered in sequence. Much of what a Mac does is manage the scraps of data in those little memory cubbyholes, shuffling them from one to another at high speeds. The first three DS errors have to do with problems in *memory addressing*, such as when the Mac looks for information in the wrong box.

When the Type 01 error appears, the Mac has tried to access memory that doesn't exist — for example, the program you're using assumed that the Mac has more RAM available that it actually does. As mentioned in FAQ 18-1, the problem is usually that you're using out-of-date software.

ID=02: Address Error

Mac Plus and SE only: Your processor chip has tried to access an odd-numbered memory location when it should have accessed an even-numbered one.

ID=03: Illegal Instruction

Your processor has a fixed, specific vocabulary; if the software issues an instruction using lingo your processor doesn't understand, you get this error message.

ID=04: Zero Divide Error

When programmers test their works in progress, they might deliberately instruct the computer to divide a number by zero, to see how well the program handles errors. Trouble is, they occasionally forget to take this instruction *out*. You are the lucky benefactor.

ID=05: Range Check Error

The software checked to see if a number — part of some internal calculation — is within a certain range. It wasn't.

ID=06: Overflow Error

The Mac allots a certain amount of space for each number it processes. You see this error if a number was too big for the space the software allotted for it.

ID=07: Privilege Violation

For programmers only: Your Mac attempted to process a command in User mode instead of Supervisor mode. Bad move.

ID=08: Trace Mode Error

When they are debugging their newly-written software, programmers sometimes walk through it, line by line, using something called Trace mode. If you see this message, your processor chip has accidentally switched into Trace mode.

ID=9 and ID=10: Line 1010 & 1111 Trap

Once again, the software has issued an instruction that the processor chip doesn't understand.

ID=12: Unimplemented Core Routine

As with the ID=04 error, this results from a leftover instruction from the debugging process.

ID=13: Uninstalled Interrupt

An *interrupt* is a moment during the running of a program when an external device, such as the keyboard or the disk drive, asks for attention. If there aren't any instructions in RAM that tell the Mac how to talk to that device, you get this error message.

ID=15: Segment Loader Error

To conserve memory, a non-Power Mac program is loaded into RAM in se*gments* as needed. A piece of system software called the *segment loader* oversees this swapping process. If, for some reason, the segment loader can't do its thing, this error results.

ID=26–27, 30–31: Missing Packages

A *package* is a ready-to-run set of system software instructions that handles a particular task, such as initializing a disk. If a package is damaged, one of these messages tells you so. You need to perform a "clean reinstall" of your System Folder, as described in Appendix C.

ID=25: Memory Full Error

You've probably run out of memory, although this message may appear erroneously.

ID=26: Bad Program Launch

The Mac couldn't open the program you tried to launch. Try reinstalling it.

ID=20: Stack Ran into Heap

Just as in ID=25, you've probably run out of memory, although this message may appear erroneously.

Negative Error Codes

There are many more negative-numbered error messages than positive. Furthermore, they make even less sense to the nonprogrammer. (Example: "Packet too large or first entry of the write-data structure didn't contain the full 14-byte header." Thanks a bunch.)

Table 18-1 provides the general categories for each number range, along with a few that actually make sense to human beings (such as "bad floppy disk").

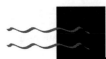

Table 18-1

Negative-numbered errors

Error number	What causes it
0 through –8	General system errors
–9 through –21	Color Manager errors
–17 through –61	System errors involving files and disks (I/O, or *input and output*)
–34	The disk is full.
–35 disk	No such disk, or the Mac can't find the it's looking for.
–37	Something is wrong with the name of a file (for example, the name includes a colon).
–39 is	A corrupted file is on the disk, or the disk having problems.
–41	The file is too big to fit in memory.
–42	Too many files are open.
–44 and –46	The disk is locked.
–53 through –57	Something's wrong with the request for a disk.
–60	Something's wrong with the disk directory.
–64 through –66	Font problems
–64 through –90	Problems reading disks (timing and track troubles).
–91 through –99	AppleTalk errors
–108 through –117	Various memory allocation errors
–120 through –127	HFS errors (disks, directories)
–126 through –128	Menu problems
–130 through –132	More HFS errors
–147 through –158	Color management problems
–185 through –199	Resource Manager errors (problems managing data)
–200 through –232	Problems with sound or sound files
–250 through –261	Problems with the MIDI Manager (music data, used with synthesizers)

"You do not have enough access privileges." Why not?

 Apple is trying to save your System Folder from disaster.

If the problem is what I think it is, you have either a Performa or System 7.5. In both cases, the "not enough privileges" message appears when you try to drag something out of, or into, the System Folder. In families with out-of-control children, this System Folder-protection feature can be a blessing.

If you find this feature annoying, however, it's easy to defeat. Open your Control Panels folder. If you see an icon called Performa, double-click it; otherwise, open the one called General Controls.

In either case, you'll see a checkbox like the one shown in Figure 18-2. Click it so that the X no longer appears. Congratulations: You now *do* have enough access privileges.

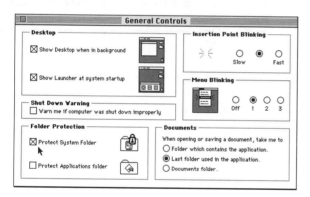

Figure 18-2: The "Protect System Folder" checkbox (lower-left) is what's been annoying you.

Incidentally, there are two less-common circumstances in which you might see this warning. The first is if you keep your programs in a folder called Applications; there's also a "Protect Applications folder" checkbox in the General Controls panel, as you can see in Figure 18-2. When this feature is on, you can't change the Applications folder's contents. Finally, if your Mac is on a network, "access privileges" may refer to permission to examine the hard drives of other people on the network. See FAQ 25-1 for details on giving other people access to your Mac.

I'm double-clicking an icon, but the Mac says "The original item could not be found."

▽   **You're double-clicking an alias, but you've thrown away the original.**

An alias, of course, is a duplicate of a file's *icon,* which lets you, in effect, put one file in more than one place on your hard drive. Whenever you double-click an alias icon, the original, actual icon — wherever it may be — opens.

Trouble is, occasionally people get confused about what's an actual icon — the one that contains actual information — and what's an alias. (For the record: An alias's name always appears in italics, as shown in Figure 18-3.)

Figure 18-3: When an icon's an alias, the name appears in italics.

If, in this state of confusion, you *throw away* the original file, the alias remains stranded on your desktop, a pointer to nowhere. If you double-click this orphaned icon, the Mac displays this error message. There's nothing you can do about it except throw away the useless alias.

[ ]   See also FAQ 2-5, "How do I put stuff in the menu?"

[ ]   See also FAQ 5-11, "What's an alias for?"

"Not enough memory"

▷   [ ]   See FAQ 6-1, "What should I do about these 'not enough memory' messages?"

"System 7.1 won't run on this machine. A newer version is required." What the —?

▽   **You're missing the enabler file for your Mac model.**

Until System 7.1, your System Folder needed exactly two files to run the computer: the System file and the Finder. If either of these was missing, the Mac wouldn't even start.

With the invention of System 7.1, a third essential file was born: the *enabler*. A couple years' worth of Mac models contained *three* files in the System Folder, each of which was necessary for the computer to operate — System, Finder, and the enabler for that particular model.

What the "a newer version is required" message means is that your System Folder is missing the correct enabler file. (The wording of the message, of course, is somewhat hilarious — at the time, System 7.1 *was* the latest version!) To solve the problem, you must start up the computer from the Disk Tools floppy disk that came with it. From the System Folder on that disk, copy the enabler file into your hard drive's System Folder. Alternatively, you can reinstall your System Folder, as described in Appendix C.

With the release of System 7.5, fortunately, the need for enablers disappeared for all models manufactured before 1995. (Models introduced in 1995 and later once again require enablers, even with System 7.5.)

Can't I turn off that "The Mac wasn't shut down properly" message?

 Yes. The on/off switch is in your General Controls control panel.

Actually, the Mac is only trying to be helpful (System 7.5 and Performas only) — it's reminding you not to turn the Mac off by pulling the plug, punching the on/off switch, and so on. It wants to teach you to use the Shut Down command.

I get a sad-Mac icon when I turn on the Mac!

 It's probably a SCSI, System Folder, or RAM-chip problem.

When the Mac is turned on, it takes a minute or so before the Desktop appears. Part of the delay is the ritual of self-testing the Mac performs. If it detects a problem that prevents the startup process from continuing, you see the dreaded little frowning-Mac-with-X's-for-eyes icon.

The first possibility (the most common, in my experience) is that something is wrong with your SCSI chain — gadgets plugged into the back panel such as CD-ROM player, scanner, extra hard drive, and so on. If you haven't carefully followed the rules of SCSI (see Appendix C), or if all of the devices haven't been turned on, you may get the sad Mac icon at startup. Here's a quick way to see if this is the problem: Unplug any SCSI devices from the back of your Mac. Check to see if the problem has gone away.

Another possibility is that one of your RAM chips is defective. You'll know if this is the explanation, because you'll see the sad-Mac icon immediately after installing new memory SIMMs. Often the problem isn't a broken SIMM — just an improperly installed one. (The little numbers underneath the sad Mac actually identify *which* chip is bad.) Anyway, it's easy to open the Mac again and reseat the memory boards.

A third possibility is that something is wrong with your System Folder. Start up the Mac with your Disk Tools floppy; if it starts up now, you've isolated the problem. Reinstall your System Folder.

If none of these syndromes — bad SCSI, bad memory, or bad System Folder — seems to be at work, it's possible that another hardware malfunction haunts you. Unfortunately, at this point, only a technician can help you.

See also Appendix C, "Troubleshooting Cheat Sheet."

What is "zero K needed, zero K available"?

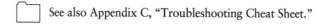 **It's an America Online downloaded file that has been corrupted by static on the line.**

18-15

Sign onto AOL and use keyword *credit* to get a reimbursement for the time you spent downloading the file. Then delete the file and download it again.

See also FAQ 28-2, "What's a keyword?"

See also FAQ 28-6, "How do I resume an interrupted AOL (or eWorld) download?"

CHAPTER

19

Frequently Cursed Glitches

*T*he previous chapter explored dozens of error messages. Of course, an error message means that some programmer anticipated the problem you'd someday have.

The problems in this chapter, however, probably never arose in the early Macintosh design meetings. Today, they hit somebody somewhere every 15 seconds.

This Mac keeps crashing. Is it a lemon?

▽ **Almost certainly not; it's probably a software thing.**

Most of the time, mysterious crashes are caused by memory shortages, extension conflicts, or corrupted system software. The solutions to all three are listed in Appendix C.

The other common cause of mysterious glitches is SCSI problems. The short-term fix is to detach anything plugged into your SCSI jack — CD-ROM, scanner, whatever. The long-term fix is to apply the rules of SCSI, also as described in Appendix C.

FA Q
19-1

19-2

My screen is frozen! What should I do?

▽   **First try "force quitting." Then press the reset switch.**

If you've been running more than one program, it's sometimes possible to escape from the frontmost one — the one that crashed — and still save your unsaved work in the other programs. This technique involves *force quitting* the frozen program. Here's what to do:

1. While pressing the ⌘ and Option keys, press the Esc key.

   A message appears, asking if you're sure you want to force quit. Unfortunately, sometimes it asks about the *wrong program;* that should give you some insight into the multitasking nature of the Mac. (In other words, at the exact moment you pressed the keystroke, the program in front *wasn't* the one getting the Mac's attention.) Further unfortunately, if you *are* asked about the wrong program, the whole process has pretty much backfired — clicking Cancel usually doesn't work. You now must restart the computer, as described below.

2. If the correct program is named in the "force quit?" dialog box, click the Force Quit button.

   If the fates are smiling, the frozen program now collapses into nonexistence. Switch to each of the remaining programs, save your work in each one, and then restart the Mac normally.

   If clicking the Force Quit button merely locks up your Mac further, give up. Press the reset switch (read on).

If you don't particularly care about saving your work in other programs, or if the force-quit business doesn't work, you have only one remaining option — restart the computer. But since it's frozen, you can't exactly choose Restart from the Special menu.

Instead, you need to find your *reset switch*. Apple never seems satisfied with its placement of this important button; it appears in a different spot on every Mac model. One thing remains constant: There are always two switches, side by side, somewhere on every Mac. The button marked by a left-pointing triangle is the reset switch. It performs the same function as turning the Mac off and on again — but more safely and conveniently than ripping out the power cord.

✦   On the Mac SE and most of the II series, the reset switch is one of the two buttons that come on a Mac-colored, plastic piece that you're supposed to install yourself. It goes on the lower side or front of the case.

- On recent higher-priced models, such as the 7100, 8100, most Quadra and Centris models, two small round buttons are on the front or back panel.

- On PowerBook 100-something models, look for two tiny holes on the Mac panel. To "push the button," push a pin or a straightened paper clip into the appropriate hole.

- On all other models — those without visible external buttons — you set off the reset function by pressing a keystroke, not a switch. That keystroke is ⌘-Control-power key (the key on the keyboard with the big left-pointing triangle).

 See also Appendix C, "Troubleshooting Cheat Sheet."

How come all my icons show up as blank pieces of paper?

▼ **Probably because your Desktop file is corrupted.**

The Desktop file is the invisible database where the Mac stores the icons for all your files — as well as the relationship information (which kind of document gets which icon). If this file gets damaged or confused, as it sometimes does, it gives up on your icons. All document files show up looking like blank pieces of paper, and all programs look like generic diamonds.

Fortunately, slapping the Desktop file back into coherence is simple. The process is called rebuilding the desktop, and it's described in Appendix C.

 See also FAQ 4-20, "What's the Desktop file?"

See also FAQ 19-18, "I can't rebuild the desktop if At Ease is installed!"

Where'd all my text go?

▼ **Maybe you accidentally replaced it; maybe its window got hidden.**

Both of these strike virtually every first-time Mac user. You're typing away on your masterpiece. Suddenly, unexpectedly, everything you've typed disappears.

Possibility #1: Accidental replacement

Few beginners recognize the danger inherent in selecting a big swath of text. Of course, on the Macintosh, highlighting text is the equivalent of "overtype mode" on other computers. Anything you type doesn't get *inserted* into your document — it *replaces* whatever was highlighted. It's perfectly possible, therefore, to highlight a 50-page manuscript (by choosing the Select All command, for example), and then to *wipe it all out* by pressing a single key. Figure 19-1 shows this principle.

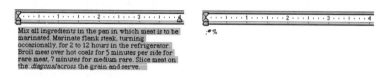

Figure 19-1: Highlight some text (left). Type anything, or fall accidentally onto your keyboard, and you have just replaced everything that was highlighted (right).

If this ever happens to you, you have exactly one chance to recover that deleted text: Choose Undo from the Edit menu. In most programs, the Undo command only retracts the last thing you did — so if you don't discover your mistake immediately, it may be too late. Microsoft Word version 6 and the Nisus word processor are exceptions. Each lets you "take back" dozens of your last word-processing steps. If you're aware of this feature, losing text accidentally is a much rarer occurrence.

Actually, you *do* have one more chance to recover the deleted text: Close the window without saving changes. Figure 19-2 shows how this technique could save you.

Possibility #2: Hidden-Window Syndrome

Maybe the window you were typing into got hidden — that is, sent to the back of your other windows (see Figure 19-3). If that's the case, recovering your words is as easy as using your application menu. (That's the tiny icon in the upper-right corner of your screen, to the right of the question mark.)

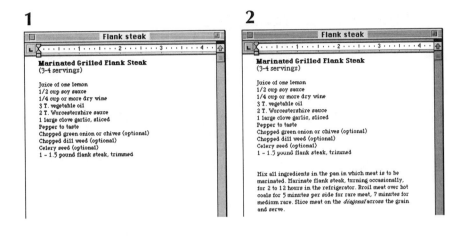

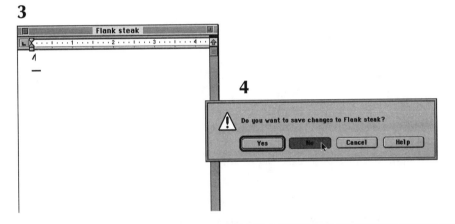

Figure 19-2: (1) You were doing well; you saved the document. (2) You typed some more. (3) Before you had had a chance to save, you accidentally deleted everything. (4) Close the window. When the Mac asks if you want to save changes, click no. When you open the document again, it will be as it was in step 1. This technique means that you lose the additional stuff you had typed in step 2; at least you recover some of your work.

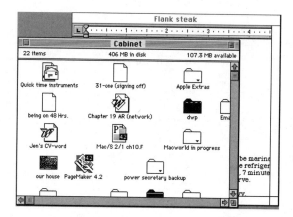

Figure 19-3: Because your programs are like overlapping pieces of paper, one errant click can send your word-processor window to the back, to be covered up by, say, a Finder window. The solution: Choose the name of your word processor from the application menu.

Because Possibility #2 struck so many people, Apple created the option shown in Figure 19-4. When the checkbox *isn't* selected, whatever program is in front can *never* accidentally disappear behind Finder windows. This neat feature is available on System 7.5 and later, as well as on every Performa ever made.

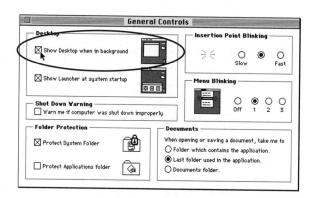

Figure 19-4: When you turn off this checkbox, the Finder disappears when you launch any other program. On recent Performas and in System 7.5, this option is in the General control panel. On older Performas, it's in the Performa control panel.

See FAQ 4-5, "What's the application menu?"

Where did my file go?

See FAQ 1-1, "Help! I typed something, and saved it, but now I can't find it."

See FAQ 1-2, "How can I avoid losing files in the future"?

Where'd all my memory go?

▷   ⬜   See FAQ 6-3, "Where'd all my memory go?"

Where'd all my Power Macintosh memory go?

▷   ⬜   See FAQ 14-4, "Why do Power Mac programs require so much more memory?"

Why is my system taking up 10MB of memory?

▷   ⬜   See FAQ 6-7, "Why is my system taking up 10MB of memory?"

My mouse is jerky and sticky. Do I need a new one?

▽   No — just clean the one you have.

The instructions for cleaning out a mouse are exactly the same as cleaning a PowerBook trackball. See FAQ 15-11.

Why can't I empty the trash?

▽   Because your Mac is convinced that something in there is locked, busy, or corrupted.

If a locked file is in the trash, just press the Option key while choosing Empty Trash from the Special menu.

If the trash still won't empty, the Mac may think that one of its contents is in use by a program. (Microsoft programs are famous for clinging, behind the scenes, to documents you've already closed.) Quit all your open programs and try again.

If *that* doesn't work, then perhaps you have the famous "folder from hell" syndrome, in which nothing you do will get rid of a folder in the trash. One of the following steps is guaranteed to solve the problem:

✦ Rebuild the desktop (see Appendix C) and try again to empty the trash.

✦ Turn on the Mac with your Disk Tools disk (or CD-ROM disc) in the drive. Try to empty the trash now that a different System Folder is in charge.

✦ If, incredibly, you still can't get rid of that stubborn folder, do a "clean re-install" of your System Folder; this will definitely work. Again, the instructions are in Appendix C.

Why is my Mac so slow?

▽ **I don't know for sure, but here are some likely suspects.**

Each of the following features exists, of course, for a reason. But when your Mac wakes up one morning feeling unusually sluggish, turning them off can give your work a welcome speed boost.

✦ Open your Memory control panel. Make sure the feature called Virtual Memory is turned off.

✦ Open your Views control panel. Make sure the feature called Calculate Folder Sizes is turned off.

✦ Open your File Sharing control panel. If the button there says Stop, click it. (If it says Start, never mind.) You just cut yourself off from the network, but at least you've gained some speed.

✦ If your Mac has an '040 processor inside (such as a Quadra, Centris, or PowerBook 500-something), open the Cache Switch control panel. Make sure that it's set to its Faster setting.

If your Mac still feels strangely slow, consider *zapping your parameter RAM, rebuilding your desktop,* and *defragmenting your hard drive.* Appendix C describes the first two techniques, and FAQ 8-1 covers the third.

Why can't I eject my CD-ROM?

▽ **Because File Sharing is on.**

For the moment, visit your File Sharing control panel, click the Stop button, eject your cartridge (or CD-ROM disc), and turn File Sharing back on.

For a long-term solution, get System 7.5.1 (which is to say, get System 7.5 and then install System 7.5 Update #1, which is available from America Online and other online services). It forever eliminates the hassle of ejecting cartridges and CDs while File Sharing is on.

   See also FAQ 1-32, "Where do I get Apple software updates?"

See also FAQ 28-3, "How do I find a file I want to download?"

My Mac's clock keeps going back to 1904 or 1956.

▽ **Your lithium backup battery is dying.**

You need to contact an Apple technician to replace it.

Oh no! I think I have a virus!

▽ **Actually, probably not. But if you do, Disinfectant will take care of it.**

Viruses on the Mac have never been as plentiful, nor as destructive, as on DOS machines. In fact, there has never been a Mac virus that actually destroys your data — all of them so far have just made mischief (random beeps, etc.). In today's Mac society, it's pretty hard to *get* a virus, too; you can no longer get one from an online service (they pre-scan every single file). You can't get a virus from a *document*, either, even if it's handed to you on a floppy disk. A virus can live only in a *program*.

Yet when some mysterious glitch inhabits your Mac, it's easy to leap to conclusions. Before becoming hysterical, remember that whatever ails your Mac is probably something much less exotic. Blank document icons, sudden sluggishness, a clock that resets itself — all might make you think that a virus is at work. These are actually just cues that it's time for you to do some housecleaning. Appendix C shows you how.

If those steps don't restore your Mac to health, sign onto America Online and download the free antivirus program called Disinfectant. It should clean out whatever you've got. If you spend a lot of time handling floppy disks given to you by other people, or if you spent a lot of time dialed into local, homemade bulletin boards, then you may even want to consider buying a commercial virus program.

See also FAQ 28-3, "How do I find a file I want to download?"

Why can't I rename my hard drive?

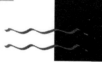

See FAQ 8-10, "How come I can't rename my hard drive?"

19-15

RAQ: Rarely Asked Question

Why is my Mac acting so weird?

A true tale from a true repair center:

A customer called us to say that his computer was acting "funny." The customer said that he couldn't understand why his Mac should be acting up — "After all," he told us, "the Mac says that it's OK!"

That last comment made us wonder. We asked him exactly *how* the Mac was communicating that it was OK.

"It's right there, that the top of every window," was the reply.

It was then that we realized that the computer actually said "zero K" — the customer's hard drive was completely full!

What does the blinking question mark mean?

▽ **It means that there's no working System Folder on board.**

See Appendix C for instructions on re-installing your System Folder.

My keyboard typesssss likkkeeee thissss!

▽ **If it's a PowerBook Duo, it's a keyboard problem. If not, adjust your Keyboard control panel.**

See FAQ 16-4 for details on the quirks of Duo keyboards. If you don't have a Duo, then perhaps you're lingering a little too long on the keys as you press them. (Don't forget that on a Mac *every* key is a repeating key like the X on an electric typewriter.)

To adjust your keyboard's sensitivity, open the Keyboard control panel. See where it says Delay Until Repeat? Select a setting closer to the Long button — or even turn it off completely.

I can't rebuild the desktop if At Ease is installed!

▽ **You're right, especially in System 7.5. Here's the workaround.**

Rebuilding the desktop, as described in Appendix C, is an important troubleshooting technique. It's also a feature of the *Finder*. If you're using the child-proofing Apple software called At Ease, your Mac doesn't *go* to the Finder when you start up — it jumps into At Ease instead. You could hold down the rebuild-the-desktop keys (⌘ and Option) until doomsday, and the desktop would never be rebuilt.

If you have System 7.5:

1. Turn At Ease off. For version 1.0, open the At Ease control panel; for version 2.0, double-click At Ease Setup. In either case, click the Off button.

2. Restart the Mac.

3. While the Mac is starting up again, hold down the space bar. If everything is installed properly, you'll see a list of extensions appear, courtesy of the Extensions Manager control panel.

4. By clicking the names of the extensions in this list, turn off all the extensions *except* Macintosh Easy Open.

5. Close the Extensions Manager window.

6. As the startup process continues, hold down the ⌘ and Option keys. Eventually, you'll be asked if you want to rebuild the desktop. Say yes.

7. After rebuilding the desktop, open the Extensions Manager control panel; by clicking their names, turn your extensions back on.

8. Turn At Ease back on by reversing step 1 above. Restart the Mac. You're back in business!

If you have any other version of System 7:

1. Turn At Ease off, as in step 1 for System 7.5. Restart the Mac.

2. As the Mac begins to start up again, press the Shift key to turn extensions off.

3. After you see the "extensions off" message, hold down the ⌘ and Option keys to rebuild the desktop.

Oh no! I spilled milk on my keyboard!

▽   This will sound insane, but here it is: Soak it.

That's right — detach your keyboard, and completely immerse it in tap water. Then set it aside to dry. Don't use it again until it is *completely* dry, even if it takes days. This technique, while certainly not endorsed by any keyboard company, has rescued many a keyboard. After all — what have you got to lose?

The volume is all the way up, but my speaker is still too quiet.

▽   You need to find the secret panel of the Sound control panel.

In 1993, Apple changed the design of the Sound control panel. The slider you adjust at the main screen only affects the *error beep* volume. To adjust the speaker volume for everything else, you must choose Volumes from the popup menu at the top of the screen. Figure 19-5 makes it all clear.

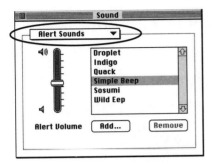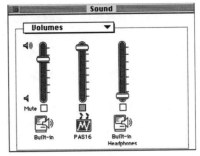

Figure 19-5: At left: The new Sound control panel as it appears when you first open it. If you choose Volumes from the circled popup menu, you get the screen shown at right. Use it to adjust your speaker's overall volume.

The point is, of course, that you can now set the volume of your error beeps independently of the general speaker volume.

 See also Chapter 13, "Speech, Multimedia, and CD-ROM."

How can I fix the speaker on my IIsi?

▼ **Tweak the volume, clean the contacts, or use external speakers.**

In most Macs, a wire connects the built-in speaker to the main circuit board. In a IIsi, however, the speaker's contacts rest directly on the circuit board's contacts. Those contacts often become dirty or slightly corroded, leading to the famous IIsi sound dropout problem.

For some people, just opening the Sound control panel and changing the volume level (and playing a sound) seems to help. For others, nothing works except opening the Mac and cleaning the contacts. (A pencil eraser will do; the pros buy an electronics cleaner called Cramolin.)

My keyboard doesn't work, and I'm getting funny sounds.

▽   **Easy Access is probably turned on.**

Easy Access is a control panel that makes the Mac easier to use for physically disabled people. It lets you operate the mouse by pressing keys on the keyboard. The little chirpy sound signals you that you've just turned Easy Access on or off.

To turn it off for good, take Easy Access out of your Control Panels folder and restart the Mac.

I have a program that requires an FPU. Am I out of luck?

▽   **No. Software FPU may help.**

Software FPU is a clever system extension that tricks your software into thinking that your FPU-less Mac actually has an FPU (a math coprocessor chip). The Power Mac version is available only from the author (John Neil, P.O. Box 2156, Cupertino, CA 95015); it costs $20. The non-Power Mac version is available as shareware on America Online and other services.

Software FPU doesn't give your Mac any mathematical speed boost, as a real math chip would. It does, however, let FPU-dependent programs *run,* period.

> See also FAQ 4-31, "What's an FPU?"

> See also FAQ 18-6, "Why do I get 'No Co-Processor Installed' errors? My Mac *has,* an FPU!"

My custom hard drive icon went generic.

▷   See FAQ 8-11, "When I try to give my hard drive a new icon, I get this message: 'This command cannot be completed because it cannot be found.'"

Why is my Apple menu black instead of striped colors?

▼ **Either your monitor setting or your system installation is responsible.**

Possibility #1: Ever experimented with your Monitors control panel? That's where you choose a color setting for your screen: black-and-white, grayscale, or color.

What's especially weird is that you can't set your monitor to more than 256 *grays*. If you try to select Thousands or Millions of grays, your monitor goes right back to displaying in color!

Well, almost. The menu remains a solid black logo, not colored, under those circumstances. Change the Monitors setting to Colors, or down to 256 grays, and normalcy will return.

Possibility #2: When you install your system software, some versions (such as System 7.1) offer you a Minimal option. It installs as small a System Folder as possible.

Among the frilly extras you don't get with that installation is, sure enough, the colored Apple logo. Do a complete installation, and it will return.

My Mac keeps starting in black and white.

▼ **If you don't mind my saying so, your PRAM needs zapping.**

PRAM, geekese for *parameter RAM,* is a little piece of battery-sustained memory in every Mac. It keeps your clock accurate, remembers many of your control panel settings, and so on. Like any bank of RAM, its contents can become scrambled.

If that happens, you'll see funny symptoms like your color monitor going black-and-white against your will. To fix it, "zap your PRAM," as described in Appendix C.

If that doesn't solve the problem, try these four last resorts:

✦ Open the System Folder; then open the Preferences folder. Locate the file called Finder Preferences — and drag it into the trash. (You won't be allowed to empty the trash, however. Not yet.) Restart the Mac, open your Monitors control panel, switch it to color, and the problem is gone.

✦ Open your Monitors control panel. Click from black-and-white to color, from 256 to 16 colors, and on. This action sometimes works to slap some sense into your system.

✦   Perform a "clean reinstall" of your System Folder, as described in Appendix C.

✦   Replace your Mac's lithium backup battery.

19-27

I found this "rescued items" folder in my trash. What is this?

▽   **They're the Mac's attempt to recover from an unfortunate crash.**

Some programs, especially Microsoft programs, create invisible temporary files on your hard drive — sort of a scratch pad for themselves. Normally, when you quit such a program, it deletes those files.

But if you don't quit normally — in other words, if you have a system crash, or you force quit, or you just switch off the Mac without shutting down properly — that program doesn't have a chance to delete its temporary files. The Mac thinks it's doing you a favor: When you restart the next time, it puts those temp files into that Rescued Items folder. Sometimes you can even recover some unsaved typing by opening one of those temporary files. Otherwise, just empty the trash and forget about it.

19-28

Where can I turn for troubleshooting help?

▽   **You can call or e-mail Apple.**

Either way, you reach the same group of experts, who have an exceptional record for solving problems and answering questions. By phone, you can call them at (800) SOS-APPL (6 a.m. to 6 p.m., PST, weekdays). By e-mail, you need a membership on eWorld; call (800) 775-4556 for a free ten-hour starter disk. Once you're online, do this:

1.   Choose Go to Shortcut from the Places menu.

2.   Type **Apple** and press Return. You arrive at the Apple screen.

3.   Click the Apple Technical Support button; on the following screen, click the Ask Apple USA icon.

At long last, you arrive at what many people thought would never exist — an actual bulletin board, full of questions and answers, staffed by actual Apple technicians!

While you're at the Apple area, you might also consider searching the Apple Tech Info Library. It's Apple's official technical support database, filled with thousands of mini-articles about a wide range of Apple products, past and present. The search blank lets you type in, for example, **PowerBook** and **batteries** to see articles about that pair of topics.

20

Startup Snarls

Y ou wake up, you shower, you sit down zestfully before your Mac. You turn it on, discover a blinking question mark — and realize that the first hour of your day will be spent troubleshooting. There's nothing worse.

With this chapter's help, may these frequently annoying startup problems leave you forever.

The Mac crashes during startup. What should I do?

 For now, press the Shift key. Then solve your extension conflict.

Your problem is an extension conflict. If you just want to start the Mac and get on with your life, restart the computer (press the reset switch, as described in FAQ 19-2). This time, as the computer starts, hold down the Shift key until a message says "extensions off." To solve the problem for good, you have to find out which extensions are clashing. See Appendix C.

20-1

Yikes! I heard a car-crash sound!

▽   **Either something is wrong with your RAM chips, or something is pressing your Interrupt switch.**

Every Mac model offers a different, fascinating sound when it detects a RAM problem. The Mac II series plays four single musical notes; Quadra AV models play a drum solo; the LC series gives you a flute solo; and the Power Mac plays a hideous recording of a car wreck.

These sounds are more often heard *accidentally,* however. You can hear your Mac's bad-RAM sound any time you want. Just press the Interrupt switch during that moment, at startup, when your screen is black. (See FAQ 19-2 to locate your model's Interrupt switch.)

Trouble is, sometimes something — the keyboard, for example — is pressing this interrupt switch when you don't even know it. (That's more likely on some Mac models — the 650 or 7100, for example — than others.) If you're hearing startup error sounds, the keyboard-pressing-the-switch is certainly a less expensive problem to fix.

My desktop spontaneously rebuilds!

▽   **Macintosh Easy Open is probably in action. Or you have a folder called Desktop.**

Possibility #1: Macintosh Easy Open is the ingenious control panel (of System 7.5) that eliminates the "application not found" message forever. (See FAQ 18-4.)

To do its thing, Easy Open must know exactly what programs you *have.* It does that detective work by rebuilding your invisible desktop file at startup. Once. Thereafter, every time you install a new program, Easy Open makes a note of it.

The problem arises when, for one troubleshooting reason or another, you press the Shift key during startup. This, of course, turns off all your extensions — including Easy Open. Then, the *next* time you start the Mac, Easy Open panics. "Whoa, hold up," it says. "I was unconscious last startup. I wasn't paying attention to what programs you might have added to the hard drive. You might have slipped something by me." Now that it's reactivated, Easy Open — you guessed it — rebuilds the desktop, without consulting you, to bring its database up to date.

Possibility #2: Do you, by any chance, have a folder on your desktop or hard drive *called* Desktop? If so, it may be triggering those automatic desktop-file rebuilds, too.

 See also FAQ 4-20, "What's the Desktop file?"

See also Appendix C, "Troubleshooting Cheat Sheet."

Why does it say, "Need later version. System 7.1 is not the latest"?

20-4

 See FAQ 18-12, "'System 7.1 won't run on this machine. A newer version is required.' What the —?"

At startup, my menu bar is blank, the cursor twitches, and everything freezes. What to do?

20-5

▽ **Press the Option key during startup.**

When you press the Option key as the Mac starts up, it automatically closes any Windows that were left open. In your case, that's a good idea — the Mac has become confused about the location of one window. As a result, your Mac is stuck in a loop.

How can I identify the extension icons at startup?

20-6

▽ **Buy Conflict Catcher.**

This program (from Casady and Greene) is an extensions manager; see Appendix C to find out that it's really for solving mysterious system crashes caused by conflicting extensions. Among its neat features: It shows the names of your extensions as they load (see Figure 20-1).

 See also FAQ 4-29, "What's an extension?"

Figure 20-1: Conflict Catcher shows the names of your icons as the Mac starts up.

20-7

My Geoport icon has an X through it at startup. What should I do?

▷ ⬜ See FAQ 27-15, "My Geoport icon has an X through it at startup. What should I do?"

20-8

My AudioVision icon has an X through it at startup. What should I do?

▷ ⬜ See FAQ 9-17, "The AudioVision icon has an X through it at startup. How come?"

20-9

How come my extension icons don't load in neat rows?

▽ **Icon wrapping isn't a feature of every extension.**

When extensions were invented in the 80's, they weren't something Apple had planned for; they sort of appeared, courtesy of America's programmers. Each programmer was responsible for programming his extension icon's position during startup. Some programmers made their icons smart enough to begin a second row of icons if necessary, for example. Others didn't. Bottom line: If your icons don't wrap to a new row on your monitor, or if gaps appear as they load, one of your extensions is responsible.

⬜ See also FAQ 4-29, "What's an extension?"

21

System 7.5 Snafus

*I*t's the first version of the System Folder that can't fit on a floppy disk. It's the first System you can't drag manually from your installation disks to your hard drive. It consumes more disk space and memory than any previous System.

Yet System 7.5 is the fastest and most functional Mac operating system. The new desk accessories are the greatest — how did we live before we could type little notes into Stickies? Can you believe people used to have a Find command that only showed one icon match at a time? And it's great to have the features formerly available only on Performas: The Finder can hide itself when you launch another program, the Launcher can display frequently launched icons, and the Protect System Folder feature can prevent little hands from rendering your Mac inoperable.

I heard that System 7.5 requires 8 megs of RAM and 20 megs of disk space. Is it worth getting?

 Yes. Apple overstates the requirements.

21-1

System 7.5 requires a Mac with 8 megs of memory *only* if you install PowerTalk and QuickDraw GX.

PowerTalk is an advanced networking system for people in offices with high-horsepower Macs. QuickDraw GX is powerful new printing software whose best features lie untapped until today's programs are upgraded. For some reason, Apple advertises those requirements assuming that people *will* install them, but few people do. Therefore, the average person's System 7.5 System Folder takes up only a few hundred K more memory than the System 7.1 System Folder did, and claims far less than 20 megs of disk space. (If you omit PowerTalk, QuickDraw GX, and the Macintosh Guide help system, a full installation requires about 10 megs.)

If you ask me — yes, it's worth it. Not only do you get overall boost in speed, especially in things like opening programs and emptying the trash, but you get all kinds of cool new features.

The new Find File

This fast, efficient file-finding feature alone is worth the upgrade to System 7.5. See Figure 21-1 for details.

Macintosh Guide

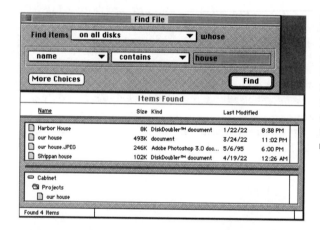

Figure 21-1: The System 7.5 Find command shows everything on your hard drive (bottom window) that matches what you looked for (top window). From here, you can double-click any found file to open it normally.

Macintosh Guide is the cool new help system under the Help menu (question mark menu) of the System 7.5 Finder. Choose a help topic, such as "How do I print?", and the Mac walks you through the process, step by step, highlighting menus and icons with a fat red animated magic marker to illustrate.

Macintosh Drag & Drop

Instead of copying and pasting, you can drag any selected text or graphics from one place to another. You can drag this material within the same document, from one window to another, or even from one *program's* window into another. At this writing, Apple's

System 7.5 programs do the Macintosh Drag & Drop thing (SimpleText, the Jigsaw Puzzle, Desktop Patterns, Scrapbook, Note Pad, and so on), as does WordPerfect. Someday, with luck, other software companies will see the light and upgrade their programs.

New desk accessories

The new Note Pad lets you resize your pages, add more than eight pages, and search for text. Stickies is the world's best desk accessory — it's an electronic version of Post-It Notes, in the same line of charming pastel colors.

New control panels

The new control panels include:

+ The long-overdue Desktop Patterns, which lets you select from among dozens of desktop backgrounds far more colorful and textured than those in previous system versions. You can even paste in your own graphics.

+ A new Date & Time control panel that (at last!) puts a clock on your menu bar.

+ The updated General Controls panel, which has inherited three useful features from the Performa line: the Documents folder option (creates a Documents folder on your desktop that automatically collects any new documents you create, which means you'll never again lose a file); the "Show Desktop when in background" checkbox lets you automatically hide the Finder — with its clutter of windows and icons — whenever you're in another program; and the Launcher, as Performa owners well know, is a floating window containing your favorite document and program icons. Just one click suffices to open any of them.

WindowShade

Finally, there's WindowShade, the best window-management tool since the close box. When you turn on WindowShade, you can double-click the title bar of any window — and it collapses. Nothing remains except the title bar itself, floating there like a window amputee. Double-click again to restore the full window. It's a great way to manage a lot of windows on a smallish screen.

See also FAQ 4-42, "What's Macintosh Guide?"

See also FAQ 4-60, "What's PowerTalk?"

See also FAQ 4-62, "What's QuickDraw GX?"

See also Chapter 17, "Performas and Other Special Macs."

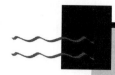

TAQ: Technically Asked Question

Before I installed System 7.5, I could switch resolutions on my Quadra AV's multisync monitor. How come I can't now?

It's a glitch. The workaround: Open your Monitors control panel. While pressing the Option key, click the Options *button*. You'll be shown the complete list of available resolutions.

My Mac came with System 7.1 installed, but a System 7.5 Installer is in a folder on the hard drive. Should I install it?

▷   See FAQ 21-1, "I heard that System 7.5 requires 8 megs of RAM and 20 megs of disk space. Is it worth getting?"

What's the Shutdown Items folder for?

▽   **Backup programs and funny sound files, mainly.**

When you choose Shut Down or Restart from the Special menu, your Mac launches anything you've put into the Shutdown Items folder. (These items *won't* be launched if you choose Shut Down from the menu, interestingly enough.)

I can think of only a couple uses for this feature. First, you could put an automatic backup program (or alias of one) into that folder, so that your stuff is automatically backed up at the end of the day. Second, you could put some witty sound file in there — Bones from "Star Trek" saying, "It's dead, Jim," comes to mind.

See also FAQ 5-11, "What's an alias for?"

I installed System 7.5, and now my Mac doesn't know its own model number.

21-4

▽ **You noticed!**

It's true: If you choose About This Macintosh from the ⌘ menu, the resulting window no longer identifies your Mac by model. Instead, it just identifies the general class, such as Macintosh, Power Macintosh, or Macintosh PowerBook. (Actually, this is true if you perform a "clean install" of System 7.5. If you install it normally onto a Mac running a previous system, your model information remains.)

Apple wrote System 7.5 so that it would hide the model information out of concern for the future. First of all, Apple frequently builds the identical logic board (the main circuit board inside) into several different Mac models — for example, the Performa 6115 and the Power Mac 6100. Furthermore, Apple's logic boards are now available in *other* companies' Mac clones. In both cases, Apple wanted to prepare for the day when logic boards had nothing to do with the computer models that contained them.

Of course, to find out your Mac's model name, you *could* just read what's painted on the front panel.

Every time I start my Mac, the desktop rebuilds. How come?

21-5

▷ See FAQ 20-3, "My desktop spontaneously rebuilds!"

How can I make Stickies stop crashing?

21-6

▽ **Install the System 7.5 Update.**

The original Stickies desk accessory had a bug. If you had collapsed a note window (using the System 7.5 WindowShade feature), you'd get a Type 1 error the next time you opened Stickies.

The inconvenient solution: Just don't collapse your Stickies. The convenient one: Install System 7.5 Update #1, which fixes the bug. (It turns your system into System 7.5.1 in the process.)

 See also FAQ 1-32, "Where do I get Apple software updates?"

 See also FAQ 18-1, "What's a Type 1 error?"

How come Macintosh Guide doesn't work in At Ease?

▽ **It's not supposed to.**

Macintosh Guide, the new System 7.5 help feature, only works if somebody has bothered to write Guide text for the program you're using. That explains why there's no Macintosh Guide under the Help menu in, for example, Photoshop or Microsoft Word — nobody has written one yet. As it happens, Apple hasn't written any Guide material for At Ease. They're working on it.

You may well then ask, "Then how come, when I switch from At Ease to the Finder, the Macintosh Guide command doesn't *reappear* under the Help menu?"

It's a bug. They're working on it.

 See also FAQ 4-42, "What's Macintosh Guide?"

 See also FAQ 21-1, "I heard that System 7.5 requires 8 megs of RAM and 20 megs of disk space. Is it worth getting?"

I installed System 7.5. Now the light on my AudioVision monitor doesn't work, and I'm missing part of the Sound control panel.

▽ **Download the AudioVision Installer version 1.0.2 or later — and install it.**

 See also FAQ 1-32, "Where do I get Apple software updates?"

When I type on my keyboard, weird characters appear on the screen.

 You must have switched accidentally to a foreign keyboard layout.

System 7.5 offers a new keyboard-switching feature that lets you flip your entire keyboard into, say, a Swahili key arrangement. Trouble is, Apple got a little overzealous about foisting this feature on us: It selected ⌘-space bar, about the most easily mistriggered keystroke on the entire keyboard, to switch your Mac from one keyboard layout to another.

To solve the problem, open your Keyboard control panel. Select *U.S.*

To prevent any further trouble, quit every program. Open your System Folder. Double-click the System *suitcase* icon; inside, you'll see icons that represent all the foreign keyboard layouts. Drag all of them (except U.S.) to the trash. (This problem was solved in System 7.5.1.)

22

Frequently Used Software

To the whiners who complain that there isn't enough software for the Mac — guess what? There are now only about 10,000 applications.

That makes a chapter that covers the most-frequent questions about the most-popular programs more challenging than ever. But here they are, in no particular order.

Should I upgrade to Word 6?

 Not unless you have a Power Mac and a *lot* of disk space.

Microsoft Word 5.1 was a pretty darned good word processor: quick, smallish on the disk, and fairly easy to figure out (at least, for a Microsoft program). Word 6, on the other hand, is an enormous, bloated, creaking behemoth, clumsily adapted from the Windows version. Even if you get the 6.0.1 upgrade, Word 6 is still slow; too slow for everyday use on anything but a Power Mac, if you ask me.

Word 6 has lots of nice features. For example, it can automatically capitalize the first word of each sentence. And it can automatically expand abbreviations that you type (turning *bdhc* into *Barney the Dinosaur Hate Club*, for example). But WordPerfect does that first feature better, and the shareware program TypeIt4Me does the second feature better.

And meanwhile, Word 6 has a lot of less attractive features. Customizing the menus is much more difficult than in version 5; no word processor should add *five* extensions to your System Folder; those inane toolbars cover up more than half your typing area (and it's too many steps to turn them off); and above all, the whole thing looks and feels like you're using a PC, not a Mac. (See Figure 22-1.)

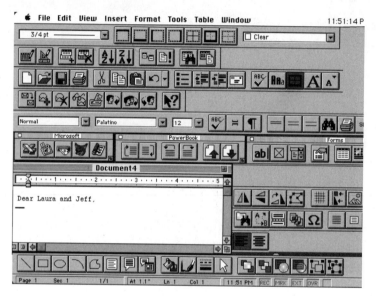

Figure 22-1: This is not a spoof. This is not a spoof. According to Microsoft, it's a word processor. Only thing missing: a place to type.

If you have Word 5-point-something, keep it. If you're shopping for something new, check out WordPerfect — or, if you can find it on sale, get Word 5.1.

   See also FAQ 23-17, "Where can I buy stuff?"

Can Word 5 read Word 6 files, and vice-versa?

▽   **Word 6 reads Word 5 files directly. Word 5 needs the free translator file.**

The translator file, called *Word 6.0 for Windows&Macintosh,* must be placed in the Word Commands folder, in the same folder as Word 5 itself. You can get this translator for free from America Online and other services. (Word 4, Word 5, and Word 5.1 files, by the way, are freely interchangeable.)

See also FAQ 28-3, "How do I find a file I want to download?"

Oh, my God, Word 6 is so SLOW! Helllp!

 Get version 6.0.1; remove some of your fonts and extensions; and tweak your memory settings.

If you legitimately own Word 6, the slightly faster 6.0.1 version is yours for the asking from Microsoft. The company also suggests that Word 6 runs faster on Macs with very few fonts and system extensions.

Microsoft further suggests that you give Word 6 more memory (using its Get Info box, as described in Appendix C). Finally, try these memory tweaks:

If your Mac has 4 megabytes of RAM

1. Launch Word 6. From the Tools menu, choose Customize. Click the Menu tab.

2. Under Categories, select Tools. Under Commands, select ToolsAdvancedSettings. (I thought they stopped leaving spaces out of things in 1970!) Click the Add button. Click the Close button.

3. If you don't work with graphics much, from the Tools menu, choose Advanced Settings. In the Categories box, choose Microsoft Word.

4. In the Option box, type **BitMapMemory**. In the Setting box, type **512**. Click Set and then OK.

   If the steps above *don't* seem to help the speed problem, repeat step 3; then, in the Options box, click the BitMapMemory setting, and then click the Delete button. Click OK.

5. Repeat step 3. In the Option box, type **CacheSize**. In Setting, type **128**. Click Set and then OK.

If your Mac has 8 or more megabytes of RAM

If your documents use a lot of graphics, do steps 1, 2, 3, and 4 as just described — but type in a higher number in step 4. If you have 8 megs of RAM, you can set the BitMapMemory as high as 2048K.

If you work with large documents, do steps 1, 2, 3, and 5, as just described — but in 5, change the CacheSize setting to 256K. If that doesn't help, increase it even more — all the way up to 1024K.

Be aware that both of these steps sap away even more memory from your Mac. Don't do *both* of the two steps above, either; just one or the other, depending on which works.

And *I* suggest that you get a Power Mac — and maybe a different program.

How do I get rid of the person's name on Word's startup screen?

  It isn't easy — but it can be done.

Of course, the smartest thing to do is, upon buying a new program, duplicate all the master disks. Use the free program called DiskCopy (available from America Online and similar services) to do it, to make sure the copies are *exactly* identical to the masters. If you do this, you will never be forced to confront some ex-spouse's name every time you start up that program.

The next smartest thing is to type spaces or asterisks into the Your Name blank whenever you install a program, so that *no* name appears on the startup screen.

But if it's too late and some unwanted name appears on your Microsoft Word welcome screen, you can download the free program called Anonymity. It comes with complete instructions.

See also FAQ 28-3, "How do I find a file I want to download?"

Why does Word say "Not enough memory to run Word?" I've got 32 megs!

It's a bug. Wait 30 seconds after your Mac has started up before launching Word.

If Word 5 is the first program to launch immediately after startup, it may tell you that there's "not enough memory." It lies. Just wait for a moment and then try launching it again.

Why don't the keys on my number pad work in Microsoft Word?

They're supposed to be used for navigating your document.

For example, the 9 and 3 keys scroll up and down one screen, respectively.

To switch those keys back to typing numbers, press the Clear key in the upper-left corner of the pad (Word 4 or 5) or Shift-Clear (Word 6). Hit that combination again to switch back to navigation mode.

See also FAQ 1-8, "I have all these extra keys like F1, Del, and Esc. What are they for?"

What's the best way to make a play or movie script?

▽ **Use your word processor's style-sheet feature.**

Most of today's word processors let you define *styles* — predefined sets of paragraph formatting (bold, double-spaced, centered, and so on) that can be applied to a paragraph with one keystroke. Word, WordPerfect, ClarisWorks 4, and other word processors all let you create styles.

To create a script, define styles as shown in Figure 22-2. These are only examples — your preferred format may differ — but the point is that style sheets are definitely the way to go.

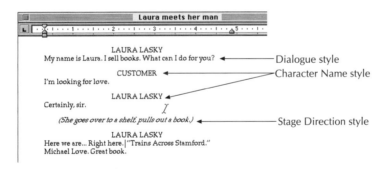

Figure 22-2: The beauty of style sheets is that one style can be programmed to switch to another automatically — when you press the Return key. For example, after you type the character name, press Return, and you are automatically deposited into the Dialogue style.

Unfortunately, using your word processor as a screenwriting program has one major drawback. At the end of a page, a character's speech may break and continue on the top of the next page. Hollywood tradition dictates that *(continued)* indications appear at the bottom and top of such pages — which is a difficult feat for a word processor. If you add or delete a paragraph, all your *(continued)* indications throughout the screenplay get thrown out of position!

If you care about such things, consider buying the copy-protected, but terrific, screenwriting program called Final Draft from Mac Toolkit, (310) 395-4242.

I just sorted my FileMaker (or ClarisWorks) database, and now all my records are gone!

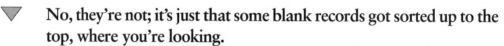 No, they're not; it's just that some blank records got sorted up to the top, where you're looking.

Blanks, when sorted alphabetically, come even before the letter A. If you scroll down far enough, you'll see your other records.

Is there any way to make my FileMaker database stay sorted?

▽ Yes — but there's no *easy* way.

As you've noticed, FileMaker (and ClarisWorks) databases don't seem to stay sorted after you've sorted them. As soon as you start working with the database, they seem to be instantly out of order.

The only way to keep your records permanently sorted is to sort them; export them, using the Import/Export command in the File menu; delete all the records from the database; and then reimport the data you exported.

Sometimes when I launch FileMaker, it says a file must be recovered. How come?

▽ Because the program was unexpectedly terminated last time.

To gain speed, FileMaker keeps some of your information in memory, and only occasionally saves it back onto your hard drive. If your system crashes while FileMaker is running (or if something else makes FileMaker quit unexpectedly), the program gets worried about your data. The *next* time you open that file, FileMaker checks to make sure that all your data is safe.

Can I open my ClarisWorks database in FileMaker?

▽   **No. You can transfer the data, but not the layouts.**

You would think, since ClarisWorks and FileMaker are both made by Claris, that the database files might be mutually compatible. They're not. You can transfer the information between programs using the Save As and Import commands. But your layouts, macros, and font selections can't be transferred.

How the heck are you supposed to delete database records in ClarisWorks?

▽   **Click to the left of a record to select it; then use the Cut or Clear command in the Edit menu.**

How come my ClarisWorks (or FileMaker) fields aren't sliding to eliminate gaps?

▽   **Maybe they aren't perfectly aligned — or they aren't the right widths.**

You realize, of course, that this slide-to-eliminate-gaps feature only works in *printouts*, not on the screen. In FileMaker, you can use Preview mode to see the effect, but in ClarisWorks 3.0 and earlier, even Page View doesn't reflect the way the printout will look.

In both programs, the fields must be perfectly aligned. For example, the Zip Code field won't slide up against the end of the State information if it is even slightly higher or lower on the screen. Use the Align command to make them square with each other.

Finally, an object won't slide unless it's *smaller* than the object it's sliding toward. To slide left, a field must be shorter than the field to its left. To slide up, it can't be wider than the object above it.

22-14

Isn't there any way to change the font permanently for all my ClarisWorks documents?

▽   Yes. Create a blank stationery document called ClarisWorks WP Options.

In other words, create a new word processor document. Change the font to something you like. (Change everything else while you're at it — the margins, the line spacing, and so on.) Choose Save from the File menu. In the next window, click the Stationery button. Give your new document the name *ClarisWorks WP Options,* and save it into the ClarisWorks folder.

From now on, every time you create a new word processing document, it will have the font you want.

Bonus hint: You can create stationery default documents for the other ClarisWorks document types, too. Follow the same steps; but in place of the WP (for word processing), type GP for graphics, DB for database, SS for spreadsheet, and so on.

22-15

Help — I'm stuck in Myst!

▽   All the help you need is online.

On America Online and similar services are hint sheets aplenty. Dial up, search the software libraries for *Myst,* and cheat away!

☐   See also FAQ 28-3, "How do I find a file I want to download?"

22-16

How come After Dark has no modules?

▽   Your After Dark Files folder is lost or missing.

It's not enough to have the After Dark control panel — you also need the folder filled with its individual modules. It should be in your System Folder, but not inside any other folder. If it's not there, After Dark won't do any of its usual dazzling stuff; it will just show that boring skyline-at-night screen saver.

Use your Find command. Search for *After Dark Files.* If it doesn't turn up, reinstall After Dark from its original disk.

Why does my PageMaker document keep getting bigger on the disk?

 PageMaker is trying to save you time.

In an effort to take less time when saving, PageMaker saves your latest work by appending it to the end of the file. As a result, your file takes up more disk space every time you save it.

Version 5 and later lets you turn off this behavior. In the Preferences menu, choose either Faster or Smaller saving.

In either case, creating a small-as-possible version of your document is easy. Just use the Save As command (in the File menu), and give your document a different name. PageMaker will be forced to create a fresh, compact copy of your file.

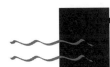

AAQ: Actually Asked Question

Help! Toasters!

A verbatim report from an Apple help center technician:

The caller was concerned about occasionally seeing flying toasters on her screen. She wanted to know if this was normal. She was familiar with fish occasionally appearing on her screen, but thought something might be wrong when the flying toasters appeared.

I told her that the Flying Toaster is a normal phenomenon and inherent in her screen saver technology.

She started giggling uncontrollably and hung up.

22-18

I just bought Photoshop 3.0, and it tells me I have an "expired beta version." What the — ?

▽ That's a little surprise left over from the testing process. Get the Photoshop 3.0.1 updater.

It's available on America Online or another service.

See also FAQ 28-3, "How do I find a file I want to download?"

22-19

What's the difference between TeachText and SimpleText — and do I need both?

▽ SimpleText is newer and has more features. You don't need both.

Every time you get a new program, the manufacturer includes a tiny text file (a Read Me file) with last-minute instructions. Trouble is, that manufacturer doesn't know for sure what word processor you own. So, to make sure that you have *some* program that can open that Read Me file, the manufacturer also gives you a copy of SimpleText, the world's most stripped-down word processor.

SimpleText, which debuted with System 7, is nothing more than a beefed-up version of its processor, TeachText. Those beef-ups include QuickTime movie playing, sound recording, free selection of typefaces, the ability to open more than one document at a time, and so on. SimpleText can even read to you, as mentioned in FAQ 13-19.

Not only don't you need both TeachText and SimpleText, but you only need *one* of one of them. Use your Find File command; I'll bet you have several copies cluttering up your hard drive. Throw the extras away.

PART 5

How to Spend
Your Money

There really ought to be a book on this topic alone. How do you know what to buy, and where to buy it? Every catalog ad looks great; every new Mac model looks tastier than the one you already have.

But most of us have wallets of limited thickness. Sure, we're resigned to the fact that we have embraced one of the world's most expensive hobbies; but that doesn't mean that we shouldn't do our best to make purchases wisely. May the following chapters be your guide.

23

Gear Bought and Sold

An Apple survey showed that 60% of all Mac users buy a newer, better Mac every two years. Frightening, isn't it?

May these words of wisdom guide you into the frenzied, ever-changing Mac marketplace.

Should I get a Performa or a regular Mac?

 With a couple of exceptions, the Performa is almost always a better deal.

Equipment-wise, most Performa models are 100 percent identical to non-Performa models. Table 23-1 shows some equivalent models.

"Performa" means that everything's included in one box — monitor, keyboard, fax/modem, software, the works. When you buy a non-Performa, you have to buy every one of those items separately. When you add up the prices, you'll have paid more than the Performa's all-inclusive price.

A *non*-Performa is a better idea in only these three cases:

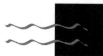

Table 23-1

Performa/non-Performa equivalents

Performa model	Identical model
6115	Power Mac 6100
630	Quadra 630
475	Quadra 605
575	LC 575
405	LC III

+ You already own software or some of the hardware (monitor, keyboard, and so on), so the Performa package wouldn't represent much savings.

+ You want a bigger or better monitor than the standard one that comes with the Performa.

+ You work with mathematical, structural modeling, or analytical scientific software. You may therefore prefer a Mac that contains a *math coprocessor* (FPU) chip, which speeds up number crunching in certain programs. Performa models generally don't include an FPU chip, whereas their mainstream Quadra equivalents usually do. (This guideline applies to three-digit models only. The four-digit Performas are the same as Power Macs, FPU and all.)

See also FAQ 4-32, "What's an FPU?"

See also Chapter 17, "Performas and Other Special Macs."

Should I get a Macintosh clone?

▽ **Probably, yes.**

Reviews of the first Macintosh clones — from companies like Power Computing and Radius — indicate that they're 100 percent Macintosh, in compatibility and speed. They're about 10 percent less expensive than Apple machines, available in your choice of configuration, and warrantied exactly as long as Apple Macs. About all you lose is access to the (800) SOS-APPL hotline — and the Apple logo.

And you don't have to worry that you're showing disloyalty to Apple — they *want* you to buy a clone. They get a cut of every clone's price.

Should I buy my computer from a local dealer or from a mail-order place?

 There are rotten apples in both barrels. Ask around.

Buying Apple equipment from mail-order places isn't as risky as it once was, now that Apple has said it's OK. I've heard horror stories of El Cheapo hard drives secretly swapped into new Macs, and of demo units sold as new. I've heard chilling tales about things going wrong, when the outfit that sold the Mac wouldn't lift a finger to help. The thing is, I've heard those stories about *both* mail-order and retail stores.

Chalk up one more reason to join a Macintosh user group, where you can ask around for recommendations.

 See also FAQ 1-28, "How do I find a nearby Mac users' group?"

Where do I sell my Mac?

 Locally is best, but don't forget about online possibilities.

A user-group newsletter is the ideal place to advertise — it's inexpensive, local, and targeted directly at Mac users. To find the user group nearest you, call Apple at (800) 538-9696.

Your next best bets are the local newspaper, library/grocery bulletin boards, and so on.

Finally, remember that America Online and other online services have enormous and often-visited classified ad sections. And, of course, the Internet has its own gigantic classified ad area — the newsgroups called **comp.sys.mac.wanted** or **alt.forsale.computers.mac**. Computers sold this way are usually sent C.O.D, which minimizes the risk of outright ripoff for both sides.

 See also FAQ 1-28, "How do I find a nearby Mac users' group?"

 See also FAQ 29-1, "What is the Internet?"

What should I charge for my old Mac?

▽   **Unfortunately, less than you think.**

A computer loses its value at a sickeningly fast rate. To find out how little yours is worth today, look at *Macworld* or *MacUser* magazine's monthly list of going used-Mac prices. If you're online, visit your online service's classified ad section to see what people are charging. (*Macworld*'s contents are also available on eWorld and America Online; *MacUser*'s online edition is on eWorld and CompuServe.)

When I sell my Mac, what about the software on it?

▽   **Let your conscience be your guide.**

When you sell your Mac, the buyer may well look forward to inheriting all the cool programs on it, and may even be willing to pay more for it. Just so you know: Legally, if you sell your Mac and your programs go along with the ride, you're supposed to hand over the manuals, too — and not keep any copies of those programs for yourself.

Where can I see Apple's complete list of current models and prices?

▽   **There's no such list — officially. But you can get pretty close.**

Just calling the nearest Apple dealer is probably the easiest route, of course. If it's the middle of the night, and you have access to the Internet, try Apple's World Wide Web address: **http://www.info.apple.com/product/product.html,** which usually has plenty of good information.

See FAQ 20-9, "What's the Web?"

The ad says "66/33 MHz" processor. Which is it — 33 or 66?

▽   **For your purposes, it's 33.**

In 1994, Apple started this new twist in advertising the Macs based on the 68040 processor chip (Quadra models, for example). (IBM-clone manufacturers had been listing speeds this way for years.) The higher number refers to the data speed *inside the processor;* the lower number is how fast data moves through the computer itself. For the sake of comparison with other Macs, the lower number is what counts.

Is it worth buying an extended warranty like AppleCare?

 No, except maybe for PowerBooks.

You almost never come out ahead, financially speaking, by buying an extended warranty on desktop computer equipment. Even if something does go wrong in, say, five years, the repair cost probably won't be as much as you'd have paid in AppleCare for those five years.

If you carry your PowerBook around a lot, a service plan *may* make more sense; these are more fragile computers, and they're subject to a lot more abuse.

Where do I take a broken, out-of-warranty Mac?

Apple is one possibility; local repair shops are another.

Apple will still repair your out-of-warranty Mac; you just have to *pay* for the work. Call (800) SOS-APPL to set it up.

If you live in a reasonably-sized city, repair outfits are probably all around you. About the only safe way to find a good one is to ask at your local user group.

 See also FAQ 1-28, "How do I find a nearby Mac users's group?"

Can I trust the reviews in the Mac magazines?

 If you mean, "Are the reviews free from advertiser influence?", then: yes.

This answer is based primarily on my experiences writing for *Macworld,* but I imagine things are much the same at other Mac publications.

In fact, reviewers are *never* told whether or not the company (whose product is being reviewed) is an advertiser. At *Macworld,* the lengths to which the editors go for objectivity's sake is amazing; I once wrote the manual for a sheet-music program. For *five years* after that, I wasn't allowed to review *any* music programs.

On the other hand, you may definitely pick up a bias in one particular *writer* or another. Some are more demanding critics; some don't use the software the same way you might. The point is, then, that — if possible — don't rely on a magazine review alone. And always buy stuff from a place that will let you return it.

See also FAQ 23-17, "Where can I buy stuff?"

I've got to rent a Mac for a month. Where do I go?

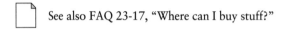 **Check the yellow pages or call GE Rents — and prepare for sticker shock.**

Renting a Mac is *incredibly* expensive. At the rates you'll pay, you could generally buy the computer after only about four months.

Still, if you're desperate, the phone book lists plenty of places only too happy to rent you gear. You may not always find the configuration or model you're looking for, however, unless you contact a reputable national agency. For example, GE Rents has virtually every Mac model available on very short notice. Reach them at (800) GE-RENTS.

Are triple-speed CD-ROM players worth the money?

▽ **No.**

Triple- and quadruple-speed CD-ROM drives are designed to accelerate triple and quadruple speed *discs.* Only one problem — there aren't any. That's one bandwagon CD-ROM publishers didn't jump on; they kept on producing regular double-speed discs. Unfortunately, a triple- or quadruple-speed CD-ROM drive actually plays normal CDs *slower* than a standard double-speed drive! Until your favorite CD-ROM titles are released in triple-, quadruple-, or even sextuple-speed formats, save your money and just by a double-speed drive.

Do I need a surge protector?

▽ **No, not even if you live where power fluctuations are common. (In that case, you need something heftier.)**

The Macintosh has its own surge protection circuitry that's at least as good as the cheapo ones you buy at the hardware store. Neither will protect your equipment from a direct lightning strike, however.

On the other hand, if you live in a rural area where brownouts are everyday events, you might want to invest in the surge suppresser's big brother, the uninterruptible power supply (UPS). This baby keeps your Mac happily and safely humming even if the power goes out completely. On the other hand, a UPS costs several hundred dollars.

Should I get speakers?

▽ **Sure — treat yourself. Just be sure they're designed for the Mac.**

Multimedia computer speakers, like those sold by all the Mac mail-order catalogs, have special shielding. If you make the mistake of using *regular* stereo speakers, you'll wreak all kinds of magnetic havoc with your monitor and your hard drive.

Anyway, if you work with CD-ROMs, games, or digital sound, speakers really make the Mac a much richer and more compelling experience.

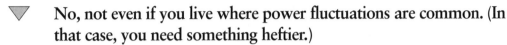 See also FAQ 23-17, "Where can I buy stuff?"

How do I connect my StyleWriter, my MIDI, and a modem all to the same jack?

▽ **Get a manual switch box for $25, or an automatic one for several hundred dollars.**

It's an age-old problem: too many gadgets, too few jacks. Several different kinds of Mac gear all are supposed to be plugged into your modem jack: the modem, MIDI synthesizers, label printers, the StyleWriter, and so on. What's a Mac fan to do?

The simplest and least expensive solution is to buy a manual A/B switch box from one of the Mac mail-order places. You can even get an A/B/C/D switch if you have a lot of gear. Just turn the knob (or punch a button) on the box to specify which gadget you want to use.

If you can't stand manually switching devices, you can buy a NuBus card that provides additional modem jacks. Or, you can get something called the Port Juggler, an external box with four modem ports. It's supposed to switch the Mac's attention from one to another automatically, depending on which program you're using. (I had trouble getting it to work with MIDI, but other people report good luck.)

Where can I buy stuff?

 From mail-order joints or local shops.

23-17

For the biggest selection and the lowest prices, order from one of the Mac overnight mail-order catalogs. In particular, you can't go wrong with Mac Connection, (800) 800-4444, or Mac Warehouse, (800) 255-6227. These catalog outfits generally don't charge sales tax, charge only $3 for shipping, and let you return software if you don't like it. They're also a good source of technical information — and Mac Connection is open 24 hours.

Local computer and software stores don't offer as much variety, especially in Macintosh gear. But at a store, you can sometimes try before you buy — at the very least, you can ask other customers their opinions before you buy.

See also FAQ 1-5, "Why is there so much more software for PC, DOS, and Windows than for Macs?"

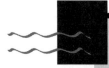

RAQ: Rarely Asked Question

What's my Mac model?

Another real transcript from the Apple 800 hotline. The customer has called to find out which Mac model he has just purchased:

Customer: Well, it's an Apple computer.

Technician: We have several computers that it might be. You can find the name on the front of the computer and the display name on its rear.

Customer: Well, it's a Trinitron with an Apple on the front of it.

(continued)

(continued)

Technician: The name of the display is on the back.

Customer: Multiple Scan 17 Display.

Technician: Okay, the computer will have its name on the front.

Customer: What do you mean, "computer?"

Technician: The box itself.

Customer: The monitor?

Technician: No, the computer is where you would put a floppy disk and plug in the keyboard.

Customer: I don't have one of those. I think that may be the problem.

Technician: What *do* you have?

Customer: I have a CD-ROM, a monitor, keyboard, a printer . . .

CHAPTER

24

Upgrading the Thing

I*t seemed so great when you bought it: fast, sleek, unlimited. And now you can't stand waiting for its pokey little wristwatch cursor.*

But upgrading — by installing an accelerator — today isn't as good a value as it was several years ago. Sure, pop in new RAM, give it a bigger hard drive. But think carefully before doing much more — it's probably less expensive just to sell the thing and get a newer model.

I need speed. Should I buy an accelerator?

 No. It almost never makes financial sense.

During the time you've owned your Mac, technology has been marching on. Today's Mac models are faster, better, and less expensive than last year's. If you're considering adding an accelerator card to your Mac, do a little math. If the cost of a new Mac, minus the money you get from selling your old one, is less than the cost of the accelerator card — well, you get the idea. It's generally cheaper to sell your Mac and buy a new model! Furthermore, the new Mac comes with a whole new warranty and updated system software.

 See also FAQ 23-5, "What should I charge for my old Mac?"

I need more RAM. What do I do?

▽ **Call a dealer, call a Mac mail-order place, or call a memory mail-order place.**

Technically, installing new memory SIMMs is a piece of cake. The hard part is figuring out what kind of SIMMs to order, learning how many you need and in what capacity, and getting the case off your Mac. There are three ways to go about it, of varying cost and simplicity:

✦ Call a local Mac dealer. *Advantages:* The dealer is responsible for figuring out what kind of chips you need, bringing the chips over, and doing the installation. Your warranty is utterly intact. *Disadvantage:* This is much more expensive than doing it yourself.

✦ Call a Mac mail-order place, such as Mac Connection. *Advantages:* This method is much less expensive than a dealer. They'll answer all your questions about what kind of SIMMs to order. They often provide instructions — or even a video. *Disadvantages:* You have to do the installation yourself; and technically, your warranty is jeopardized — Apple won't fix any problems you introduce by installing RAM yourself.

✦ Call a memory-only mail-order place, such as Chip Merchant (ads for these places appear the back of Macintosh magazines). *Advantages:* This is the least expensive way of all. *Disadvantages:* You'll get no installation help whatsoever.

See also Chapter 6, "Memory."

My hard drive is full! What should I do?

▷   See FAQ 8-3, "I'm running out of hard-drive space! What should I do?"

Can I add an FPU to my Mac?

▽ Yes, but not easily.

An FPU is a math coprocessor chip, used by a few number-crunching or scientific programs. As you'll note in FAQ 4-32, an FPU doesn't affect the speed of your Mac one bit when you use the other 95% of the world's programs.

In any case, if you turn scientist and decide you need to add a math coprocessor to your Mac, you can do so — but the possibilities depend on your model's main processor chip. See Table 24-1 to find out your model's version.

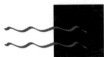

Table 24-1

Processor versions and the Macs that use them

020 chip	030 chip	040 chip
Mac II	SE/30	LC 475, 575
LC	Classic II	Performa 475, 575
	Performa 200–450	All Quadra models
	Color Classic	All Centris models
	IIfx, IIx	LC/Performa 630 series
	IIci, IIcx	
	IIsi, IIvx	
	LC II, III	
	LC 550, Mac TV	
	PowerBooks 140–230	

The 68020 and 68030 chips

Of the '020 models, the Mac II came with an FPU chip; the LC didn't. Although it makes little financial sense, you can add an FPU to the LC.

The same situation applies to the '030 models; many included a built-in FPU, but the LC, Performa, and PowerBook models didn't.

If you want an FPU for your 68020 or 68030 Mac, you can buy and install one (or hire someone to install one). Check the back pages of a Macintosh magazine to locate some companies who sell FPUs. The chip you want is called the MC68882. Remember that, technically, you violate your warranty if you perform this installation — then again, if you own a 68020 or 68030 Mac, its warranty has already expired.

The 68040 chip

Once again, some Mac models — Quadras and some Centris models — came equipped with a math coprocessor when you bought it. Others, such as the Performa and LC series, are distinctly advertised to contain something called a *68LC040* processor. You might imagine that the LC stands for *lacking chip* — the FPU chip.

If a coprocessor-free '040 Mac is your fate, getting an FPU isn't simply a matter of adding one, as it is with the previous chips. You have to replace your *entire processor chip,* taking out the 68LC040 chip and putting in a full-fledged 68040. Once again, the Mac magazines contain ads for companies who will happily send you the full '040 chip in exchange for your old one plus some money. (You still have to find somebody to do the installation.)

See also FAQ 4-31, "What's an FPU?"

See also FAQ 18-6, "Why do I get 'No Co-Processor Installed' errors? My Mac *has* an FPU!"

Can I upgrade my old Mac to be a Power Macintosh?

▽ **Yes, if it's a recent model.**

Apple, not wanting to leave millions of Mac fans in the dust, will be delighted to sell you an upgrade card that turns your early-90s Mac model into a Power Mac.

The upgrade card

For about $500, you can install a PDS accelerator card into your older Mac. The card has a new PowerPC processor that runs at *twice* the processor speed of your existing Macintosh. For example, if you have a Quadra 800, whose original chip runs at 33 megahertz, it will run at 66 megahertz with the upgrade card in place.

Owning an upgrade card has one distinct advantage over owning an actual Power Mac — you can turn it off when necessary, leaving you with the Mac you've always had. That's useful when you want to run some program that isn't available in a "native" version.

This upgrade card is available from various mail-order outfits, and you can install it easily yourself. It's available for the **Quadra 605, 610, 650, 700, 800, 900, and 950;** the **Centris 610 and 650;** the **LC 475 through 575;** and the **Performa 475 through 550.**

The complete motherboard replacement

For about $1500 (or $2000 for the AV models), you can get a completely new main circuit board into your Mac. (These boards used to be available from Apple; now they're only available from a company called Daystar.) In other words, instead of goosing the speed of your processor, this upgrade turns your older Mac into a true Power Mac 6100, 7100, or 8100. It's available for the **Centris and Quadra 610, 650, 660 AV, 800, and 840 AV;** the **Performa 600, Macintosh IIvx and IIvi;** and Apple's **Workgroup Servers.**

Can I upgrade my Power Macintosh to a newer model?

 No.

24-6

Apple continually introduces new Power Mac models that are identical to their predecessors except for a slightly faster PowerPC chip inside. For example, the Power Mac 8100/80 gave way to the 8100/100, which itself was replaced by the very scarce 8100/110.

Unfortunately, Apple doesn't offer any upgrade if you already own one of the previous models.

I've heard about these "clock-chip accelerators" for the Power Mac. Do they work?

 Usually — and if yours doesn't, they'll give you your money back or send you a replacement.

24-7

These clock-chip goosers violate the principle in FAQ 26-1 — that it never makes sense to buy an accelerator. These accelerators clip onto your Power Mac motherboard, inexpensively turning a 66 MHz machine into an 80 MHz machine. And they actually work. Well, about 80% of them work. If you get sent one that doesn't work, the manufacturer will exchange it or refund your money.

Apple, predictably, discourages you from using these, saying that they might heat up your processor too much.

Should I upgrade to System 7.5?

 See FAQ 21-1, "I heard that System 7.5 requires 8 megs of RAM and 20 megs of disk space. Is it worth getting?"

24-8

How do I copy all my stuff to the new Mac?

 See FAQ 25-1, "How can I connect two Macs?"

24-9

Will my aliases still work on the new Mac?

   ### Yes, as long as the hard drive and folders have the same names.

As you probably know, the magic of an alias is that you can move it around, rename it, rename the original icon from which it was made, and it will still work. Double-clicking the alias icon will still open the original item.

When you move your programs to another hard drive, however, they're given new, behind-the-scenes ID numbers. If the program, now copied to your new Mac, has the same name as before, is in a folder with the same name, and is on a hard drive with the same name, the alias reorients itself — and it will work once again. (Even the Mac must have the same name, by the way. You change a Mac's name by opening the Sharing Setup control panel.) Otherwise, the aliases stop working.

See also FAQ 5-11, "What's an alias for?"

Can I add a color monitor to my Plus/SE/Classic/Classic II?

   ### Yes, but why bother?

Even today, there may be some company who will sell you the necessary components to let you connect a color screen to your older black-and-white Mac. Without a doubt, however, it will cost more than a new, inexpensive Performa. Those older compact Macs simply weren't designed to accommodate such major surgery.

The Classic II is designed to *print* color, if you have access to a color printer — but it still won't *show* color. That is, if, in your graphics program, you specify that an object is blue, it will print blue. But again, adding a color screen is an expensive and difficult process.

PART 6

Making
Connections

Yes, a Macintosh provides plenty of joy and usefulness — but not half as much as when it's connected to other computers, either by network or by modem. If you don't believe it, glance at the nearest newspaper or news magazine. Every other article seems to be about the Internet, online services, or cyberspace.

Unfortunately, hooking up a Mac to the outside world is much more difficult and complicated than most other tricks it knows. Sure, it's much easier to wire up a Mac than a PC clone, but that doesn't mean it's simple. May the answers in the following five chapters make making connections as simple as possible.

25

Network City

M illions of Mac owners don't even know it's there. Yet for millions of others, networking (connecting to other computers) is one of the great things about Macs. Unlike DOS and Windows computers, networking hardware and software is built right into every Mac.

Setting up a network isn't a hard process, but it's long. Fortunately, after your network is established, connecting to other Macs requires only a double-click. Seated at your Mac, you can easily view or manipulate files on any other Mac on the network, you can send electronic mail messages to your coworkers, and you can share expensive peripheral equipment like laser printers and modems.

If your ambitions are slightly less grandiose — for example, if you have a PowerBook and you want a simple way to transfer files between it and your desktop Mac — the network can still serve you well. Keep these instructions handy, too, when you buy a new Mac. Networking is the least expensive method of transferring all your files from the old Mac to the new one.

How can I connect two Macs?

▽ Use one cable and about 50 control panels.

To wire your Macs together, you use exactly the same kind of cable you use to connect your Mac to a laser printer. That is, you use ordinary telephone wire, strung between small plastic adapters (one per machine) called *PhoneNet connectors*. (Technically, only one company — Farallon — makes PhoneNet connectors. Dozens of companies make clones. Still, people generically call them PhoneNet connectors, regardless of the actual brand, just as everybody says Jello instead of "gelatin dessert.")

Wiring the network

Doing the cabling is easy:

1. Each connector has a short, round, protruding cable that connects to your Mac's *printer jack*. Walk among your Macs and laser printers, attaching a PhoneNet connector to each.

2. Each connector also has two places to plug in the clip at the end of a telephone wire. Using individual lengths of telephone wire, string all the PhoneNet connectors together. The only rule about wiring your Macs together is that the wiring can't form a loop. Connect one Mac or laser printer to the next in a long, continuous daisy chain.

3. When you're finished, there should be one empty hole on the PhoneNet connector at each *end* of your chain. Plug this empty jack with one of the tiny plastic *terminators* that came in the PhoneNet connector package. The terminator looks like a little end-of-phone-wire clip that's been broken off.

Figure 25-1 shows the essence of how a small network might be wired.

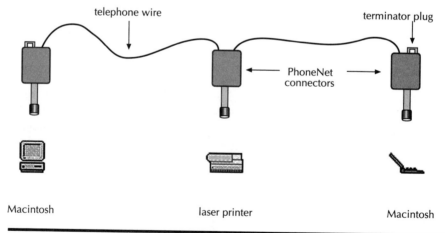

Figure 25-1: To create a network, every gadget must have its own PhoneNet connector. Join them with phone wire, and fill the empty PhoneNet jacks with terminator clips.

Now you must fuss with the software. There are two phases to this process: setting up *your* Mac so that other people on the network can have access to it; and accessing somebody *else's* Mac while seated at your own.

Making your Mac available

Making your Mac ready for public invasion requires a ridiculous number of steps. Fortunately, it's a one-time setup.

1. Open the Chooser (from the menu). Check the lower-right corner of the Chooser window and make sure that AppleTalk is active. If AppleTalk is inactive, click the upper button (*Active* or *Active on Restart*), close the Chooser, and restart the Mac.

2. Choose Control Panels from your menu. Double-click the Sharing Setup control panel. (If you're missing this or any of the control panels to come, re-install your System 7-or-later System Folder from the installation disks that came with your Mac.)

3. Figure 25-2 shows the Sharing Setup window. Type your name in the first blank and a password in the second. (This is the password *you* will need, later, when you want to get into your Mac while seated elsewhere on the network. If you aren't worried about prying eyes, skip the password.) Also give your Mac a name in the third blank (usually the model name or something).

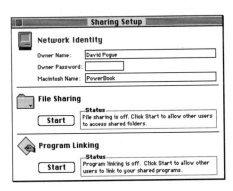
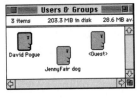

Figure 25-2: Name yourself, your password, and your Mac in the Sharing Setup control panel (left). Then create icons for your comrades in Users & Groups (right).

4. Click the Start button. When that button changes to say Stop, you're ready to plow ahead. Close this window.

5. Open the Users & Groups icon. You get a window full of icons, each representing somebody on the network. At this moment, it's probably just you and Guest, which means "anyone else."

6. For each person on your network, choose New User from the File menu to create a new icon. Name it appropriately, double-click it, and provide a password (see Figure 25-2 once more). Again, this is the password that person will need to invade *your* Mac.

   Repeat this process for each person to whom you're giving permission to sign onto your machine. Remember to do the same for Guest, keeping in mind that Guest has no password. Permitting Guest access makes life easier if you have no worries about security.

   Close the control panel and all windows, saving when you're asked to do so.

7. Fortunately, you don't have to make your *entire* digital life available for ransacking by the local network thugs. You can specify individual folders that you'd like to make public. Keep all your private stuff in *other* folders.

   Highlight a folder you'd like other people to be able to access. (Or, if you're not paranoid, highlight your *hard-drive* icon.) From the File menu, choose Sharing. In the window that appears, click to select the "Share this item and its contents" checkbox. (Ignore the other settings.) Close the window. When the Mac asks if you want to save, click OK.

   If you're doing this on a folder-by-folder basis, repeat this step for the other folders you're making public.

Your Mac is now network-ready, network-friendly. Go now to another Mac on the network, and play the role of somebody trying to get at your stuff.

Opening your Mac from elsewhere

Once you're seated at another person's Mac, do this:

1. Choose Chooser from the menu. Click the AppleShare icon. (If there *is* no AppleShare icon, reinstall your System software.) If everything is properly wired and control-paneled, your Mac's name should show up on the window's right side. (See Figure 25-3.)

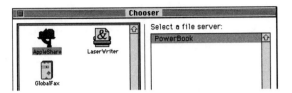

Figure 25-3: This is how someone else on the network would first see your network-friendly PowerBook.

2. Click the name of the Mac you want, and click OK. In the next window, type your name and password. Unlike other situations on the Mac, in the password's case, capitalization *does* matter. (If you had previously turned on access to the Guest icon in the Users & Groups control panel, here's a shortcut: In this window, just click the Guest button. No password necessary.) See Figure 25-4.

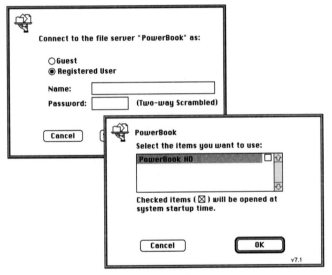

Figure 25-4: First you identify yourself (left). Then you identify the hard drive you want to invade (right).

3. Click OK. Yet another window appears, displaying the name of your hard drive. Click OK yet again.

4. Close any lingering windows, and look at the upper-right corner of your screen (see Figure 25-5).

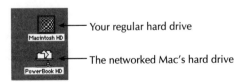

Your regular hard drive

The networked Mac's hard drive

Figure 25-5: Though it may be down the hall, or even in another building, the hard drive of the distant Mac shows up on your screen as though it's just another floppy disk.

You've finally brought your Mac's hard drive onto the screen of this other computer (where you're now sitting). Its "server" icon is the tipoff that it isn't directly attached to your current machine. Nonetheless, you can double-click this icon, view its contents, and manipulate them exactly as you would if you were still sitting at your original Mac. And, of course, you can *copy* files between the networked Mac and yours — one of the most useful aspects of this whole affair.

Doing things across this kind of a network, by the way, always takes longer than it would if you were accessing a Mac directly. Copying is slower, and launching or opening files that are on a distant Mac is *much* slower. Upgrading to System 7.5.1 increases the speed substantially.

When you're finished using the networked hard drive, drag its icon to the trash to "disconnect" from it.

Saving time next time

You're probably hoping you don't have to go through all those steps every time you want to access another Mac. Fortunately, you don't.

Highlight the networked hard drive icon after it appears on the screen. From the File menu, choose Make Alias. A duplicate of the hard drive's icon appears, with its name italicized — an alias. The *next* time you want to bring that Mac's icon online, just double-click its alias. Instantly the remote hard drive's icon pops up (after asking for a password, if you set things up that way). You've just bypassed all of those steps.

See also FAQ 5-11, "What's an alias for?"

How do I set up e-mail in our office?

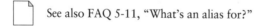

There's a cheap way and a good way; take your choice.

Once your network is established, *file sharing* (the process described in FAQ 25-1) isn't the only neat new collaborative feature you've added to your Mac. You have also opened the possibility of in-office *e-mail* — onscreen messages, delivered instantly to the screens of your office comrades.

First, of course, you have to wire your office Macs together into a network. See FAQ 25-1 again.

Now you can choose an e-mail software kit. Most of the business world uses Microsoft Mail, QuickMail (CE Software), or Lotus cc:Mail. If those commercial products whet your interest, call a mail-order place and place your order.

There is, however, a less expensive alternative built right into the latest system software. It's called PowerTalk, and it comes free with System 7.5 and later. Unfortunately, PowerTalk takes up a lot of memory. And it isn't simple to figure out. You don't even get a manual to help you — you're supposed to rely on the onscreen instructions of PowerTalk Guide (which magically appears in your Help [question-mark] menu after you install PowerTalk). But here are the basics:

1. Install PowerTalk. This involves finding your System 7.5 CD-ROM or floppy-disk set. PowerTalk normally isn't installed when you install System 7.5; you must specifically request it, using a separate installer on your system disks or CD.

2. On your hard drive, you'll find about 17,000 new extensions, control panels, desktop icons, and other junk. To establish a simple e-mail system, begin by choosing Unlock Key Chain from the Special menu. You'll be asked for your name and a password. Type away.

3. Make sure that everyone else on the network also installs and sets up PowerTalk.

4. You're now finally ready to send some actual e-mail. In the Apple Extras folder on your hard drive, inside the PowerTalk folder, is a new program called AppleMail. When you double-click it, you'll see something like Figure 25-6. Type your message in the lower part, type in a short phrase to serve as the Subject, and indicate the recipients by clicking the icon identified in Figure 25-6.

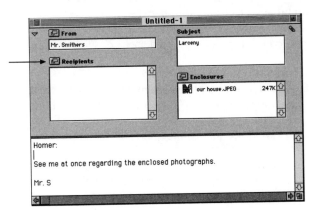

Figure 25-6: To address your e-mail, click the Recipient icon. In the window that appears, double-click the name(s) of the person(s) to whom you want to send this missive.

5. To send the finished memo, choose Send Mail from the Mail menu. The message, "New mail has arrived" appears on your recipient's screen. That person must double-click the Mailbox icon to see your note.

PowerTalk is much more than this simple e-mail system, of course. It holds fantastic potential for simplifying the rat's nest of passwords, e-mail, online services, faxes, and other electronic correspondence. While many of those features require that you buy special new software, several programs (ClarisWorks, WordPerfect, Word 6, for example) already come complete with a Send command. When you're finished working on something, choose Send — and your entire *document* appears in the recipient's Mailbox.

See also FAQ 4-60, "What's PowerTalk?"

What's the difference between LocalTalk and Ethernet?

▽   Speed and cost — LocalTalk is slow and free.

The Mac's built-in file sharing feature, as described in FAQ 25-1, is called LocalTalk. It's fantastically inexpensive, convenient, and easy to figure out. Unfortunately, it also has some limits. The maximum number of Macs you can hook up this way is about 30, and the wires can't be longer than a total of about 500 feet (unless you get special shielded cable, which could buy you another 1000 feet or so). And LocalTalk isn't terribly fast, either. Anyone who has ever tried to copy a giant graphics file from one Mac onto another that's connected by LocalTalk can tell you how long the wait can be.

If your network's speed is bothersome, you can use an alternative wiring system called *Ethernet*. This system of wires and connectors lets you hook together more Macs and farther apart Macs, and Ethernet transfers stuff between them about three times faster than LocalTalk. Of course, Ethernet also costs more than LocalTalk; each Mac or laser printer needs an Ethernet connector, and you need special cables to connect them.

It used to be that you'd have to buy a $150 Ethernet *card* and a $75 *connector* for every Mac on the network. Fortunately, each of today's high-end models (the more expensive Quadras, all Power Macs, and the pricier PowerBooks) comes with built-in Ethernet circuitry. The fancier laser printer models also have Ethernet jacks. All you have to add to these Macs and printers are those $75 connectors (and the Ethernet wiring).

Then, too, wiring Ethernet networks is much more complex and difficult to troubleshoot than LocalTalk, the old standby. Networking experience is definitely a prerequisite.

I read that I can access my office Mac from home, over the phone line. How?

▽   You need fast modems and the program known as Apple Remote Access.

Remember from FAQ 25-1 how it feels to bring another Mac's icon onto your screen — over the network? Imagine opening your Chooser, clicking the AppleShare icon, and being shown a list of all the other Macs and printers on your network ... which is *3000 miles away.*

That's exactly what Apple Remote Access (ARA) lets you do, via modem. You can sit with your PowerBook in Dallas, plug your modem into the phone jack, dial the phone number of your network in Ottawa, and have complete access to all the Macs and laser printers on that distant network.

There are two versions of the ARA software. The *client software* is what you need to dial *in* to a network; it's free from Apple and is included with most new Mac models. The *server software* is what your office technician uses to prepare the network for access by the outside world of modems. It costs a couple hundred dollars.

Anyway, if you want to set up your own ARA system so that you can dial into your home Mac while on the road, you'll have to buy the server software. You'll also have to equip both your Macs with fast modems — 14.4 kbps is about the minimum speed to prevent the sluggishness from driving you mad.

Finally, you'll probably need some means of ensuring that your home Mac is *on* when you call in. A device called the PowerKey Remote, in conjunction with the regular Power Key, can switch a Mac on when the phone rings, and then turn it off again after a specified interval. (Actually, the Mac that's calling will probably hang up before connecting — because your home Mac will probably take a minute or two to start up, depending on how many extensions it has to load. In real life, you may have call your home Mac *twice* — once to turn the Mac on, and again a minute later to make the connection.)

See also FAQ 23-17, "Where can I buy stuff?"

I've set up a LocalTalk network, but I can't bring the other Mac online.

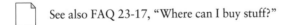 The problem can only be one of two things: hardware or software.

First, check the wiring. Remember that your chain of Macs must never form a loop, and that the PhoneNet connectors at either end of the chain must be equipped with a terminator. (See FAQ 25-1 for a refresher.) Also be aware that phone wire is the most temperamental of cables. One little crimp and your network is dead. On the other hand, phone wire is certainly cheap to replace.

Second, check the software. Every Mac on the network should have the usual assemblage of extensions and control panels in the System Folder necessary for file sharing, outlined in Table 25-1.

Table 25-1

Extensions and control panels needed for file sharing

Extensions	Control Panels
AppleShare	File Sharing Monitor
File Sharing Extension	Network
Mailbox Extension	Sharing Setup
Network Extension	Users & Groups
PowerTalk Extension *	
PowerTalk Guide *	
PowerTalk Manager *	

(* Needed for PowerTalk only.)
If you're missing any of these items, reinstall from your original system disks.

Remember, too, that AppleTalk must be turned on in the Chooser, and that the PhoneNet connectors must be connected to the *printer* ports of the Macs, not the identical-looking modem ports.

Last thing to check: Open your Network control panel. Make sure that the correct network type is selected — LocalTalk or EtherNet.

26

PCs and Macs

"*R*un your favorite DOS applications on your Mac!" The ads have been saying it for years. Only recently, however, has that fantasy become real (if using DOS can be said to be a fantasy). Today, you can indeed sit at your Mac, merrily puttering away in your favorite DOS and Windows programs.

A true Mac bigot, of course, wonders why on earth you'd want to do that. The answer is: Software. Thousands more programs are available for the PC than for the Mac. Not that sheer numbers are worth anything — but among those thousands are a few programs that would be nice to have on the Mac. And a few PC CD-ROM discs might be worth trying, too.

Can I use this PC disk in my Mac?

 Yes. It's much easier, though, if you have System 7.5.

Every Macintosh made since 1988 has had a special kind of floppy drive called a SuperDrive. Its big feature is that it can read both Mac and PC 3.5-inch floppy disks. And yet, as you may have discovered, inserting a PC floppy into a Mac generally produces nothing but an error message: "This is not a Macintosh disk."

The big unspoken fine print is that you need *software*, too, to read PC disks. On all versions of the system software before System 7.5, you were supposed to dig up the program called Apple File Exchange. It came on the system floppy disks that came with your Mac (often on the one called Tidbits). Launch Apple File Exchange *first*, and then insert your PC disk. Its contents appear on the right side of the screen, and your hard drive appears on the left. You're supposed to transfer each file from the PC disk to your Mac by clicking its name (on the right side), and then clicking the Translate button. (You can move files from your hard drive to that floppy, too; just click the file's name on the *left* side, then click Translate.)

Fortunately, there's an easier way. It's a control panel called PC Exchange. It used to be sold separately by Apple, and it's now included with System 7.5. It permits the Mac to perform a simple miracle: When you insert a PC disk, its icon shows up on your desktop, exactly as though it were a Mac disk. The PC disk behaves exactly like a Mac disk, whether you're copying, trashing, erasing, renaming, whatever — except that it's slightly slower than using a Mac disk. In fact, I know people who have been using PC disks for months — *accidentally*. They purchased the wrong kind of disks from a computer store. But because PC Exchange does its job so well, these Mac users never even discover their mistake.

Oh, by the way: If you're asking about using those big, old, floppy, 5.25-inch PC disks, you have two less-attractive options:

✦ Take them to a local computer-printing shop and ask them to copy the disks' contents onto Mac disks.

✦ Buy a 5.25-inch disk drive for your Mac. It's sold by Dayna for $600.

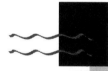

FAQ: Facetiously Asked Question

What does IBM stand for?

I suppose it depends on which bumper sticker you prefer:

✦ I Bring Manuals

✦ I Bought Macintosh

✦ In Bed with Microsoft

Can I use a Mac disk in a PC?

 Yes. You need TransferPro for Windows.

Call Digital Instrumentation Technology at (505) 662-1459.

My friend gave me a PC disk with an important manuscript on it. How do I open it?

 Launch your word processor. See if the Open command will do the trick.

First, of course, you must make sure that your Mac can even *read* the PC disk; see FAQ 26-1.

Once the *disk* problem is solved, you still have to overcome the *file format* hurdle. Just as you can't play an audiocassette in your CD player, you can't open a Word for Windows file with SimpleText.

Fortunately, many Mac word processors can automatically translate documents from many PC word processors. For example, Microsoft Word can open WordPerfect documents created on a PC. WordPerfect (on the Mac) can open documents from dozens of both Mac and PC word processors. A set of specialized *translator files* does this conversion; if you're missing the translator files, the conversion won't happen. (Re-install your word processor if that's your situation.)

In all cases, however, you won't get far simply double-clicking the PC document's icon. Instead, do this:

1. Launch your Mac word processor.

2. From the File menu, choose Open. If there's a popup menu in the dialog box that appears, play with it. Choose the most general setting; for example, in Microsoft Word, the popup menu should say All Documents, not Word Documents.

3. If the PC document shows up in the Open File dialog box, you're in luck. Double-click its name to open and convert it into your word processor's format.

If using the Open command doesn't work, your PC-owning correspondent may have to give you a fresh disk. This time, ask him or her to save the file in a different format, one that *your* word processor can open.

If in doubt, ask the friend to convert the manuscript to Rich Text Format (RTF), a special conversion type that preserves most of the formatting — bold, italic, font, or type-size information, for example. Most self-respecting word processors can both open and create RTF files.

Finally, if even that idea fails, here's a sure-fire last resort: Ask for the file as a *plain text file*. This kind of file has no formatting at all, like bold or italic — it's just pure typing. But at least your word processor will be able to open it — guaranteed.

How do I run DOS and Windows programs on the Mac?

▽ **Use emulator software (SoftWindows) or special hardware (a card from Apple, Reply, or Orange Micro).**

SoftPC and SoftWindows, both from Insignia Solutions, are software programs that turn your Mac into a PC clone. SoftPC, which runs on almost any Mac, lets you run DOS programs — not Windows — somewhat slowly. To run Windows (the Microsoft program that PC users install to make their computers more like a Mac), you need SoftWindows. It runs only on the Power Mac, and it has the speed of a standard 486 PC clone. It's important to note that version 1.0 doesn't run in Windows enhanced mode, which means that you can't run many modern Windows programs. (Version 2, scheduled for a late 1995 release, removes that limitation.)

If you prefer better speed and more-complete compatibility, consider installing a PC-emulation circuit board into your Mac. Apple sells what it calls "DOS compatible" cards for the 630 series, certain LC models, and certain Power Macs (such as the 6100). For other Mac models, Reply and Orange Micro make similar cards.

All of these cards add an actual PC, complete with Intel processor, to your Mac. Press one key, and your screen fades — to be replaced by the traditional black screen of DOS. At this point, you can launch Windows or run any program you'd run if you owned an actual PC.

If you've only used Macs, take a deep breath before investing in one of these products. You're about to leave the comforts and simplicity of the Macintosh world — and enter the more technical, chaotic world of the PC. Good luck to you.

Can my Macintosh play CD-ROM discs for a PC?

▼   **Yes. You may not hear the sound, though.**

If you have equipped your Mac with a DOS card (see FAQ 26-4), you should be in good shape. You can play CD-ROM discs designed to run on PCs only.

If you're running SoftWindows, however, you probably won't hear the sound or music. At least in version 1, SoftWindows doesn't emulate the popular SoundBlaster sound board, which a PC needs to produce music.

If you have neither a DOS card nor SoftWindows, the answer is no — you can't use PC CD-ROM discs on your Mac.

Can I use a PC printer with my Mac?

▼   **Yes, if you buy PowerPrint.**

PowerPrint is a terrific little cable-and-software kit. It lets your Macintosh connect to, and print on, any of 1200 non-Macintosh printers. It really works.

   See also FAQ 23-17, "Where can I buy stuff?"

Can I use a PC monitor with my Mac?

▼   **Yes; you just need the proper adapter.**

In fact, many "Macintosh" monitors sold today are just PC monitors with a Mac adapter already attached to the cable. If you have an old PC monitor but no adapter, stores and catalogs from Radio Shack to Mac Connection sell VGA-to-Mac adapters for under $20.

When I open a file from a PC or Internet, there are Returns at the end of every line!

▽ **Ugly, isn't it? Easy to fix, though, with shareware.**

In the olden days, non-Mac computers weren't smart enough to wrap your text when your typing reached the end of a line. Instead, there were two invisible characters — a Return character and a *linefeed* — at the end of each line within a paragraph. The Mac, enlightened machine that it is, has no use for those strange characters; it displays them as little boxes along the margin, or breaks the lines of text in peculiar places, or both.

America Online and other services are crawling with programs that can clean up those weird-looking text files — PlainText or Deskzap, for example.

📄 See also FAQ 28-3, "How do I find a program I want to download?"

Is there a way to switch programs from the keyboard, like in Windows?

▽ **Sure. A little shareware will do the trick.**

Visit America Online or another service; download Program Switcher, ProSwitch, or any of the other shareware programs that do the same thing: Let you switch to the next running program by pressing a couple of keys.

📄 See also FAQ 28-3, "How do I find a program I want to download?"

Can I get a PC virus?

▽ **Yes, but only if you have equipped your Mac to run PC software.**

It sure is handy to be able to run PC programs on your Mac (see FAQ 26-1). Adding a PC compatibility card or SoftWindows opens up your Mac to a world of new software titles. Unfortunately, it also opens up your Mac to a world of PC viruses.

If you download games and other programs from public BBSs, you are indeed vulnerable to viruses that thrive on PC compatibles. If you're worried, buy a PC virus-checking program and run *it* on your Mac, too.

CHAPTER

27

Modems, Faxes, and Lines

O*wning a Mac, no doubt, is the most fun you've ever had (that you can tell your mother about). And yet — without a modem, you're only experiencing* half *the fun you could be having.*

These days, nobody sells modems. Everybody sells fax/modems — *gadgets that turn your Mac into a true fax machine* and *act as a traditional modem.*

What if I only have one phone line?

▽ **No problem. A Y-jack costs $3 at Radio Shack.**

Actually, you may not even need a Y-jack to accommodate both your modem and your telephone. Most external modems today already *have* a jack for your phone. You can use the telephone exactly as you always have, completely ignoring the modem. Life goes on sweetly, provided you never try to talk on the phone and use the modem at the same time. (Doing so thoroughly interrupts whichever kind of call was placed first.)

If you use your Mac to receive faxes, you'll probably want to buy a fax/voice switcher. This $100 device automatically handles incoming calls, routing them to your fax/modem or your telephone as appropriate. (Outgoing calls need no such device; as mentioned above, whichever device — you or your modem — dials first determines what kind of call it is.)

Of course, if you do a lot of talking, faxing, and modeming, the ultimate solution is to call the phone company to request a second line. You'll have one for humans and the other for your Mac.

How do I connect my modem and MIDI and StyleWriter at the same time?

See FAQ 23-16, "How do I connect my StyleWriter, my MIDI, and a modem all to the same jack?"

What do V.32, V.42, bis, MNP, etc., mean?

▽ **They're tech-talk for various modem speeds and features.**

In the early days, you were cool if you owned a modem at all. This amazing gadget could pump an impressive 300 bits of information — about six English words — *per second* to another computer over the phone lines.

Today, you can't *give away* a 300-bps modem (and nobody much wants 1200- or 2400-bps models, either). 9600-bps, 14,400-bps, and now 28,800-bps modems have come our way, making it possible to transfer stuff from computer to computer in less time than ever. Each faster speed was brought to us by a different technological breakthrough, and each breakthrough has been given a name. Table 27-1 shows how they correspond.

Incidentally, one modem model may have more than one designation — one may be V.32, V.42, *and* V.42bis, for example (many probably are). Such a modem would have 9600-bps speed, with built-in error correction and data-compression features.

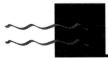

Table 27-1

Secret modem code names

Code name	English translation
V.22bis	2400-bps modems
V.32	9600-bps modems
V.32bis	14,400-bps, also known as 14.4-Kbps, modems
V.42	*Not* a code name for a particular speed. Instead, a modem with this code on its feature list uses a special *error correction* technique. That means that if static garbles the transmission when your modem is sending information, your modem automatically resends the lost data. The result is a more efficient transmission.
V.42bis	Once again, this code doesn't refer to a particular speed. Instead, it indicates that a modem can speed up data transmission by *compressing* it during the sending process.
V.fast	During the competitive early 90s, modem makers frantically worked to invent the next level of modem speed: 28.8 Kbps (otherwise known as 28,800 bps). Eventually, a few companies began selling modems that came pretty close. They were designated V.fast modems. Imagine those companies' horror when, a year later, the rest of the industry settled on a *different* technological 28.8 Kbps standard (called V.34). V.fast was an aborted, nonstandard type of 28.8 Kbps modem.
V.34	Newer 28.8-Kbps modems

Why does one 28.8 modem cost three times as much as another?

 It's all in the packaging, included software, and technical help.

27-4

Here's a little secret: Inside almost every one of the 200 modem brands on the market is the exact same communications chip. The only difference between one modem brand and another is what the modem company has *added*. Those goodies include the modem housing, the included fax software, the manual, the telephone support personnel, and so on. The quality of those add-ons varies dramatically — along with the corresponding price.

When using the modem as a plain old modem, the cheapest may do as well as the most expensive. It's when you start faxing, needing help, and trying new things that you'll discover what the higher price paid for.

 See also FAQ 27-12, "Rats! My fax software messed up again!"

What do all the blinking modem lights mean?

▽ **Generally, very little.**

When troubleshooting or trying to learn about telecommunications, however, the little status lights might come in handy. Table 27-2 shows what the little labels stand for.

Table 27-2

Modem status lights deciphered

Abbreviation	Meaning when lit
HS (High Speed)	Your modem has connected at whatever it considers a high speed. This is fairly meaningless.
AA (Auto Answer)	Your modem is ready to answer a call, such as to receive an incoming fax.
CD (Carrier Detect)	Your modem has heard the annoying squeal of a remote modem's *carrier tone*. Until both modems detect carrier, no other communication can pass between them.
OH (Off Hook)	Your modem has taken the phone line off the hook and is ready to dial a number and connect to another modem. If you're not sure whether you're connected to something, check this light. If it's not lit, you're not connected.
RD or RX (Receive Data)	This light blinks once for each bit of data your modem receives. If the online service you're using seems to slow to a crawl, check this light. If it's blinking, be patient — you're receiving data.
SD or TX (Send Data)	This light blinks once for each bit of data your modem sends. To see this light in action, connect to an online service, keep an eye on this light, and type some characters. The light should blink once for each character you type.
TR (Data Terminal Ready)	Your modem is on and is on speaking terms with your Mac.

Abbreviation	Meaning when lit
MR (Modem Ready)	Your modem is plugged into a power source and is turned on.
ARQ, EC, or Error Control	Your modem detected an error-control signal from the other modem, and is working in error-control mode.
LB (Low Battery)	Your modem's battery is low (portable modems only).

What's the difference between baud and bps?

 Today, bps is the more accurate term.

27-6

The original 300-baud modems were so called because they could send 300 bits of information per second. (Eight bits = one byte = one typed character.) It worked by warbling rapidly between two tones — high and low; each change from high to low represented one bit.

Today, however, modems achieve their higher speeds by packing more information into each warble. For example, a modem might warble only 600 times per second — 600 baud — but each tone change represents *four* bits of information, resulting in a net transfer of 2400 bits per second.

In such a case, obviously, most people couldn't care less about the baud rate. What really matters is the bottom line — how many bps they get.

 See also FAQ 27-3, "What do V.32, V.42, bis, MNP, etc., mean?"

My stupid call-waiting feature keeps disrupting my modem sessions!

 Learn the secret of the *70 code.

27-7

In most parts of the country, you can turn off call-waiting for a particular call by dialing *70 before dialing the number. Fortunately, the same code works when the *modem* will be making the call — you just have to figure out where to type that code. In America Online, at the startup screen, click the Setup button; then select the "To disable call waiting" checkbox. Ditto for eWorld, except that the button is called Edit Local Setup.

In most other modem programs — Zterm, ClarisWorks, CompuServe, and so on — just add the code, followed by a comma, in front of the phone number. (If the *70 code doesn't seem to work, contact the phone company — it may be an added-cost service in your area.)

27-8

How do I send a file to a friend over the modem?

▽ **If you both have an online-service membership, use e-mail. Otherwise, you each need a telecom program.**

If you and your friend are both, say, America Online members, transferring a file is easy. Just prepare an e-mail message in the usual way — but before you send it, click the Attach File button. Specify which file(s) you want to send, and the service does the rest when you send your e-mail.

If you don't subscribe to one of those services, you can dial your friend directly. To pull this off, you each need a piece of *telecom software,* a program dedicated to conversing over the phone lines. Examples: ClarisWorks, Zterm, White Knight, Microphone, SmartCom, and so on. It helps if you both use the *same* telecom program — you'll each find the settings in the same places when setting up the call — but it's not necessary.

What *is* necessary is that your settings, of which there are dozens, match. Spend five minutes on the phone with your friend before beginning this process, and make sure that all your modem-software settings are the same. Keep in mind that if your modems are different speeds, the slower one's speed is what you'll get.

If there's a Connect or Dial command, use it; if not, just type **atdt 555-1234** (or whatever the phone number is), and press the Return key. Your friend, having launched the telecom program at the far end, should have used the Wait for Call command (or typed **ata,** and pressed Return). You'll both hear the squealing sounds of your modems connecting. You should both press the Return key. You should now be able to type to each other. Anything either of you types shows up on both your screens.

Finally, look for a Send File or Transfer File menu command. If you're offered a choice of "protocol," or transfer method, the one called *Zmodem* is superior. If that's the way you send the file, your friend doesn't even have to do anything to receive it (as long as the receiving telecom program supports Zmodem, too).

If your program doesn't offer Zmodem, use Xmodem. In this case, however, your friend must begin the receiving manually by choosing a Receive Xmodem File command. (The point is: Whatever protocol you use must be available in both telecom programs.)

That *should* be all there is to it, except that modeming is a crazy, complex stunt, invented by decidedly non-Macintosh people.

See also FAQ 28-15, "How do I exchange files with my friends?"

I've connected, modem-to-modem, with my friend. How come nothing appears when I type?

 You must turn on Local Echo.

27-9

You'll find the Local Echo setting somewhere in every telecom program. Look for a menu command called Settings, or Terminal, or Preferences, for example. Turn Local Echo on if nothing is appearing when you type. Conversely, turn it *off* if your typing produces ddoouubbllee lleettttteerrss.

Which should I get: an internal or external modem?

 External.

27-10

In fact, you'd be hard pressed to *find* an internal modem-on-a-card for a non-laptop Mac, even though they're common on PCs. The exception: the Apple Modem Card, which is only available for a few specific low-cost Mac models, such as the 630 series or the LC (or Performa) 5200. That modem, because it relieves your desk of so much clutter and wiring, might be worth considering. Just remember — you won't be able to sell it very easily when you want something faster.

My wife cuts off my connection every time she picks up the extension downstairs. What I can do?

 Buy a Radio Shack Teleprotector, Item #43-107.

27-11

It makes all other phone extensions go dead when you are — or your modem is — using the phone.

Rats! My fax software messed up again!

 Welcome to the club!

27-12

When programmers write, say, a screen saver, it has to be compatible with merely 90 Mac models. When they write fax software, though, it has to work with 90 Mac models *and* the 200 fax/modem models that might be attached, *and* the thousands of quirky, aging fax machines they're supposed to dial, *and* the billions of software programs you might be using. No wonder life with a fax modem is fraught with dropped connections, lost faxes, and other electronic headaches.

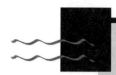

IAQ: Improbably Asked Question

Why won't this disk eject?

Yet another true story from an Apple repair center:

A customer brought in a Macintosh SE with a floppy disk stuck in the disk drive. Even pushing a straightened paper clip in the manual-eject hole would not eject the disk.

Upon disassembling the disk drive, I discovered why. The customer had a fondness for carrying Mac disks in his front shirt pocket. He had also put his Visa Gold Card in his front pocket that day. It had managed to lodge itself on the back of the disk by slipping under the metal shutter. The customer had inadvertently inserted the disk, Visa and all, into the drive.

And yes, to pay for the repair, he charged it.

For example, no matter which fax software you wind up with, you will not be able to fax PostScript graphics. This means you, Freehand, Illustrator, and QuarkXPress fans. Your PostScript and EPS artwork generally faxes as a blank spot, a blotch, or a system crash. Furthermore, every fax/modem program conflicts with one system extension or another. And sooner or later, a fax machine somewhere won't be able to talk to your fax/modem at all.

You aren't utterly helpless, however. You don't have to stick with the fax software that came with your modem. For example, Delrina Fax Pro, a fax program that works with almost every modem alive, solves the fax headache for many people. Global Village software is also excellent, although it works only with Global Village modems.

If you use Apple's Express Modem (for PowerBooks) or the GeoPort adapter (for Power Macs and other recent models), make sure that you have the latest version of the Express Modem software. (Apple updates it all the time. You can get it from eWorld or other online services.)

And if your business depends on fax transactions, consider the ultimate fax paradise: Get a fax machine. This way, you can *send* faxes using your fax modem (which look twice as sharp as faxes scanned in by a fax machine). And you can *receive* faxes on paper, whether your Mac is turned on or not, with none of the uncertainty or riskiness of receiving faxes on the Mac.

See also FAQ 1-32, "Where do I get Apple software updates?"

My Express Modem faxes are all white-on-black, like a negative.

▽   It's a glitch. Set your Monitors control panel to 256 colors.

What do they get when I fax photos or colors from my Mac?

▽   Depends on your fax software.

If you're using a not-so-hot fax program, gray shades and darker colors appear in the final fax as blotches of solid black. Modern fax software, such as Global Village version 2.6 or later (for that brand modem only) or Delrina Fax Pro, instead converts the photo or artwork into a reasonable grayscale image. The recipient will at least get the general idea of what you sent.

My Geoport icon has an X through it at startup. What should I do?

▽   You're missing some important files; reinstall your GeoPort software from the original disks.

I'm having trouble connecting to an online service with my GeoPort.

▽   Upgrade your GeoPort software to 2.0 or later.

This much more stable software is available for free from the usual sources of Apple upgrades.

See also FAQ 1-32, "Where do I get Apple software updates?"

CHAPTER

28

America Online and Company

Having acquired a modem, but not the chutzpah necessary to tackle the wild electronic underbrush of the Internet, you could do a lot worse than sign up for an online service. America Online (AOL) is the biggest and easiest to use; eWorld is the smallest, but is based on the America Online software, so all America Online answers also apply to it.

This chapter, and the next, were cowritten by a special guest author: Leslie Jones, author of the popular (and free) AOL FAQ document, which you can download from AOL (of course) for 200 onscreen pages of more detailed questions and answers.

I can't get online! I hate this!

 You and the other billions of eWorld and AOL members! Everybody dials in between 9 p.m. and midnight.

The AOL and eWorld computers are constantly been upgraded to handle the additional demands of exploding numbers of subscribers. Unfortunately, SprintNet, the network that carries the call from your local access number all the way to AOL headquarters in Virginia (or eWorld headquarters in California), isn't being upgraded quite so agressively. Particularly if you live in a populous city, that carrier's lines may simply be busy.

Here are some ways to beat the system:

✦ Don't waste your time trying to connect during peak evening hours. Dial during the day or in the wee hours; you'll be almost certain to get through.

✦ Dial in on a slower-rated access number. As people switch to faster modems, all those older phone lines (rated for a maximum of 2400 bps) aren't used as much, and you'll have better luck getting through. (Use keyword *access* to find out what those numbers are, or call the service's 800 help line.)

✦ If you're desperate, consider dialing an access number that *isn't* local. For example, if you're in New York, look up one of the less-trafficked Connecticut access phone numbers. Yes, you're now paying long-distance charges, but at least you can get an emergency session in if your work depends on it.

America Online, at least, is trying to alleviate the problem by developing its own network of local access numbers. This new network is called AOLNet. At this writing, there are AOLNet access numbers in about 50 cities; more will be in place with every passing month. Use keyword *AOLNet* online to find a local number.

See also FAQ 27-3, "What do V.32, V.42bis, MNP, etc., mean?"

See also FAQ 28-2, "What's a keyword?"

What's a keyword?

▽ **A shortcut for jumping directly to a particular feature of your online service.**

On Prodigy, it's called a jump word; on CompuServe, it's a Go word; but the idea is the same. Here's how it works:

✦ *America Online:* Choose **Keyword** from the Go To menu (or press ⌘-K).

✦ *eWorld:* Choose **Go to Shortcut** from the Places menu (or press ⌘-G).

✦ *CompuServe Information Manager:* Click the little stoplight icon on the floating toolbar.

In each case, a little window appears in which you can type the keyword you want, and then press the Return key to go there. Typical keywords are things like Help, Weather, Mail, and so on — but each service offers its own list of several hundred.

See also FAQ 28-22, "Is there a list of all AOL keywords somewhere?"

How do I find a file I want to download?

 Use the appropriate keyword or use the menu.

28-3

Each of the three popular Mac services — AOL, eWorld, and CompuServe — has a Find feature that helps you locate the piece of software you're looking for. That's handy, since the file libraries on these services contain tens of thousands of programs, shareware, Apple software updates, clip art, and whatever.

✦ **America Online** — Choose **File Search** from the Go To menu (or use keyword *file search*).

✦ **eWorld** — Choose **Find Software** from the Places menu.

✦ **CompuServe Information Manager** — Click the stoplight icon on the floating toolbar. In the window that appears, type **Macff** and press Return. (Nobody ever said CompuServe was user-friendly.)

In each case, a window appears. There's a blank where you can type what you're looking for. You can search for a file based on its name, the date it was uploaded, the category it was placed in, and so on. Searching by the file's name is easiest, but make sure that you spell the name correctly. You may have to search several times, experimenting with spellings and spacing.

When you're searching, don't forget that — on AOL and eWorld — you can use words like *and* and *or*. For example, if you're trying to find a font that contains little pictures of animals, search for *animals and fonts* — searching for just *animals* or just *fonts* would produce hundreds of matches, but using the *and* produces quickly and exactly what you're looking for.

See also FAQ 28-2, "What's a keyword?"

What's .sit, .hqx, etc.?

 See FAQ 29-16, "What's .sit, .hqx, etc.?"

28-4

What am I supposed to do with these ".image" files I downloaded?

 Use Disk Copy or ShrinkWrap to access them.

When software is complicated enough to require an installer program, it's stored online as a *.image* file. When you download such a file, you must convert the file into a floppy disk using Apple's Disk Copy program. (Disk Copy is available online. So is ShrinkWrap a less complicated program that lets you access *.image* files without requiring floppy disks.) You can then install the program from the floppy disk.

Here's how to use Disk Copy:

1. Launch Disk Copy. Click the Load Image File button, and open the image file you downloaded. Disk Copy reads the file into memory.

2. Click the Make a Copy button and insert a floppy disk. The floppy disk must have the same capacity (800K, for example) as the image (which will be identified on the screen).

3. After copying the disk image, Disk Copy ejects the floppy disk.

4. Quit Disk Copy. Insert the floppy disk you created and install the software on it as usual.

When you're creating high-density disks, Disk Copy may report "There is not enough available memory to work with a disk that size." In that case, increase its memory allotment to 1500K, as described in Appendix C.

 See also FAQ 29-16, "What's .sit, .hqx, etc.?"

How do I resume an interrupted AOL (or eWorld) download?

 Don't move the half-finished file; then use the Download Manager.

In fact, don't do *anything* with the partially-downloaded file. Don't move it, rename it, or trash it. Launch the America Online application and choose Download Manager from the File menu (in eWorld, the command is called Files to Get).

If you now click the Start Download icon, AOL (or eWorld) completes the download automatically.

Why do my downloads get interrupted?

  Any of the following intrusions may be responsible.

If you have call waiting, turn it off (see FAQ 27-7). If the download got interrupted while you were away from the computer, look for programs that kick in when the computer is idle, such as background compression programs and screen savers. FaxSTF and older versions of After Dark and CP TrashBack have caused problems, too.

Where are the files I downloaded?

  They're probably in a Downloads folder in the online service's program folder.

For example, files you download from America Online (or eWorld) normally land in the Online Downloads (or eWorld Downloads) folder, which is inside the America Online (or eWorld) folder. If you use CompuServe Information Manager, you'll find a similar folder in the MacCIM folder. If you still can't find a file you downloaded, use your Find command.

If you can't remember the file's name, here's a trick that works in AOL or eWorld. Choose Download Manager from the America Online File menu (or Files to Get from the eWorld File menu); click the Show Completed Downloads icon. You'll see the names of the last 50 files you downloaded. Make a note of the missing file's name, and use your Find command to search for it. (Leave off extensions like *.sit* and *.sea,* which may have changed when the file was decompressed.)

   See also FAQ 1-2, "How can I avoid losing files in the future?"

Who is the host, and why won't he respond?

  The host is the America Online computers, which are overloaded.

America Online's computers sometimes get bogged down. When that happens, you may get the "Host has failed to respond" message. It's not your fault. The problem is on AOL's end — too many members, too little capacity. Wait a few minutes and try again.

How can I stop the spinning beach ball?

 Double-click an AOL (or eWorld) text file or mail file.

28-10

Sometimes, while waiting for the "Host has failed to respond" message, the cursor turns into a spinning beach ball (sometimes described as a BMW logo). Pressing ⌘-period doesn't stop the beach ball, and you can't *do* anything while it's spinning.

To stop the spinning beach ball and regain control of your software, switch back to the desktop and double-click an AOL (or eWorld) text file or mail file that you had previously saved onto your hard drive. You may as well prepare for your next beach-ball experience right now — choose New Memo from the File menu and save the memo onto the desktop.

When the beach ball starts spinning, click on the desktop to switch to the Finder, then double-click the memo. (If you *can't* switch to the Finder, you probably have the Finder Hiding feature turned on. See FAQ 19-4.)

Handy trick: Save this blank memo into your Apple Menu Items folder — in your System Folder. Now you can just kill the beach ball by choosing that memo's name from your menu.

In either case, stopping the beach ball cursor doesn't get you where you were trying to go — it doesn't let you read the message you were trying to open, for example. However, it does return control to you, so you can go do something else until the host feels more responsive.

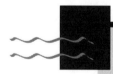

RAQ: Rarely Asked Question

When I first signed up as Xerxes, AOL suggested Xerxes9487. Are there really 9486 other people named Xerxes?

No. Actually, if you have the same name as somebody else, the AOL computer just adds enough extra digits to make your new screen name ten characters long (the maximum).

How can I turn my modem speaker off?

▽ **Add M0 to your configuration string.**

Your *modem configuration string* is a series of command codes that your communications program (such as the AOL, eWorld, or CompuServe software) sends to your modem each time you use it. You'll almost never need to change these codes — but silencing your modem's shrieks and squeals is a tempting exception.

> ✦ **America Online and eWorld** — Launch the AOL (eWorld) software and click the Setup button (Edit Local Setup button). Make a mental note of which modem type is selected and close the window. Now choose Open from the File menu and navigate to the Online Files (eWorld Files) folder. (It's inside the America Online [eWorld] folder). Open the modem type you're using. Add M0 (that's a zero) to the end of the Configuration string and click the Save Changes button. (M0 is a standard Hayes command to silence your modem's speaker.)

> ✦ **CompuServe Information Manager** — From the Special menu, from the Settings submenu, choose Connection. In the next window, click the Modem button. Add M0 (that's a zero) to the end of the Init string.

What's my Internet address?

▽ **Your Internet e-mail address is your screen name plus a special suffix.**

If you're sending mail to somebody else on your own service, such as from one America Online member to another, you just type that person's *screen name* (such as Ski Bunny or TomSmith7) into the *To:* blank of the e-mail screen.

If people who *aren't* on your service want to write to you, however, they must add the appropriate codes to the end of your screen name. Their mail will travel, via the Internet, into your e-mail box; therefore, if you are on an online service, you already have an Internet address.

Table 28-1 shows how to figure out your Internet address (or somebody else's) if you have an online service account. (Spaces aren't allowed in Internet addresses, so remove any spaces.)

A couple of notes: Make sure that you change the comma in the CompuServe address to a period. Also, if you are sending the e-mail from America Online, you may use shortened forms of those suffixes: just *@cis* for CompuServe, *@apple.com* for AppleLink, or *@genie* for GEnie.

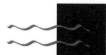

Table 28-1

How to send mail to other online services

Your screen name	Your service	Your Internet address
SkiBunny	America Online	SkiBunny@aol.com
SkiBunny	eWorld	SkiBunny@eWorld.com
SkiBunny	AppleLink	SkiBunny@applelink.apple.com
12345,6789	CompuServe	12345.6789@compuserve.com
S.Bunny	GEnie	S.Bunny @genie.geis.com
abcd12a	Prodigy	abcd12a@prodigy.com

How do I send e-mail to somebody on the Internet?

▽ **The same way you send any other e-mail.**

On America Online, for example, choose Compose Mail from the Mail menu. Type your correspondent's entire Internet address, no matter how many @ signs or periods it takes, into the To: field. The same applies if you're using eWorld. It's the same on CompuServe, except that you have to type **INTERNET:** in front of the Internet address. (Sending Internet mail is free on America Online and eWorld, but costs 15 cents each on CompuServe.)

My friend is on the same service. How do I find his screen name?

▽ **Choose Member Directory from the Members menu.**

(On eWorld, the menu is called Membership. On CompuServe, it's called Mail.)

On AOL and eWorld, searching the member directory only works if your friend has filled out a *member profile* (by using keyword *profile*). That also means that no one will be able to find *your* screen name in the member directory if you haven't filled out a member profile.

How do I exchange files with my friends?

 If your friends are on the same service, use e-mail file attachments.

For example, on AOL, choose Compose Mail from the Mail menu and write your friend an e-mail. (On eWorld, choose New Message from the eMail menu.) Before sending the e-mail, click the Attach File button to select a file. When your friend receives the e-mail, he'll see a Download Now button at the bottom of the message.

If your friend *isn't* on the same online service as you, you'll have to send the file via the Internet, which is much more difficult. It involves converting the file into a special, all-text gibberish format, sending it as e-mail, and requiring your friend to reverse the process on the other end.

From your service's file libraries, download the program called UULite (version 2.0 or later). Launch that program; choose Encoding Preferences from the File menu; and choose the America Online Compliant option. Then tell UULite to encode the file into text. You'll have to copy and paste each resulting chunk of text into a separate e-mail message, and your friend will have to reassemble the pieces with either UULite or (if your friend is using a PC) WinCode.

See also FAQ 28-3, "How do I find a file I want to download?"

See also FAQ 29-16, "What's .sit, .hqx, etc.?"

Where can I check my bill?

 On AOL, use keyword *billing*.

A window appears, offering a list of information sources. Double-click the one that says Current Month's Billing Summary. It shows your current and previous months' bills and how many of your five free monthly hours are left. (On eWorld, choose Check Connect Time from the Places menu to accomplish the same thing.)

Use keyword *clock* to see how long you've been logged on for the current session. Keyword *clock* shows the total time for the current session, including time spent in free customer support areas. You are not charged for time in free areas.

28-17

How can I reduce my online-service bill?

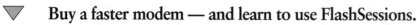

Buy a faster modem — and learn to use FlashSessions.

A fast modem makes downloading, reading messages and e-mail, and browsing the World Wide Web much faster, so you spend less time online. In most American cities, for example, you can connect to most online services at speeds up to 14,400 bps — in some cities, even 28,800 bps. Since it doesn't cost any more to connect at faster speeds, your bill drops according to the speed of your modem.

A *FlashSession* is an automated AOL session. (It's called Automatic Courier on eWorld.) At a specified time, the program logs on, sends any e-mail written while not connected, receives mail that's waiting for you, and downloads any files you had marked for future delivery. You save money by reading and writing e-mail offline. You can schedule FlashSessions to run automatically and sign off when they're complete.

Writing mail offline is easy. For example, launch AOL, but don't sign on. Choose Compose Mail from the Mail menu, write your message, and click the Send Later button. To read mail you've downloaded, choose Read Incoming Mail from the File menu.

Automating your sessions on CompuServe can also save you money. Unfortunately, this act requires a complex, programmable program called Navigator, which you must purchase separately.

28-18

Whenever I quit AOL, it says I have "information to be sent and/or received." What's that about?

Apparently, you haven't read (or sent) all your e-mail yet. Or you haven't downloaded the files you wanted.

Do you see the message shown in Figure 28-1 every time you try to sign off AOL? It's a reminder that you have files or e-mail to upload or download: You haven't read all your incoming mail yet, or you haven't sent all the mail you've written offline, or you've marked some software for future downloading but haven't retrieved it yet.

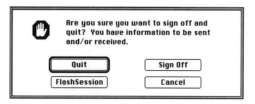

Figure 28-1: Either you haven't read or sent your mail, or you haven't transferred the files you marked for delivery.

Here's how to clear out all three of these information types:

✦ **E-mail not yet read** — Choose Read New Mail from the Mail menu.

✦ **E-mail not yet sent** — Choose Read Outgoing Mail from the Mail menu.

✦ **Software not yet downloaded** — Choose Download Manager from the File menu.

What does "serial port in use" mean?

▽ **Some other piece of your software — probably your fax software — is using the modem jack.**

You have only one modem port. If America Online (or another modem program) tries to dial while the port is already busy, this "serial port in use" message results. Usually, the offending program is your fax software. Sometimes you can eliminate this conflict by turning off your fax software's auto-receive feature (Delrina and Global Village software work this way). Other times (as in FaxSTF), you have to click the OK button every time you launch AOL (or download the shareware program from AOL called FaxState, which lets you turn FaxSTF on and off without having to restart the Mac).

Or try this: Choose Preferences from the Members menu of the America Online program; turn off the Ask to Reset Serial Port option. From now on, AOL won't even bother asking you about resetting the port — it will just do so automatically. (This option is available only in AOL version 2.5 or higher.)

See also FAQ 28-3, "How do I find a file I want to download?"

I got an e-mail with typing in different colors and type styles. How'd they do that?

▽ They used the Font, Style, Size, and Color commands in the Edit menu (AOL or eWorld only).

How do you make those sounds in an America Online (or eWorld) chat room?

▽   **Choose Sound from the Chat menu.**

(On eWorld, choose Send a Sound from the Conference menu.)

This menu only appears when you are actually *in* a chat room, by the way. Also remember that everybody *else* in the room will only hear the sound you send if that sound is installed on their computers. Which means that the only sounds you can be sure everybody will hear are the basic Mac error beeps — Wild Eep, Indigo, Quack, Simple Beep, and so on — plus the familiar America Online sounds like Welcome and Goodbye. (eWorld comes equipped with a handful of additional useful sounds that every eWorld member has — a cheer, a laugh, and so on.)

And people who don't *have* Macs won't hear your Mac beeps at all.

Is there a list of all AOL keywords somewhere?

▽   **Yes. Download the file from AOL called Ultimate Keyword List.**

What are freeware, shareware, and so on?

▽   **They refer to ways of distributing and paying for noncommercial software.**

There is megabyte upon megabyte of software online — both on the Internet and on online services — waiting for you to download. Technically, however, not all of it is free; in some cases, you're supposed to pay for the programs according to the honor system. Here's a summary of the terms you're likely to see:

- ✦ **Public domain** — The author of this software has given up all rights to the software. It's free. Use it as you wish.

- ✦ **Freeware** — The programmers of this software copyright it and maintain ownership. However, you can use and distribute the program for free.

✦ **Shareware** — Shareware is try-before-you-buy software. Shareware authors ask that you send them money if you like the software. (Generally, the programmer has provided a mailing address — you're supposed to send a check.) You aren't charged for shareware when you download it; nice people pay for the shareware they use.

How do I get on the Internet from America Online?

▽ Use keyword *Internet,* then click the icon for the Internet feature you want.

See also FAQ 28-2, "What's a keyword?"

See also FAQ 29-3, "What can you do on the Internet?"

How do I sign up for an online service?

▽ Call the toll-free number for a free starter kit.

America Online is at (800) 827-6364, eWorld is (800) 775-4556, and CompuServe is (800) 848-8199.

29

Planet Internet

O*n a list of today's 100 most frequently asked questions, 25 of them are probably about the Internet.*

Which immediately explains one pertinent point about this mother of all computer networks — it's confusing as all get-out. It represents the absolute opposite of Macintosh-style friendliness. You can't make a move without hearing — and being forced to use yourself — terms like TCP/IP, FTP, and ftp.ucs.ubc.ca. While this was supposed to be a user-friendly book, all bets are off when discussing this arcane, anarchic rat's nest of tangled computers and cables.

What is the Internet?

 A network of computer networks.

The Internet is a network of computers that speak a common language, known in geek-speak as *TCP/IP* (Transfer Control Protocol/Internet Protocol). Because they use the same language, all of these computers can exchange information — over the world's telephone wires.

No one person or organization owns the Internet. The networks that compose the Internet are an exotic mix of educational, government, and commercial organizations. The Internet encompasses most of the inhabited globe, and spans a broad spectrum of beliefs, nationalities, languages, politics, and laws.

Where did the Internet come from?

▽ **It was created by the U.S. government in the 1960s.**

During the Cold War, the U.S. built a national computer network that could survive even if some of the cities on the network were destroyed by an atomic bomb. The network was originally named *ARPAnet* (Advanced Research Projects Agency network). In the decades that followed, the Internet grew beyond the United States but was still used mostly by educational and government agencies.

The Internet grew explosively in the 90s after it was opened to commercial access. Companies could use the Internet. They could also *sell* access to the Internet, which opened the Internet to ordinary Joes like us.

What can you do on the Internet?

▽ **Exchange e-mail, get files, read public discussions, do research, type in live conversations, and explore the World Wide Web.**

The Internet isn't One Big Thing. It's divided into different services (or resources), which use different software.

✦ **Electronic mail** is the most useful Internet service. You can send e-mail to a friend anywhere in the world for pennies. Your e-mail arrives in minutes. FedEx must hate this.

✦ **File Transfer Protocol (FTP)** means software you can download from *FTP sites* around the world. For example, Apple's latest software updates are always posted to an area called **ftp.apple.support.com**. You can use FTP as almost any part of speech: "I'll FTP the file tonight."

✦ **Usenet newsgroups** are the Internet equivalent of public bulletin boards. Newsgroups give the Internet its color and sense of community. There are thousands of newsgroups, on every conceivable topic — the weirder, the better. A warning, though: Keeping up with the hundreds of newsgroup messages that are added daily will quickly suck your life and time away.

✦ **Gopher** is a menu-based system for retrieving information from databases. Some university libraries have made their card catalogs available through Gopher.

✦ The **World Wide Web** integrates text, pictures, sound, and video into convenient, point-and-click *pages* (screens). See FAQ 29-6 for details.

✦ **Internet Relay Chat** (IRC) lets groups of people type messages to each other in real time, like an Internet CB radio. Different *channels* discuss different subjects.

How do I get connected?

▽ **The easy way: Sign up for an online service. The macho way: Find an Internet access provider.**

If you'd rather not spend your first weekend of Internet exposure mucking around in codes and technical settings, sign up for America Online, eWorld, or CompuServe. To varying degrees, each offers easy, safe access to most Internet features.

For example, America Online lets you access most of the features described in FAQ 29-3: The Web, Internet e-mail, software from FTP sites, Gopher databases, and newsgroup discussions. (Only the live chat is missing — and America Online itself offers plenty of that.) And for occasional use, an online service (usually $10 for five hours) is less expensive than a genuine, direct Internet account (for example, about $35 per month, flat fee).

If the smooth, paved access road of an online service is too sissified for you, you can also subscribe directly to the Internet. This involves finding a local or regional company that's an *Internet service provider*. In exchange for a monthly fee, this company provides you with more complete Internet access than the big online services. You provide your own software and knowledge of how to use it.

Realize, however, that these companies offer no content of their own — no *Time* magazine; no encyclopedia; no stock quotes; none of the organized, popular features of online services. A direct Internet connection is also, needless to say, harder to use than an online service.

So how do you find a local Internet service provider? Easy: Look it up on the frequently updated text file called *PDial*. To get the PDial list, send e-mail to **info-deli-server@netcom.com** — yes, that's the address; and if you make one little punctuation error, this won't work. (Welcome to the Internet.) In the body of your e-mail message, type only this: **SEND PDIAL**.

Of course, the dumb part is that you can't *send* e-mail unless you *already* have an Internet (or at least online-service) account! That's part of the problem with starting with a local access provider. You can always call directory assistance to find a service provider in your area.

Prices vary wildly; if you're lucky enough to live in a city with a so-called *Freenet*, you get *free,* or nearly free, access. Most service providers offer two options: a dialup account (sometimes called a *shell account*), and a *SLIP* (Serial Line Internet Protocol) or *PPP* (Point-to-Point Protocol) account. A dialup account uses a *command-line interface* (no icons or graphics — you have to type computer codes to get anything done) and usually requires that you learn some UNIX. It's not pretty, and it's not easy to use, but it's usually cheap.

A SLIP or PPP account allows your computer to become one of the computers on the Internet, at least for the duration of the phone call. With a SLIP or PPP account, you can use programs like NewsWatcher, Eudora, and Fetch that put a graphic, point-and-click interface on the Internet.

As you've probably gathered by now, online services charge for Internet access by the hour. If you start spending a lot of time online, you may want to switch to an Internet service provider. Most offer flat-rate billing option (unlimited hours for one monthly fee).

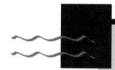

UAQ: Understandably Asked Question

What do you mean, I can get the Web from AOL?

If you're an America Online subscriber, you may have done a double-take to read that AOL provides access to the most popular Internet feature of all — the World Wide Web.

To access this neat new feature, you must upgrade your AOL software to version 2.6 or later. To do so, use keyword *WWW*; you'll find the two programs you need, complete with instructions, there.

Caution: For now, AOL's Web-browsing feature is actually a separate program, requiring 3000K of memory *in addition to* the 2500K required by the original AOL software. If your Mac doesn't have at least eight megs of RAM, this avenue to the Web is blocked.

Where do I find good Macintosh information?

29-5

 Visit newsgroups whose names begin with *comp.sys.mac.*

There are dozens of discussion groups about the Mac. Every single one's name is in the form *comp.sys.mac.____*, where the topic goes in the blank.

And here are some topics to fill that blank: *advocacy, announce, apps, comm, database, digest, games, hardware, hypercard, misc, oop.macapp, oop.misc, portables, programmer, scitech, system,* and *wanted.*

Where do I find all the good Macintosh programs on the Internet?

29-6

 At *sumex-aim.stanford.edu* and *mac.archive.umich.edu.*

If you're on the Internet, I'll assume that you know how to find a particular software area (*FTP site*). *Sumex-aim.stanford.edu* and *mac.archive.umich.edu* are the worldwide Internet centers for Macintosh shareware and other files.

Trouble is, though there are millions of people on the Internet, only a few hundred can use these two sites at a time. These two sites are often crowded full and impossible to get into.

To get around this problem, many FTP sites *mirror* the most popular sites. Every day, for example, the **sumex** and **umich** computers send copies of their downloadable files to other computers — mirror sites — to make them more widely available. Use the mirror sites whenever possible. You'll save wear and tear on sumex and umich, and you'll have a better chance of getting in. Tables 29-1 and 29-2 show the American and Canadian mirrors of those two popular Macintosh software sites.

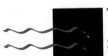

Table 29-1

Sumex-aim and its mirrors

FTP site	Directory
sumex-aim.stanford.edu	info-mac
amug.org	info-mac

(continued)

Table 29-1 (continued)

FTP site	Directory
ftp.ucs.ubc.ca	pub/mac/info-mac
ftp.hawaii.edu	mirrors/info-mac
grind.isca.uiowa.edu	mac/infomac
wuarchive.wustl.edu	systems/mac/info-mac

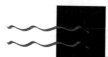

Table 29-2
Umich and its mirrors

FTP site	Directory
mac.archive.umich.edu	mac
grind.isca.uiowa.edu	mac/umich
wuarchive.wustl.edu	systems/mac/umich.edu

Here's a frequently asked one: Where are the pornographic FTP sites? Essentially, there aren't any — they all get shut down within hours.

What are some other cool FTP sites?

▽   **From among the thousands, here are a few useful ones.**

Remember: FTP means, essentially, *software you can download*. From America Online, you get there by using keyword *FTP*. If you're accessing the Internet directly, you are, as always, on your own to figure out how to get to this stuff.

✦ **ftp.support.apple.com** — Apple Computer. The premier source of new and updated Apple system software and utilities.

✦ **cathouse.org** — The Cathouse. Fun and unusual stuff here. There are directories for David Letterman, Rush Limbaugh, humor, urban legends, and song lyrics.

✦ **ftp.etext.org** — This is the Internet equivalent of a magazine stand, with hundreds of electronic magazines. You'll also find texts from Project Gutenberg, which puts classic, public-domain works in text format. The Gutenberg library is still small, but includes the Bible, the 1911 edition of Roget's Thesaurus, the CIA World Fact Book, and classic literature.

✦ **naic.nasa.gov** — The National Aeronautics and Space Administration. In the directory called *pub/images* are space photos you can download.

What software do I need to connect?

 It depends on how you connect to the Internet.

29-8

If you connect to the Internet through an online service, you just use the software provided by that service. For a dialup account — you techies know who you are — a terminal emulator like ZTerm is all you need.

To connect to a SLIP or PPP account, you'll need **SLIP or PPP software** and Apple's **MacTCP control panel.** MacTCP comes with System 7.5. (It also comes with several Internet books, such as *Internet for Macs for Dummies* and *The Internet Starter Kit for Macintosh*.) You'll also need individual programs for each of the Internet features you hope to use: Eudora for email, NetScape for the World Wide Web, and so on. Collecting all of this software from scratch is tricky, unless you already belong to an online service.

What's the Web?

 It's something like a global, democratic America Online, where anybody can have his/her own screen.

29-9

Each screen contains icons and highlighted text phrases; click one, and a related screen appears. If you've used America Online or eWorld, where clicking an icon makes a new screen appear, you get the general idea (see Figure 29-1).

You can spend hours on the Web, doing nothing but clicking buttons and reading. You'll quickly discover that the vast majority of *web pages,* as they're called, are intensely boring — badly spelled accounts by 11-year-olds about what they had for lunch and what their dogs' names are.

Here and there, though, you'll find some Web pages worth visiting. At the top of your screen, you'll see its address — its *URL (Uniform Resource Locator).* No matter which program (which *Web browser)* you're using to access the Web, somewhere you'll find a command for storing the worthwhile URLs you encounter. Most Web browsers offer a menu known as a *hot list* — of your favorite Web pages.

You can access the Web from America Online (version 2.6 or later); other online services are furiously working to offer Web features. Otherwise, for Web access, you'll have to sign up for Internet access through a *service provider,* as described in FAQ 29-4.

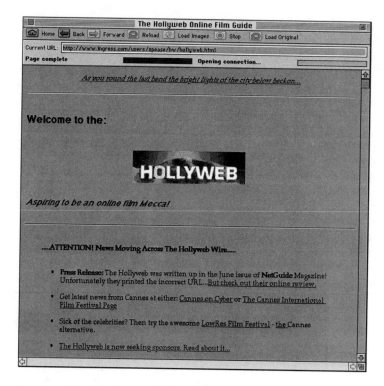

Figure 29-1: A sample Web page, as viewed from America Online. See the pieces of underlined text? Click one to bring up another screen — which may be running on a computer halfway around the planet.

Caution: You need a *very* fast modem to serve the Web, or else you'll wait forever for the graphics on each screen to appear.

And where do you find good Web URLs? From friends, from articles, and so on. Here are a few to get you started.

✦ **http://www.yahoo.com/** — The **Yahoo** page is like a World Wide Web librarian. Yahoo organizes thousands of web pages by subject. When you find the page you want, it's only a mouse click away.

✦ **http://gagme.wwa.com/~boba/pick.html** — **Spider's Web Pick of the Day** tirelessly scours the net looking for the very best pages. Every day, Spider chooses one page that's outstanding because of its design, content, or concept.

✦ **http://turnpike.net/metro/mirsky/Worst.html** — And now we have the exact opposite of Spider's pick of the day: **Mirsky's Worst of the Web.** Every day, this page features the ugliest, silliest, most vain, and most tasteless Web pages Mirsky can dig up.

✦ **http://www.eg.bucknell.edu/~boulter/crayon/** — You've probably heard the hype: One day you'll be able to create your own newspaper with just the news you're interested in. Another AT&T commercial, right?

Wrong. You can do it now with **CRAYON**: *CReAte Your Own Newspaper.* CRAYON lets you pick and choose from news pages all over the Web: national news, world news, sports, weather, entertainment, and even comic strips. The only limitation is that the news has to be on the World Wide Web, and it has to be free. Even with those limitations, CRAYON is fantastic and points to a new age of information gathering.

+ **http://www.apple.com** — Apple's beautifully-designed page contains links to pages with new product announcements, Apple's tech info library, product data sheets, and pointers to other Apple resources on the Internet.

+ **http://lycos.cs.cmu.edu/** — The Lycos web searcher at Carnegie Mellon. Allows you to search for Web pages by keywords.

What are some good newsgroups?

 Here are a few to get you started.

For information about newsgroups themselves, visit these three:

+ **news.announce.newusers** — A good one to read if you're new to newsgroups. Highlight: "Emily Postnews Answers Your Questions on Netiquette."

+ **news.newusers.questions** — Frequently asked questions about newsgroups.

+ **news.answers** — The FAQ documents for many newsgroups are found here. Lots of good, well-edited information.

For an extensive list of newsgroups, read the List of Active Newsgroups, posted to the *news.lists* newsgroup. The one-line descriptions in Table 29-3 are from that list.

Table 29-3

Cool newsgroups

Newsgroup	Description
alt.fan.douglas-adams	The author of "Meaning of Life" and other fine works
alt.fan.letterman.top-ten	The nightly *Late Show* Top 10 List
alt.tv.mst3k	Hey, you robots! Down in front!
comp.graphics	Computer graphics, art, animation, image processing
misc.jobs.misc	On employment, workplaces, and careers
news.answers	Repository for periodic Usenet articles (moderated)

(continued)

Table 29-3 (continued)

Newsgroup	Description
news.newusers.questions	Questions and answers for users new to the Usenet
rec.arts.movies	On movies and moviemaking
rec.humor.funny	Jokes
rec.music.phish	Discussing the musical group Phish
rec.sport.baseball	On baseball
rec.startrek.misc	General discussions of *Star Trek*
rec.woodworking	Hobbyists interested in woodworking
sci.engr	Technical discussions about engineering tasks
sci.med	Medicine and its related products and regulations
soc.penpals	In search of net.friendships
soc.roots	Discussing genealogy and genealogical patterns
talk.politics	All aspects of politics

See also FAQ 29-5, "Where do I find good Macintosh information?"

How do I use the files posted in newsgroups?

▽   **It's StuffIt Expander to the rescue.**

29-11

While it may seem odd to discuss *files* among newsgroups — which are normally associated only with *discussion* — some newsgroups do indeed offer files to download. These newsgroups's names contain the word *binaries*.

So how do people post a file — a picture, sound, or software program — in an area that generally contains only text? By converting it to text, of course, as described in FAQ 28-15.

To use a file from a binaries newsgroup, save the message onto your hard drive. Large files have been split into multiple messages, so make sure that you get all of the parts, usually labeled "Part 1/5, Part 2/5," and so on. Now combine the messages into one big text file. You *can* use copy and paste to combine the parts, but it's easier to use a shareware program like BBEdit Lite (use the Concatenate Files command). Finally, drag the text file onto the StuffIt Expander icon to convert it into a genuine Mac file. (Get StuffIt Expander from an online service or the Internet itself, if you can find it.) Nobody ever said the Internet was easy.

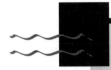

RAQ: Rarely Asked Question

Who's Craig Shergold, and why should I send him a card?

Craig Shergold, the story goes, is a seven-year-old boy who's dying of cancer. His last wish is to get into the Guinness Book of World Records for having received the most Get Well cards. It's a touching story, and it's true.

Or at least, it *was* true — a decade ago. Craig had surgery and is in complete remission. He turned 16 in January of 1995. And he did get into the Guinness Book of World Records. Trouble is, the story continues to spread on the Internet, and people keep sending cards. His family receives five sacks of unwanted mail a day.

Then there was the Good Times e-mail virus hoax. And there was the "for every e-mail this computer company receives, they'll make a donation to a cancer charity" hoax.

In other words, the Internet can sometimes be the *mis*information superhighway. Remember, nobody runs the Internet; nobody looks over the information that appears there. Don't believe everything you read.

What's a mailing list?

 It's a cross between a magazine and e-mail.

29-12

You "subscribe" to a mailing list by sending a special e-mail to a special address; more on this in a moment. A computer program (such as *LISTSERV*) processes your request and adds you to the mailing list. Thereafter, each message in the ongoing flood of conversation comes to you as an e-mail. It's like an Internet newsgroup, except that instead of going to *it*, the discussion comes to *you*.

For an extended directory of mailing lists, read Stephanie De Silva's Publicly Accessible Mailing Lists, available in the *news.lists* newsgroup. Also visit *http://www.yahoo.com/ Computers/Internet/Mailing_Lists/* on the World Wide Web for links to information about mailing lists.

Meanwhile, here are a few to get you started, along with instructions for subscribing. *Note:* When you've been added to the mailing list, you'll receive e-mail confirming your subscription. Be sure to save that e-mail — it contains instructions for *unsubscribing* from the list. That information may be useful when you discover exactly how hard it is to keep up with 100 messages per day! (If you need help with a mailing list, or if you forget how to unsubscribe, send e-mail to the listserver with the word HELP by itself in the body of the message.)

In the instructions below, substitute your first and last name (e.g., Bob Smith) for YOURFULLNAME. You can put anything in the subject line.

- ✦ **TidBITS** — Adam Engst's weekly magazine about the Macintosh and the Internet. Send e-mail to *listserv@ricevm1.rice.edu* with SUBSCRIBE TIDBITS YOURFULLNAME in the body of the message.

- ✦ **In, Around, and Online** — Robert Seidman's excellent newsletter covers developments on the major online services and the Internet. Send e-mail to *listserv@clark.net* with SUBSCRIBE ONLINE-L YOURFULLNAME in the body of the message.

- ✦ **David Letterman Top 10 List** — The mailing list version of the alt.fan.letterman.top-10 newsgroup. Send e-mail to *listserv@listserv.clark.net* with SUBSCRIBE TOPTEN YOURFULLNAME in the body of the message.

- ✦ **Humor** — Send e-mail to *listserv@uga.cc.uga.edu* with SUBSCRIBE HUMOR YOURFULLNAME in the body of the message.

- ✦ **TV Tonight** — Listings of network and cable TV shows. The poor man's TV guide. Send e-mail to *majordomo@netcom.com* with SUBSCRIBE TV2NITE-L in the body of the message.

- ✦ **X-files** — Discussions of Fox's strange and wonderful TV show. Send e-mail to *listproc@uel.ac.uk* with SUBSCRIBE X-FILES YOURFULLNAME in the body of the message.

How can I avoid looking like a complete moron?

▽ **Lurk before participating, and read every FAQ you can get your hands on.**

Unfortunately, Internet veterans are notoriously impatient with newcomers. Say the wrong thing, ask a dumb question, and you're likely to be yelled at in vulgar typewritten tones.

Before you speak up — in a newsgroup discussion, for example — hang out for a while. See how things are done. Better yet, read the FAQ for a newsgroup before posting a message there. That's right: Just about every discussion group, software site, or other Internet feature has been written up into an introductory Frequently Asked Questions document.

Here are some good places to find FAQs:

+ In the file libraries of your online service

+ On the **news.answers** newsgroup on Usenet

+ Via FTP from **rtfm.mit.edu** in the pub/usenet directory

+ On the World Wide Web at ftp://rtfm.mit.edu/pub/usenet/

What's netiquette?

▽ **Netiquette means online etiquette — more rules to avoid nasty e-mail from irritated veterans.**

Here are three things to avoid:

+ DON'T TYPE IN ALL CAPITAL LETTERS LIKE THIS. ALL CAPS IS HARD TO READ AND VERY RUDE. IT'S LIKE SHOUTING IN SOMEONE'S EAR. AREN'T YOU GLAD THIS WHOLE BOOK ISN'T IN ALL CAPS?

+ Don't post Make Money Fast and other pyramid schemes. These schemes violate federal fraud laws. What's more, they annoy the heck out of almost everyone. By the way, the scams don't work, because no one sends money, and the participants cheat by putting their names at the top of the list.

+ Don't send unsolicited advertisements. The only newsgroups where you may post advertisements are in the **biz.marketplace** or **for-sale** newsgroups. Even then, you should limit the number of groups you post to. Posting the same message to dozens of newsgroups is called *spamming*, after the Monty Python skit where a group of Vikings drown out conversation by chanting "spam, spam, spam, spam, spam." Spamming will make a lot of people mad and can result in the loss of your Internet account.

29-15

What's an LOL and a :-)?

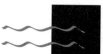 **LOL is an abbreviation, and :-) is a smiley face turned sideways.**

To save typing online, many people abbreviate expressions like *laughing out loud* and *for what it's worth*: LOL and FWIW. When people want to let you know they're kidding (or serious), they use little smileys, also known as emoticons. The classic smiley is :-) , which, if you rotate your head 90 degrees to the left, looks like a smiley face.

There are zillions of abbreviations on the Internet, and twice that many smileys. You can buy entire books filled with smileys, but Table 29-4 lists all of them you'll ever need.

Table 29-4

Abbreviations and smileys

Symbol	Meaning
BTW	by the way
HAND	have a nice day
HTH	hope this helps
IMHO	in my humble opinion
IMO	in my opinion
LOL	laughing out loud
ROTFL	rolling on the floor laughing
RTFM	read the f&%*&!! manual
TIA	thanks in advance
YMMV	your mileage may vary
:-)	Smiley
:-(	Frowney
;-)	Winkey
:-|	Seriously

What's .sit, .hqx, etc.?

 Those letters at the end of a file name tell you what kind of file it is.

If you've spent much time online, you know that most files are stored in a *compressed* format so they take less time to download. You also know that there are several different compression formats, with StuffIt being the most common for the Macintosh. You can tell that a file has been compressed with StuffIt — the file's name ends in *.sit*.

Hold on to your hat: There are many other compression programs on the Internet. What's more, some files have been encoded into *text*. The encoding process converts a typical Macintosh-format data file into a long, gibberish-looking *text file* that can be transferred through computers that wouldn't understand a Mac file format. A piece of software that has been thus converted into text is said to have been *binhexed*.

Most of the files at Macintosh FTP sites have been binhexed. If you open a binhexed file in your word processor, you'll see that it begins with the line "*(This file must be converted with BinHex 4.0)*." There *is* a program called BinHex 4.0, but it has some bugs. Use the free program called StuffIt Expander instead. You can get it from an FTP site, or very easily from an online service.

In fact, there are many more forms of file compression and text conversion. All you need to know is that StuffIt Expander, along with the accompanying DropStuff with Expander Enhancer, can restore them to normal Mac files. Including any format listed in Table 29-5.

Table 29-5

Common filename extensions for compressed and encoded files

Name suffix	Compression method
.arc	arc
.zip	PKZip
.sit	StuffIt
.cpt	Compact Pro
.Z	UNIX compress
.gz	GNU Zip
.hqx	binhex
.uu	uuencoded

You may also encounter filename suffixes that have nothing to do with compression. For instance, **horn.wav** is a sound in WAV format (a PC format). You'll learn these things as you go along.

 See also FAQ 28-5, "What am I supposed to do with these '.image' files I downloaded?"

29-17

How do I find someone's e-mail address?

 Call them.

Believe it or not, the easiest way to find a friend's e-mail address is to pick up the phone. It sure would be nice if there were some kind of up-to-date, electronic, worldwide directory of Internet participants. Trouble is, the Internet's millions of members change hourly—trying to maintain an accurate directory would be a futile task. There are some ways to search for e-mail addresses—there are even entire books, called "Internet White Pages" — but none of them is very good.

29-18

Where's the bold command, the tab settings, and the ® symbol?

 Not on the Internet, I'm afraid.

Text on the Internet is decidedly unfancy. Remember—you use a Mac. You're spoiled. The rest of the world doesn't have such luxuries.

For the most part, text on the Internet is limited to the 128 symbols in the set of *ASCII* (*American Standard Code for Information Interchange*) text set — some of which are carriage returns and other control characters. (See FAQ 4-7.) Strange things can happen when you copy a non-ASCII character from your word processor and paste it into a modem program. For instance, the word *don't* (with the nice curly apostrophe) becomes donUt, because the nice curly apostrophe isn't an ASCII character.

How do you know which characters on your keyboard will be OK on the Internet? If you have to press the Option or ⌘ keys to make the character, it's not ASCII. Curly quotes and apostrophes aren't ASCII, either.

If ASCII text can't even create those basic symbols, you can probably guess that it doesn't know a thing about bold, italic, and underline, or font or margin settings. Page layout in ASCII is Spartan indeed. People just put a blank line between paragraphs and leave it at that. (**Hint**: if you really want people to read your messages, break them up into short paragraphs.)

Why does this Internet text look so funny?

 Because you're communicating with much less sophisticated computers than yours.

In the early days, people accessed the Internet through dumb terminals (that's really what they were called). These crude computers showed lines of text 80 characters wide. Many people still use these terminals; therefore, when you read Internet messages, if your window isn't wide enough to accommodate all 80 characters across, you'll find that lines of text break off in strange places (see Figure 29-2).

Font choice plays a part, too. Most fonts, like Times and Helvetica, are *proportional* — different typed characters have different widths (compare the narrow letter I and the wide letter M in this font, for example). When you read e-mail and newsgroup messages from the Internet, everything will be much more readable if you use the Monaco or Courier font. Like the font used on dumb terminals, these fonts are *monospaced*, so characters — no matter what their normal widths — line up in neat vertical columns. Figure 29-2 should help you understand why.

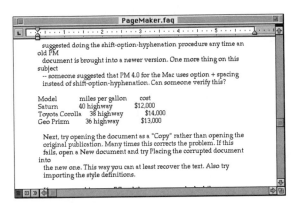

Figure 29-2: At top: This text from the Internet is a disaster. The columns in the table don't line up, and the lines wrap in funny places. Solution (bottom): Make the margins wider and the font smaller — and switch to a monospaced font like Courier.

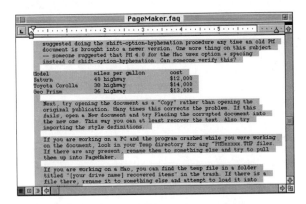

A small shareware mini-word processor can take the headache out of all these text rules. For example, BBEdit Lite can wrap lines to a specified length, get rid of non-ASCII characters that often garble Internet messages, and much more. You can find it wherever you find Macintosh freeware and shareware.

See also FAQ 29-7, "What are some other cool FTP sites?"

What are GIFs and JPEGs, and how do I open them?

▽ **They're picture formats. Use GIFConverter or GraphicConverter.**

GIF (pronounced like the peanut butter) stands for *Graphics Interchange Format*. JPEG (pronounced *jay*-peg) stands for *Joint Photographic Experts Group*. Both graphics formats are widely used online, because they use compression to reduce downloading time.

If you have America Online 2.5 or higher, you're in luck — the program can open GIFs and JPEGs (just use the Open command in its File menu). If not, download GIFConverter or GraphicConverter (shareware graphics programs). Launch the graphics viewer and choose Open from its File menu to open the pictures.

See also FAQ 28-3, "How do I find a file I want to download?"

See also FAQ 29-7, "What are some other cool FTP sites?"

Appendixes

Appendix A lists every Mac OS keystroke you'll ever need, as well as keystrokes for many major applications. Appendix B lists the phone numbers and addresses for all the companies mentioned in this book. Finally, Appendix C helps you troubleshoot the most common Mac troubles.

What's That Keystroke Again?

H*ere they are: The bestselling programs — and the keystrokes that make them tick. I won't bother listing keyboard shortcuts that already appear in your menus; clicking a menu to remind yourself of a particular keystroke is even easier than flipping for this appendix. These pages list the* hidden *keyboard shortcuts.*

And may you never have to hunt for another manual.

System 7 Finder

Miscellaneous options

Function	Keystroke
Make the desktop active the desktop pattern	⌘-Shift-up arrow or click
Delete locked files in the Trash	Option-Empty Trash (from Special menu)
Reverse the current setting of "Always snap to grid" (in the Views Control panel) while moving an icon	⌘-drag the icon

(continued)

Miscellaneous options *(continued)*

Function	Keystroke
Erase a disk automatically when you insert it	Hold down ⌘-Option-Tab when inserting the disk
Take a snapshot of the screen	⌘-Shift-3
Hide a program's windows when you switch to another program	Option-make another program active (by choosing it from the Application menu or by clicking its windows)
Select an item in a list in the Chooser	Begin typing the name.
Make the next list active in the Chooser	Tab
Make the previous list active in the Chooser	Shift-Tab
Choose Guest when connecting to another computer	⌘-G
Choose Registered User when connecting to another computer	⌘-R
Set the language to English (if WorldScript is installed)	⌘-left arrow
Set the language to the system script	⌘-right arrow
Set the language to the next script in the Keyboard menu	⌘-Space
Set the language to the next language in the current script	⌘-Option-Space (System 7.5.1 offers option to turn off this keyboard shortcut in the Keyboard Control Panel)

During startup

Function	Keystroke
Rebuild the Desktop file	Hold down ⌘-Option.
Turn off all system extensions when starting up	Hold down Shift.
Eject floppy disk (to avoid using it as the startup disk)	Hold down mouse or trackball button.
Bypass internal hard disk when starting up	Hold down ⌘-Option-Shift-Delete.
Reset the Chooser and control panel settings (stored in parameter RAM)	Hold down ⌘-Option-P-R.

Working with icons

Function	Keystroke
Copy an icon into another folder (instead of moving it)	Option-drag the icon.
Clean up selected icons	Shift-Clean Up (Special menu)
Clean up and sort icons	Option-Clean Up (Special menu)
Select an icon by name	Begin typing the name.
Select the next icon alphabetically	Tab
Select the previous icon alphabetically	Shift-Tab
Select an icon to the left or right (icon views only)	Left arrow or right arrow
Select an icon above or below (in any view)	Up arrow or down arrow
Select more than one icon	Shift-Click the icons or drag to enclose the icons.
Select no icon (making desktop active)	Click an icon on the desktop, then click the desktop pattern.

Working with list views

Function	Keystroke
Change how items are listed	Click a window column heading.
Expand contents of the selected folder	⌘-right arrow
Collapse contents of the selected folder	⌘-left arrow
Expand contents including inner folders	⌘-Option-right arrow
Collapse contents including inner folders	⌘-Option-left arrow or Option-Click the triangle.
Expand or collapse the contents of every folder in the window	Choose Select All from the Edit menu, then expand or collapse the contents.

Working with windows

Function	Keystroke
Close all disk and folder windows	Option-Close (from File menu) or Option-click any window's close box.
Move a window without making it active	⌘-drag the window's title bar.
Open a popup menu of the folders and disk that contain this folder	⌘-point to the window title and drag through the menu.
Close a window after opening one of its icons	Option-Open or Option-double-click the icon.
Zoom a window to the full size of the screen it is on	Option-click the zoom box

Most Programs

Most programs

Function	Keystroke
Scroll the document window down	Page Down
Scroll the document window up	Page Up
Scroll to the top of a document	Home
Scroll to the bottom of a document	End
Move to next blank (dialog boxes)	Tab
Print	⌘-P
Type an optional hyphen	⌘-hyphen
Type a nonbreaking hyphen	⌘-Shift-hyphen
Type a nonbreaking space	Ctrl-Shift-Space
Type an em dash (—)	Option-Shift-hyphen
Type a copyright symbol (©)	Option-G
Type a registered trademark symbol (®)	Option-R
Type a trademark symbol (™)	Option-2
Type an ellipsis (. . .)	Option-;
Type a single opening quotation mark	Option-]
Type a single closing quotation mark	Option-Shift-]
Type a double opening quotation mark	Option-[
Type a double closing quotation mark	Option-Shift-[

ClarisWorks

General keyword commands

Function	Keystroke
Tile windows down	Option and choose Tile Windows from the View Menu
Cancel options in a dialog box	⌘-. (period)
Close dialog box	⌘-. (period)
Cancel printing	⌘-. (period)
Center align text or cell data	⌘-\
Check Document Spelling	⌘-=
Check Selection Spelling	⌘-Shift-Y
Find Again	⌘-E
Find/Change	⌘-F
Find Selection	⌘-Shift-E
Help	⌘-?, Help
Justify text	⌘-Shift-\
Left align text or cell data	⌘-[
Modify frame	⌘-Shift-I
Page View	⌘-Shift-P
Play Macro	⌘-Shift-W
Print without displaying the Print dialog box	Option and choose Print from the File menu.
Record Macro/Stop Recording	⌘-Shift-J
Right align text or cell data	⌘-]
Show/Hide Rulers	⌘-Shift-U
Show/Hide Shortcuts	⌘-Shift-X
Show/Hide Tools	⌘-Shift-T
Thesaurus	⌘-Shift-Z

Communications keyboard commands

Function	Keystroke
Open or close connection	⌘-Shift-O
Phone book	⌘-B
Save lines off top	⌘-T
Select a block of text	⌘ and drag the mouse.
Show scrollback	⌘-L
Wait for connection	⌘-Shift-W

Database keyboard commands

Function	Keystroke
Browse	⌘-Shift-B
Define fields	⌘-Shift-D
Deselect all records	Enter
Duplicate record	⌘-D
Duplicate request (find)	⌘-D
Find	⌘-Shift-F
Hide selected	⌘-(
Hide unselected	⌘-)
Insert a Tab in a text field	⌘-Tab
Insert current date (in a date field)	⌘-hyphen
Insert current record number (in a number field)	⌘-hyphen
Layout	⌘-Shift-L
Lock (a field in Layout)	⌘-H
Match records	⌘-M
New record	⌘-R
New request (find)	⌘-R
Show all records	⌘-Shift-A
Sort records	⌘-J
Unlock (a field in Layout)	⌘-Shift-H

Object editing

Function	Keystroke
Duplicate	⌘-D
Frame links	⌘-L
Lock on a tool	Double-click the tool.
Modify arc	⌘-Shift-I
Modify frame	⌘-Shift-I
Reshape	⌘-R
Rotate	⌘-Shift-R
Round corners	⌘-Shift-I
Select the eye dropper	Tab
Smooth	⌘-(
Turn autogrid on/off	⌘-Y
Unsmooth	⌘-)

Object alignment and moving

Function	Keystroke
Align objects	⌘-Shift-K
Align to grid	⌘-K
Group	⌘-G
Lock	⌘-H
Move behind	⌘-Shift-hyphen
Move toward front	⌘-Shift-+
Turn autogrid on/off	⌘-Y
Ungroup	⌘-Shift-G
Unlock	⌘-Shift-H

Spreadsheet keyboard commands

Function	Keystroke
Calculate now	⌘-Shift-=
Cancel an entry	Esc
Clear cell contents and format	Clear
Delete cell contents	Delete, Del
Delete cells	⌘-Shift-K
Fill down	⌘-D
Fill right	⌘-R
Go to cell	⌘-G
Insert cells	⌘-Shift-I
Make chart	⌘-M
Protect cells	⌘-H
Sort	⌘-J
Unprotect cells	⌘-Shift-H

Text keyboard commands

Function	Keystroke
Copy ruler	⌘-Shift-C
Insert footnote	⌘-Shift-F
Insert page break	Enter (numeric keypad)
Other (font size)	⌘-Shift-O
Plain text	⌘-T
Return to the main text area from the footnote area	Enter (numeric keypad)
Show/hide formatting (invisible) characters	⌘-;
Subscript	⌘-hyphen
Superscript	⌘-+

Microsoft Word 6

Changing text formatting

Function	Keystroke
Change the font	⌘-Shift-F, then type font name.
Change the font size	⌘-Shift-P, then type number.
Increase the font size to the next available size	⌘-Shift->
Decrease the font size to the previous available size	⌘-Shift-<
Increase the font size by one point	⌘-]
Decrease the font size by one point	⌘-[
Change the case of letters	Shift-F3 or ⌘-Option-C
Create all capital letters	⌘-Shift-A
Underline single words	⌘-Shift-W
Double underline words	⌘-Shift-D
Create small capital letters	⌘-Shift-K
Apply subscripts (auto spacing)	⌘-=
Apply superscripts (auto spacing)	⌘-Shift-=
Remove formatting	⌘-Shift-Z
Create Symbol font	⌘-Shift-Q
Make the number keypad type numbers	Shift-Clear (press again to restore navigation functions)

Setting paragraph formatting

Function	Keystroke
Single-spaced lines	⌘-1
Double-spaced lines	⌘-2
One-and-a-half-spaced lines	⌘-5
Add one line of space preceding text	⌘-0 (zero)
Remove space preceding text	⌘-0 (zero)
Center a paragraph	⌘-E
Justify a paragraph	⌘-J

(continued)

Setting paragraph formatting *(continued)*

Function	Keystroke
Left-align a paragraph	⌘-L
Right-align a paragraph	⌘-R
Indent a paragraph from the left	⌘-M
Remove a paragraph indent from the left	⌘-Shift-M
Create a hanging indent	⌘-T
Reduce a hanging indent	⌘-Shift-T
Remove paragraph formatting applied by using shortcut keys or menu commands	⌘-Option-Q

Applying styles

Function	Keystroke
Apply a style name (Formatting toolbar displayed)	⌘-Shift-S
Open the Style dialog box (Formatting toolbar not displayed)	⌘-Shift-S
Start AutoFormat	⌘-K
Apply the Normal style	⌘-Shift-N
Apply the Heading 1 style	⌘-Option-1
Apply the Heading 2 style	⌘-Option-2
Apply the Heading 3 style	⌘-Option-3
Apply the List style	⌘-Shift-L

Delete text and graphics

Function	Keystroke
Delete one word to the left of the insertion point	⌘-Delete
Delete one character to the right of the insertion point	Del (not delete)
Delete one word to the right of the insertion point	⌘-Del (not delete)

Function	Keystroke
Cut (delete) selected text	⌘-X
Cut to the Spike	⌘-F3

Inserting

Function	Keystroke
A field	⌘-F9
An AutoText entry	Type AutoText entry name, and then ⌘-Option-V
A line break	Shift-Enter
A page break	⌘-Enter
A section break	⌘-Option-Enter
A column break	⌘-Shift-Enter

Moving around the document

Move	Keystroke
One word to the left	⌘-left arrow
One word to the right	⌘-right arrow
One paragraph up	⌘-up arrow
One paragraph down	⌘-down arrow
To the previous frame or object	Option-up arrow
To the next frame or object	Option-down arrow
One column to the left (in a Table)	Shift-Tab
One column to the right (in a Table)	Tab
Up one line	up arrow
Down one line	down arrow
To the End of a line	End
To the beginning of a line	Home
Up one page	⌘-Option-Page Up
Down one page	⌘-Option-Page Down

(continued)

Moving around the document *(continued)*

Move	Keystroke
Up one screen	Page Up
Down one screen	Page Down
To the bottom of a screen	⌘-Page Down
To the top of a screen	⌘-Page Up
To the end of a document	⌘-End
To the beginning of a document	⌘-Home
Repeat Find or GoAction	Shift-F4 or ⌘-Option-Y
A previous revision	⌘-Option-Z
Go to the next document window	⌘-F6
Go to the previous document window	⌘-Shift-F6

Note: If you are using a PowerBook, the navigation keys (Page Up, Page Down, Home, and End) and buttons that move the insertion point to the beginning or End of a document are available through a toolbar. From the View menu, choose Toolbars, and then select PowerBook.

Working with menus and shortcut key assignments

Function	Keystroke
Make the menu bar active	F10 or ⌘-Tab
Cancel a menu	Esc or ⌘-. (period)
Display a shortcut menu	Shift-F10 or Option-click the mouse button.
Add a command to a menu	⌘-Option-=
Remove a command from a menu	⌘-Option-hyphen
Assign an action to a shortcut key	⌘-Option-+ (plus sign on the numeric keypad)
Remove an action from a shortcut key assignment	⌘-Option- — (hyphen on the numeric keypad)

Quicken 5

Special keys

Function	Keystroke
Decrease date or check number	– (hyphen)
Increase date or check number	+ (plus sign)
Go to register	⌘-R
Go to Write Checks	⌘-J
Launch Quicken without opening a file	Hold down Option key during launch.

Lists

Function	Keystroke
Add a new item to a list	⌘-N
Select an item on a list	First letter of item
Edit a selected item in a list	⌘-E
Delete a selected item in a list	⌘-D
Use an item in a list	Double-click it

Moving around in a window

Function	Keystroke
Next field or column	Tab
Previous field or column	Shift-Tab
First transaction in register or Write Checks	Home
Last transaction in register or Write Checks	End
Next page of transactions or next check	Page Down or ⌘-down arrow
Previous page of transactions or next check	Page Up or ⌘-up arrow
Up or down one row	up arrow or down arrow

Reports

Function	Keystroke
QuickZoom a report or graph item	Double-click it.
Memorize a report template	⌘-M
Widen or narrow a report column	Drag under the column heading.

Dates

Function	Keystroke
Today	t
First day of this month	m
Last day of this month	h
First day of this year	y
Last day of this year	r

Register and write checks

Function	Keystroke
Account, select or set up	⌘-A
Category, select or set up	⌘-L
Class, select or set up	⌘-K
Copy payee name to check address	' (apostrophe)
Delete transaction or split line	⌘-D
Find transaction, Find again	⌘-F, ⌘-G
Go to a new transaction	⌘-N
Memorize a transaction	⌘-M
Paste current date	⌘-' (apostrophe)
Print checks	⌘-P

Quick fill

Function	Keystroke
Fill in Payee/Description or Category information	Start typing in the field.
Fill in category & start subcategory	Type :.
Fill in category & start class	Type /.
Fill in payee name only	Start typing, then press Option-Tab.
Recall a memorized transaction	⌘-T
Split transaction	⌘-E
Transfer, go to	⌘-[
Transfer, select account for	⌘-L

Investments

Function	Keystroke
Decrease or increase price by $1/8$	– or +
Go to Portfolio	⌘-H
View or Enter prices for next day	Option-+
View or Enter prices for previous day	Option-hyphen
View latest known price	Option-Shift-+
View earliest known price	Option-Shift-hyphen
View next price Entered	Option-> (Option-Shift-,)

Help

Function	Keystroke
Help on current window or menu	⌘-? or Help key
Go to related Help Topic	Click bold text.

WordPerfect 3.1

Basics

Function	Keystroke
Cycle Windows	⌘-Shift-W
Cancel	⌘-., or Esc
Show/Hide Ruler	⌘-R
Show/Hide Codes	⌘-Shift-K
Numbers Lock On/Off	⌘-Shift-NumLock

Selecting

Function	Keystroke
Character	Shift-left arrow or Shift-right arrow
Document	⌘-A
To end of line	⌘-Shift-right arrow
To end of document	Shift-End

Language tools

Function	Keystroke
Speller	⌘-E
Thesaurus	⌘-Shift-T
Grammar Checker	⌘-Y

Creating documents

Function	Keystroke
Insert date/time	⌘-Shift-D
Insert page break	⌘-Return
Header/footer	⌘-Shift-H
Footnote	⌘-Shift-F

Function	Keystroke
Endnote	⌘-Shift-E
Page numbers	Option-F8

Formatting characters

Function	Keystroke
Font, size, style	⌘-H
Size up or down	⌘-Shift-> or ⌘-Shift-<
Plain text	⌘-T

Formatting lines & paragraphs

Function	Keystroke
Center line	⌘-Shift-Q
Flush right	⌘-Shift-Z
Back tab (margin release)	Shift-Tab
Indent	⌘-Shift-I or Option-Tab
Left/right indent	⌘-Option-Tab
Borders	⌘-F7

Formatting pages

Function	Keystroke
Margins	⌘-M
Center text on page	⌘-;
Columns	⌘-K
Column break	⌘-Shift-Return
Column borders	⌘-Shift-F7

Microsoft Excel 5.0a

In dialog boxes

Function	Keystroke
Select the Tab to the right in a "Tab" dialog box	Ctrl-Tab or ⌘-Page Down
Select the Tab to the left in a "Tab" dialog box	Ctrl-Shift-Tab or ⌘-Page Up
Move to the next item beginning with that letter in a list box	Letter key
Select the item with that underlined letter	⌘-letter key
Expand a dropdown list box	Option-Down arrow
Collapse an expanded dropdown list box	Esc
Choose the default command button	Enter or Return
Cancel the command and close the dialog box	Esc or ⌘-.

Within an edit box

Function	Keystroke
Move to the beginning or end of the entry	Home or End
Move one character left or one character right	left arrow or right arrow
Select from cursor to the beginning of the entry	Shift-Home
Select from the cursor to the end of the entry	Shift-End
Select the character to the left of the cursor	Shift-left arrow
Select the character to the right of the cursor	Shift-right arrow

Keys for entering data

Function	Keystroke
Activate the cell and formula bar	⌘-U
Carry out an action	Enter or Return
Cancel an action	⌘-. (period) or Esc
Repeat the last action	⌘-Y
Insert blank cells	⌘-I
Delete the selection	⌘-K

Function	Keystroke
Clear the selection of formulas and data	Del
Edit a cell note	⌘-Shift-N or Shift-F2
Insert the AutoSum formula	⌘-Shift-T
Copy a picture	⌘-Shift-C
Display the Paste Special dialog box	⌘-Shift-V
Enter the date	⌘-hyphen
Enter the time	⌘-;
Fill down	⌘-D
Fill right	⌘-R
Move down through a selection	Enter
Move up through a selection	Shift-Enter
Move right through a selection	Tab
Move left through a selection	Shift-Tab

Formatting data

Function	Keystroke
Display the style dialog box	⌘-Shift-L
Apply the general number format	Ctrl-Shift-~
Apply currency format (2 decimal places)	Ctrl-Shift-$
Apply % format with no decimal places	Ctrl-Shift-%
Apply date format (day, month, and year)	Ctrl-Shift-#
Apply time format (hour:minute, A.M. or P.M.)	Ctrl-Shift-@
Apply the 2-decimal-place format with commas	Ctrl-Shift-!
Apply or remove cell border	⌘-Option-arrow
Apply the outline border	⌘-Option-0 (zero)
Remove all borders	⌘-Option-hyphen
Apply plain text	⌘-Shift-P
Apply or remove bold, italic, underline	⌘-Shift-B, or -I, or -U
Hide rows / Unhide rows	Ctrl-9/Ctrl-Shift-(
Hide columns / Unhide columns	Ctrl-0 (zero)/Ctrl-Shift-)

Keys for working in menus

Function	Keystroke
Activate the menu bar	/ or F10
Activate the shortcut menu	Shift-F10
Cancel the shortcut menu	Esc or ⌘-. (period)
Undo the last command	F1 or ⌘-Z
Repeat the last command, if applicable	⌘-Y

When menu bar is active

Cancel the menu	Esc or ⌘-. (period)
Select the menu with the underlined letter	Letter key
Select the menu to the left or right	left arrow or right arrow

With menu displayed

Function	Keystroke
Choose the command with the underlined letter	Letter key
Choose the selected command	Enter or Return
Cancel the menu	Esc
Select the next or previous command on the menu	down arrow or up arrow
With a submenu displayed, toggle selection between main menu and submenu	left arrow or right arrow

Moving and selecting in worksheets and workbooks

Function	Keystroke
Extend the selection by one cell	Shift-arrow
Move to the edge of the current data region	⌘-arrow
Extend selection to edge of the current data region	⌘-Shift-arrow

Function	Keystroke
Move among unlocked cells in protected worksheet	Tab
Move to the beginning of the row	Home
Extend the selection to the beginning of the row	Shift-Home
Move to the beginning of the worksheet	⌘-Home
Extend selection to beginning of the worksheet	⌘-Shift-Home
Move to last cell in your worksheet (lower-right corner)	⌘-End
Extend selection to the last cell in worksheet	⌘-Shift-End
Select the entire column	⌘-Space
Select the entire row	Shift-Space
Select the entire worksheet	⌘-A
Collapse the selection to the active cell	Shift-Delete
Move up or down one screen	Page Up or Page Down
Move right one screen	Option-Page Down
Move left one screen	Option-Page Up
Extend the selection down one screen	Shift-Page Down
Extend the selection up one screen	Shift-Page Up
Select the current region	Ctrl-Shift-*
Show or hide the Standard toolbar	⌘-7
Turn scroll lock on or off	Scroll Lock

Switching windows

Function	Keystroke
Close window	⌘-F4
Move to next window	⌘-M or Ctrl-Tab
Move to previous window	⌘-Shift-M or Ctrl-Shift-Tab
Maximize or minimize window	⌘-F10
Move to the next sheet in the workbook	⌘-Page Down
Move to the previous sheet in the workbook	⌘-Page Up

Working in cells or the formula bar

Activate the cell and formula bar	⌘-U
Start a formula	=
Delete to the right of the insertion point	Del
Delete text to the End of the line	Ctrl-Option-Del
Cancel an entry in the cell or formula bar	⌘-. (period) or Esc
Complete the cell entry	Enter
Insert a carriage return	⌘-Option-Return
Complete cell entry and move to next cell	Tab
Complete cell entry and move to previous cell	Shift-Tab
Insert a tab	⌘-Option-Tab
Move one character up, down, left, or right (when in Edit mode)	arrows
Move to the start of the line (when in Edit mode)	Home
Insert the date	⌘-hyphen
Insert the time	⌘-;
Copy the value from the cell above	⌘-Shift-"
Alternate between displaying values or formulas in cells	⌘-' (single left quotation mark)
Copy the formula from the cell above	⌘-' (apostrophe)
Fill a selection of cells with the current entry	Option-Enter
Enter the formula as an array formula	⌘-Enter

QuarkXPress 3.31

For help, press ⌘-? or ⌘-/.

Formatting keys (for text boxes)

Function	Keystroke
Other (font sizes)	⌘-Shift-\
Plain	⌘-Shift-P
Bold	⌘-Shift-B

Function	Keystroke
Italic	⌘-Shift-I
Underline	⌘-Shift-U
Word underline	⌘-Shift-W
Strikethrough	⌘-Shift-/
Outline	⌘-Shift-O
Shadow	⌘-Shift-S
All caps	⌘-Shift-K
Small caps	⌘-Shift-H
Superscript	⌘-Shift-+
Subscript	⌘-Shift-hyphen
Superior	⌘-Shift-V
Character attributes	⌘-Shift-D
Left	⌘-Shift-L
Centered	⌘-Shift-C
Right	⌘-Shift-R
Justified	⌘-Shift-J
Forced justify	⌘-Option-Shift-J
Leading	⌘-Shift-E
Formats	⌘-Shift-F
Rules	⌘-Shift-N
Tabs	⌘-Shift-T

Formatting keys (for picture boxes)

Function	Keystroke
Negative	⌘-Shift-hyphen
Normal contrast	⌘-Shift-N
High contrast	⌘-Shift-H
Posterized	⌘-Shift-P
Other contrast	⌘-Shift-C
Other screen	⌘-Shift-S

(continued)

Formatting keys (for picture boxes) *(continued)*

Function	Keystroke
Fit to box	⌘-Shift-F
Fit to box (maintain aspect ratio)	⌘-Option-Shift-F
Center (middle) of box	⌘-Shift-M

Special formatting keys

Function	Keystroke
Decrease horiz/vert scale 5%	⌘-[
Increase horiz/vert scale 5%	⌘-]
Increase horiz/vert scale 1%	⌘-Option-[
Decrease horiz/vert scale 1%	⌘-Option-]
Decrease kern/track 10/200 em	⌘-Shift-{
Increase kern/track 10/200 em	⌘-Shift-}
Decrease kern/track 1/200 em	⌘-Option-Shift-{
Increase kern/track 1/200 em	⌘-Option-Shift-}
Decrease leading 1 point	⌘-Shift-:
Increase leading 1 point	⌘-Shift-"
Decrease leading 1/10 point	⌘-Option-Shift-:
Decrease size (within presets)	⌘-Shift-<
Increase size (within presets)	⌘-Shift->
Decrease size/scale (full range)	⌘-Option-Shift-<
Increase size/scale (full range)	⌘-Option-Shift->
Decrease baseline shift 1 point	⌘-Option-Shift-hyphen
Increase baseline shift 1 point	⌘-Option-Shift-+

Adobe PageMaker 5.0a

Control palette

Function	Keystroke
Display/hide control palette	⌘-' (apostrophe)
Activate control palette (toggle)	⌘-' (left single quotation mark)
Paragraph/character view (toggle)	⌘-Shift-~
Apply change or return to layout	⌘-Return
Apply change and stay at same option	Shift-Return
Selected button option on/off	Spacebar
Select different unit of measure	⌘-Option-M

Styles palette

Function	Keystroke
Display/hide styles palette	⌘-Y
Define styles	⌘-3

Colors palette

Function	Keystroke
Display/hide colors palette	⌘-K

File management

Function	Keystroke
Revert to last mini-save	Shift-Revert File
Save all open publications	Option-Save
Close all open publications	Option-Close

General layout commands

Function	Keystroke
Select all	⌘-A
Power paste	⌘-Option-V
Guides on/off	⌘-J
Rulers on/off	⌘-R
Snap to guides	⌘-U
Snap to rulers	⌘-[
Send to back	⌘-B
Bring to front	⌘-F
Place	⌘-D

Font size

Function	Keystroke
Increase one point size	⌘-Option-Shift->
Increase to next standard size	⌘-Shift->
Decrease one point size	⌘-Option-Shift-<
Decrease to next standard size	⌘-Shift-<

Alignment

Function	Keystroke
Align left, right, center	⌘-Shift-L, R, C
Justify	⌘-Shift-J
Force justify	⌘-Shift-F

Leading, width, track

Function	Keystroke
Auto leading	⌘-Shift-A
Normal width	⌘-Shift-X
No track	⌘-Shift-Q

Position

Function	Keystroke
Subscript	⌘-Shift-hyphen
Superscript	⌘-Shift-+

Type style

Function	Keystroke
All caps	⌘-Shift-K
Small caps	⌘-Shift-H
Bold, italic, underline	⌘-Shift-B, I, U
Strikethrough	⌘-Shift-/
Outline	⌘-Shift-D
Shadow	⌘-Shift-W
Normal	⌘-Shift-Space
Type specs dialog box	⌘-T

Text editing in story editor

Function	Keystroke
Find	⌘-8
Find next	⌘-,
Change	⌘-9
Spelling	⌘-L

Paragraph formatting

Function	Keystroke
Define styles	⌘-3
Paragraph	⌘-M
Hyphenation (layout view)	⌘-H
Indents/tabs (layout view)	⌘-I

Tools

Function	Keystroke
Display/hide toolbox	⌘-6
Pointer (toggle with current tool)	⌘-Space
Pointer	Shift-F1
Line tool	Shift-F2
Rule tool	Shift-F3
Text tool	Shift-F4
Rotating tool	Shift-F5
Rectangle tool	Shift-F6
Oval tool	Shift-F7
Cropping tool	Shift-F8

What's the Phone Number?

Maybe this appendix is more for me than for you. But my life is a never-ending trip to the closet to find the manual to look up the number to call for help to finish my project. I kept wishing: Why can't somebody just put all the major Mac hardware and software companies' help-line phone numbers in one place?

Here it is.

Adobe

Adobe Systems Incorporated
1585 Charleston Road
Mountain View, California 94039-7900
Sales: (800) 883-6687
Technical Support: (408) 986-6580 (Adobe Acrobat)
(206) 628-2757 (Adobe Type Manager and Type Products)
(408) 986-6515 (Adobe Dimensions, Illustrator, and Streamline)
(206) 628-4506 (Adobe Fetch)
(206) 628-4501 (Adobe PageMaker)
(206) 628-4503 (Adobe Persuasion)
(408) 986-6535 (Adobe Photoshop)
(408) 986-6510 (Adobe Premiere)

Apple

Apple Computer Inc.
1 Infinite Loop
Cupertino, California 95014-2084
Sales: (408) 996-1010
Technical Support:
(800) SOS-APPL (767-2774)

APS

APS Technologies
6131 Deramus
Kansas City, Missouri 64120
Sales: (800) 677-3294
Technical Support: (800) 334-7550

Caere

Caere Corporation
100 Cooper Court
Los Gatos, California 95030
Sales: (408) 395-7000
Technical Support: (408) 395-8319

Claris

Claris Corporation
5201 Patrick Henry Drive
P.O. Box 58168
Santa Clara, California 95052-8168
Sales: (800) 3-CLARIS (325-2747)
Technical Support: (408)727-9054

DayStar

DayStar Digital
5556 Atlanta Highway
Flowery Branch, Georgia 30542
(800) 962-2077

Delrina

Delrina Corporation
895 Don Mills Road
500-2 Park Centre
Toronto, Ontario
Canada M3C 1W3
Sales: (800) 268-6082
Technical Support: (416) 441-1026

FrameMaker

Frame Technology Corporation
1010 Rincon Circle
San Jose, California 95131
Sales: (408) 433-3311
Technical Support: (408) 922-2744

Global Village

Global Village Communication, Inc.
1144 East Arques Avenue
Sunnyvale, California 94086
Sales: (800) 736-4821
Technical Support: (408) 523-1050

Hewlett-Packard

Hewlett-Packard Company
700 71st Avenue
Greeley, Colorado 80634
Sales: (800) 752-0900
Technical Support: (208) 323-2551

Intuit

Intuit
P.O. Box 3014
Menlo Park, California 94026
Sales: (415) 322-0573
Technical Support: (415) 858-6041

Macromedia

Macromedia, Inc.
600 Townsend Street
San Francisco, California 94103
Sales: (800) 288-4797
Technical Support: (415) 252-9080

Microsoft

Microsoft Corporation
One Microsoft Way
Redmond, Washington 98052-6399
Sales: (800) 426-9400
Technical Support: (206) 635-7055

Now Software

Now Software
921 SW Washington Street
Suite 500
Portland, Oregon 97205
(503) 274-2800

Quark

Quark Inc.
1800 Grant Street
Denver, Colorado 80203
Sales: (303) 894-8888
Technical Support: (303) 894-8899

Radius

Radius, Inc.
215 Moffett Park Drive
Sunnyvale, California 94089-1374
Sales: (800) 227-2795
Technical Support: (408) 541-5700

Software Ventures

Software Ventures Corporation
2907 Claremont Avenue
Berkeley, California 94705
Sales: (510) 644-3232
Technical Support: (510) 644-1325

STF

STF Technologies, Inc.
Box 81
Concordia, Missouri 64020
Phone: (816) 463-2021

Supra

Supra Corporation
7101 Supra Drive SW
Albany, Oregon 97321-8000
Sales: (800) 727-8772
Technical Support: (503) 967-2492

Symantec

Symantec Corporation
10201 Torre Avenue
Cupertino, California 95014
Sales: (800) 441-7234
Technical Support: (503) 465-8440 (Disk
Doubler, Norton Utilities, Public Utilities,
and Suitcase)
(503) 465-8420 (Fastback and SAM)

WordPerfect

Novell Applications Group
1555 N. Technology Way
Orem, Utah 84057-2399
Sales: (800) 451-5151
Technical Support: (800) 861-2044
Sales: (800) 268-6082
Technical Support: (416) 441-1026

Troubleshooting Cheat Sheet

H*ere it is, all in one place: every single troubleshooting step you can possibly take yourself. These steps will save you a lot of time when you call for help — you'll routinely be instructed to try these before anybody will help you over the phone.*

And no wonder: trying each of the tools in this virtual toolkit will solve almost 100 percent of the following typical Mac problems:

✦ *Mysterious system crashes and freezes*

✦ *Type 1, 2, and 3 errors*

✦ *Control panel settings that don't stick*

✦ *File-copying problems*

✦ *Printing problems*

✦ *Problems with the modem, scanner, and other gear*

Follow these steps in roughly the order presented here.

Give it more memory

If you're generally having problems in one particular software program, such as freeze-ups or Type 1 errors, that program is probably gasping for breath — it needs more memory.

1. Quit the program. Return to the Finder.

2. Highlight the program's icon. From the File menu, choose Get Info.

3. As shown in Figure C-1, double-click the bottom memory box. Type in a number that's 100 or 150 higher than what's there. Close the window, launch the program, and see if there's any improvement. If not, you may need to repeat this surgery.

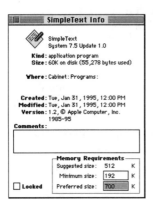

Figure C-1: In your program's Get Info box, increasing the allotted memory amount improves the reliability of almost any program.

See also Chapter 6, "Memory"

Throw out the Prefs file

This is another only-one-program-is-acting-up technique — not to be confused with the my-whole-system-is-sick solutions in the rest of this appendix.

1. Open your System Folder. In it, you'll find a Preferences folder. Open that, too.

2. Throw away the Preferences file that corresponds to the program that has been giving you grief. For example, if Quicken has been acting up, trash Quicken Prefs. (Another good one to trash when things aren't going well at the desktop level: Finder Prefs.) Don't throw away an entire preferences *folder,* such as Claris or QuicKeys — throw away only a Prefs *file.*

The next time you launch that program, it will create a brand new, fresh, virgin Preferences file, free from whatever corruptions were affecting it before.

Reinstall the program

If one particular program is still giving you trouble, reinstall it from the original master disks. In many cases, some subtle corruption has crept into the program you're using; a fresh installation solves the problem.

Turn off your extensions

If your problems don't seem to be confined to a single program — or even if they do, and the techniques above haven't worked — your thoughts should turn immediately to your extensions.

Extensions, of course, are those self-loading background programs whose icons you see marching across your screen every time you turn on the Mac. Trouble is, to make those work, programmers often have to pull some wily programming stunts. When two extensions' programming stunts run into each other, system crashes, strange freezes, and other drama may result.

When you're in a hurry to get your work printed, or to finish that manuscript, or to look up that number, you can *turn all those extensions off* with one press of a key.

While the Mac is starting up, press down the Shift key until you see the message "Extensions off" on the screen.

Once they're off, of course, they don't do you any good. You can't use your CD-ROM, or send faxes, or have your screen automatically darkened by a screen saver — because the extensions that add those features have been turned off. But at least your Mac will run, and your documents will print.

Identify the problem extensions

Of course, life without extensions is like a car without radio, air conditioning, or shock absorbers. When you have the time, the next step to troubleshooting your Mac is determining *which* extensions were causing the problem.

By far the simplest way is to use an extension detective program such as Conflict Catcher. Its purpose in life is to help you figure out which extensions are at fault. Essentially, it asks you to restart the Mac repeatedly, each time asking you if the problem has gone away yet. After several restarts, it triumphantly announces the names of the quarreling extensions.

To me, extensions are such a never-ending nightmare that Conflict Catcher is worth *buying*. But if you're broke or in a hurry, here's a cheapo way to get it. Sign onto America Online (see Chapter 28) and download the Conflict Catcher demo. It only works for three days — but that's plenty long enough for you to figure out which extensions to yell at this time.

If you aren't willing or able to do the America Online thing, you can use the manual method, which takes much longer.

1. Open your System Folder. Double-click your Extensions folder.

2. Drag half of those extension icons *out* of the System Folder — onto the desktop, say.

3. Restart the Mac. If the problem has gone away now, one of the extensions you removed was probably the guilty party. If the problem still exists, repeat the process, but this time take some more extensions out of the Extensions folder.

Through trial and error, you should be able to figure out, eventually, which extensions weren't getting along. Sometimes, just renaming one so that it alphabetically follows its enemy is enough to solve the problem.

Incidentally — if you have System 7.5, performing steps 1 and 2 above is much easier. Just restart the Mac; as it's lighting up, hold down the Space bar. You'll be shown a list (courtesy of a program called Extensions Manager) of every extension you own. As shown in Figure C-2, you can now turn extensions on or off just by clicking their names — which is a lot easier than the manual method described above.

Figure C-2: With Extensions Manager, performing a trial-and-error extension hunt is much easier. You can just click an extension's name to turn it on or off.

Do a "clean re-install" of the System

This is the software equivalent of electroshock therapy — it isn't subtle, but boy, does it produce results.

Reinstalling your System Folder is a 20-minute procedure, and it requires the original system disks (or CD-ROM, or the Performa backup disks you made) that came with your Mac. This process is terrific for wiping out an enormous variety of glitches, crashes, freezes, and other mysterious behavior. Actually, I believe in doing a clean re-install every few months, just because my Mac always feels so much better afterward.

System 7.1 or earlier

1. Open your System Folder. Drag the Finder icon to the desktop.

2. Close the System Folder window. Change the System Folder's name to, say, *Old system*.

3. Run your Installer program (on the installation disks or CD-ROM that came with your Mac). Install the System software in the usual way (an Easy Install is usually the best option).

   If it's a Performa, use the Apple Restore program on your Disk Utilities disk to re-install your System Folder.

System 7.5 or later

1. Run your Installer program (on the installation disks or CD-ROM that came with your Mac). When the welcome screen appears, click OK.

2. At the next screen, press ⌘-Shift-K. You're asked whether you want to update your existing System or build a new one; choose the second option. Continue the installation in the usual way; I recommend the Easy Install option.

When the installation is complete, your Mac will have a brand new System Folder. You'll probably be surprised at how much faster your Mac starts, launches programs, and operates. That's because you haven't added in all of your customized System Folder junk: fonts, control panels, sounds, screen savers, and so on.

That's the final step. Open your Old system folder and your new, real System Folder in side-by-side windows. Compare their contents. Carefully copy into your *new* System Folder anything it doesn't have from the old one. Pay special attention to the contents of the Extensions, Control Panels, Preferences, and Fonts folders, as well as software-company folders (Aldus, Claris, Microsoft, etc.). When possible, reinstall this kind of stuff from the original program disks. When you're finished, your Mac should be just as functional as it was before — but without the crashes.

If everything works okay now, you can throw away the stray Finder icon (if you dragged it out in step 1 above). You can throw away your Old system folder, too.

Zap the PRAM

If you have turned off your extensions, re-installed the System Folder, and trashed your Prefs file, and your Mac is *still* acting strange, try this last-resort technique.

1. Restart the Mac.
2. As it's starting to light up, press and hold these four keys: ⌘, Option, letter P, and letter R. Press them until you hear the *second* startup chime, and then let go.

You've just succeeded in *zapping the PRAM* — flushing the contents of the Mac's parameter RAM, a tiny piece of memory, maintained by battery. The PRAM maintains several Mac settings, such as the time and your control panel settings, even when the Mac is off. If this bit of RAM becomes corrupted, headaches can result.

In fact, if you have a modem, consider downloading the free program called TechTool. It does a quicker, easier, more thorough job of clearing your PRAM (and other tasks, such as rebuilding your desktop file, described next).

See also FAQ 28-3, "How do I find a file I want to download?"

Rebuild the desktop

This technique is terrific when your icons show up as blank pieces of paper, as described in FAQ 19-3. It's also useful when double-clicking a document fails to launch the correct program.

✦ Restart the Mac.

✦ As the last of the extensions are loading (their icons appearing), hold down the ⌘ and Option keys. When the "Do you want to rebuild the desktop file?" message appears, let go. Click OK.

The Mac will take a moment to re-create its internal database of your files, their icons, and their relationships to the programs on your hard drive.

The rules of SCSI

SCSI is the technology, the cable, the jack on the back of your Mac, that permits SCSI *devices* — scanners, external hard drives, CD-ROM players, and so on — to connect. They can connect not just to the Mac, but to each other, forming a chain. That's lucky — otherwise, you'd only be allowed to use one at a time.

Unfortunately, this SCSI thing is a serious nightmare. If you have no gadgets plugged into your Mac's SCSI connector, you don't know how lucky you are. There are guidelines — printed below — for making a chain of SCSI appliances work correctly. The trouble is, you must frequently *violate* one of those rules in order to make your setup work.

Always begin, however, by obeying these principles.

✦ **Termination:** If you have more than one SCSI appliance attached to the outside of your Mac, the last one on the chain must have a *terminator* plug. This three-inch, usually gray-and-silver plug goes on the empty jack of that final SCSI device. (If there's no empty jack, plug the SCSI cable into the terminator, and the terminator into the device.)

The rules are considerably more complex for PowerBooks. See Chapters 15 and 16, and see the manual for your particular model.

Incidentally, some well designed SCSI appliances, such as the Zip drive, save you the cost of a terminator plug — they have a termination on/off switch right on the case.

✦ **SCSI addresses:** Each attached SCSI device must have its own unique *address* (a number between 1 and 6, because the Mac itself is always 7, and the internal drive is always 0). Almost every SCSI appliance includes some switch or dial for changing this number. If two attached devices have the same SCSI ID number, you're asking for trouble.

✦ **The cable:** Believe it or not, the SCSI *cable* is frequently the source of SCSI headaches. Reversing a cable end-for-end often solves a mysterious SCSI problem; so does plugging it into the *other* of two SCSI connectors on a device. Replacing the cable is also a terrific idea when you've followed the first two SCSI rules but things still aren't working. (The quality counts: use heavy-duty SCSI cables, such as those from Apple or APS.)

If obeying the rules doesn't produce a working system, try breaking them. Rearrange the order of the devices. Rearrange the cables. Add an extra terminator in the middle of the chain. Try shorter cables (your total cable lengths should not equal more than 18 feet anyway).

Finally, Apple recommends that all SCSI devices be turned on whenever the Mac is on. This was optional on regular Macs — but it's critical on Power Macs.

INDEX

— Symbols —

@ (at sign), 323–324
¢, 32–33
© (copyright symbol), 32–33
– (minus sign), 98
? (question mark), 243
↓, 346
¥, 32–33

— A —

abbreviations, Internet, 344
About Apple Guide, 18
About This Macintosh
  displaying memory usage with,
    15–16, 103–105
  displaying model numbers with,
    257
Academic Computing and Network
  Services, 22
accelerators, 283, 286–287
accent marks, creating, 33
access keyword, 318
ADB (Apple Desktop Bus), 58
addresses
  in address-book programs, 38–40
  Internet, basic description of,
    323–324
  mail merge and, 41–43

memory, 105–106, 225
  printing, on envelopes, 40–41
  SCSI, 389
Adobe
  phone number/address for, 378
  Premiere, 169
  Type Manager, 60
Advanced Research Projects Agency
  (ARPAnet), 332
advertisements, 275, 343
After Dark screen saver, 21, 268.
  See also screen savers
  cursor problems and, 98
  downloading problems and, 321
  installing, 85–87
  memory consumed by, 103
  Type 1 errors and, 221
  WallZapper feature, 85–87
airports
  theft of computers in, 55
  X-ray machines in, passing
    PowerBooks through, 54, 207
aliases, 230, 288
  basic description of, 3, 94–95
  creating, steps for, 95
  of files, in the Apple Menu Items
    folder, 34
alphabetical order, viewing icons in,
  97
America Online, 3, 306, 317–329.
  See also Internet, online services

—T—

Title	Author	ISBN	Price

INTERNET / COMMUNICATIONS / NETWORKING

12/20/94

Title	Author	ISBN	Price
CompuServe For Dummies™	by Wallace Wang	1-56884-181-7	$19.95 USA/$26.95 Canada
Modems For Dummies™, 2nd Edition	by Tina Rathbone	1-56884-223-6	$19.99 USA/$26.99 Canada
Modems For Dummies™	by Tina Rathbone	1-56884-001-2	$19.95 USA/$26.95 Canada
MORE Internet For Dummies™	by John R. Levine & Margaret Levine Young	1-56884-164-7	$19.95 USA/$26.95 Canada
NetWare For Dummies™	by Ed Tittel & Deni Connor	1-56884-003-9	$19.95 USA/$26.95 Canada
Networking For Dummies™	by Doug Lowe	1-56884-079-9	$19.95 USA/$26.95 Canada
ProComm Plus 2 For Windows For Dummies™	by Wallace Wang	1-56884-219-8	$19.99 USA/$26.99 Canada
The Internet For Dummies™, 2nd Edition	by John R. Levine & Carol Baroudi	1-56884-222-8	$19.99 USA/$26.99 Canada
The Internet For Macs For Dummies™	by Charles Seiter	1-56884-184-1	$19.95 USA/$26.95 Canada

MACINTOSH

Title	Author	ISBN	Price
Macs For Dummies®	by David Pogue	1-56884-173-6	$19.95 USA/$26.95 Canada
Macintosh System 7.5 For Dummies™	by Bob LeVitus	1-56884-197-3	$19.95 USA/$26.95 Canada
MORE Macs For Dummies™	by David Pogue	1-56884-087-X	$19.95 USA/$26.95 Canada
PageMaker 5 For Macs For Dummies™	by Galen Gruman	1-56884-178-7	$19.95 USA/$26.95 Canada
QuarkXPress 3.3 For Dummies™	by Galen Gruman & Barbara Assadi	1-56884-217-1	$19.99 USA/$26.99 Canada
Upgrading and Fixing Macs For Dummies™	by Kearney Rietmann & Frank Higgins	1-56884-189-2	$19.95 USA/$26.95 Canada

MULTIMEDIA

Title	Author	ISBN	Price
Multimedia & CD-ROMs For Dummies™, Interactive Multimedia Value Pack	by Andy Rathbone	1-56884-225-2	$29.95 USA/$39.95 Canada
Multimedia & CD-ROMs For Dummies™	by Andy Rathbone	1-56884-089-6	$19.95 USA/$26.95 Canada

OPERATING SYSTEMS / DOS

Title	Author	ISBN	Price
MORE DOS For Dummies™	by Dan Gookin	1-56884-046-2	$19.95 USA/$26.95 Canada
S.O.S. For DOS™	by Katherine Murray	1-56884-043-8	$12.95 USA/$16.95 Canada
OS/2 For Dummies™	by Andy Rathbone	1-878058-76-2	$19.95 USA/$26.95 Canada

UNIX

Title	Author	ISBN	Price
UNIX For Dummies™	by John R. Levine & Margaret Levine Young	1-878058-58-4	$19.95 USA/$26.95 Canada

WINDOWS

Title	Author	ISBN	Price
S.O.S. For Windows™	by Katherine Murray	1-56884-045-4	$12.95 USA/$16.95 Canada
MORE Windows 3.1 For Dummies™, 3rd Edition	by Andy Rathbone	1-56884-240-6	$19.99 USA/$26.99 Canada

PCs / HARDWARE

Title	Author	ISBN	Price
Illustrated Computer Dictionary For Dummies™	by Dan Gookin, Wally Wang, & Chris Van Buren	1-56884-004-7	$12.95 USA/$16.95 Canada
Upgrading and Fixing PCs For Dummies™	by Andy Rathbone	1-56884-002-0	$19.95 USA/$26.95 Canada

PRESENTATION / AUTOCAD

Title	Author	ISBN	Price
AutoCAD For Dummies™	by Bud Smith	1-56884-191-4	$19.95 USA/$26.95 Canada
PowerPoint 4 For Windows For Dummies™	by Doug Lowe	1-56884-161-2	$16.95 USA/$22.95 Canada

PROGRAMMING

Title	Author	ISBN	Price
Borland C++ For Dummies™	by Michael Hyman	1-56884-162-0	$19.95 USA/$26.95 Canada
"Borland's New Language Product" For Dummies™	by Neil Rubenking	1-56884-200-7	$19.95 USA/$26.95 Canada
C For Dummies™	by Dan Gookin	1-878058-78-9	$19.95 USA/$26.95 Canada
C++ For Dummies™	by Stephen R. Davis	1-56884-163-9	$19.95 USA/$26.95 Canada
Mac Programming For Dummies™	by Dan Parks Sydow	1-56884-173-6	$19.95 USA/$26.95 Canada
QBasic Programming For Dummies™	by Douglas Hergert	1-56884-093-4	$19.95 USA/$26.95 Canada
Visual Basic "X" For Dummies™, 2nd Edition	by Wallace Wang	1-56884-230-9	$19.99 USA/$26.99 Canada
Visual Basic 3 For Dummies™	by Wallace Wang	1-56884-076-4	$19.95 USA/$26.95 Canada

SPREADSHEET

Title	Author	ISBN	Price
1-2-3 For Dummies™	by Greg Harvey	1-878058-60-6	$16.95 USA/$21.95 Canada
1-2-3 For Windows 5 For Dummies™, 2nd Edition	by John Walkenbach	1-56884-216-3	$16.95 USA/$21.95 Canada
1-2-3 For Windows For Dummies™	by John Walkenbach	1-56884-052-7	$16.95 USA/$21.95 Canada
Excel 5 For Macs For Dummies™	by Greg Harvey	1-56884-186-8	$19.95 USA/$26.95 Canada
Excel For Dummies™, 2nd Edition	by Greg Harvey	1-56884-050-0	$16.95 USA/$21.95 Canada
MORE Excel 5 For Windows For Dummies™	by Greg Harvey	1-56884-207-4	$19.95 USA/$26.95 Canada
Quattro Pro 6 For Windows For Dummies™	by John Walkenbach	1-56884-174-4	$19.95 USA/$26.95 Canada
Quattro Pro For DOS For Dummies™	by John Walkenbach	1-56884-023-3	$16.95 USA/$21.95 Canada

UTILITIES / VCRs & CAMCORDERS

Title	Author	ISBN	Price
Norton Utilities 8 For Dummies™	by Beth Slick	1-56884-166-3	$19.95 USA/$26.95 Canada
VCRs & Camcorders For Dummies™	by Andy Rathbone & Gordon McComb	1-56884-229-5	$14.99 USA/$20.99 Canada

WORD PROCESSING

Title	Author	ISBN	Price
Ami Pro For Dummies™	by Jim Meade	1-56884-049-7	$19.95 USA/$26.95 Canada
MORE Word For Windows 6 For Dummies™	by Doug Lowe	1-56884-165-5	$19.95 USA/$26.95 Canada
MORE WordPerfect 6 For Windows For Dummies™	by Margaret Levine Young & David C. Kay	1-56884-206-6	$19.95 USA/$26.95 Canada
MORE WordPerfect 6 For DOS For Dummies™	by Wallace Wang, edited by Dan Gookin	1-56884-047-0	$19.95 USA/$26.95 Canada
S.O.S. For WordPerfect™	by Katherine Murray	1-56884-053-5	$12.95 USA/$16.95 Canada
Word 6 For Macs For Dummies™	by Dan Gookin	1-56884-190-6	$19.95 USA/$26.95 Canada
Word For Windows 6 For Dummies™	by Dan Gookin	1-56884-075-6	$16.95 USA/$21.95 Canada
Word For Windows For Dummies™	by Dan Gookin	1-878058-86-X	$16.95 USA/$21.95 Canada
WordPerfect 6 For Dummies™	by Dan Gookin	1-878058-77-0	$16.95 USA/$21.95 Canada
WordPerfect For Dummies™	by Dan Gookin	1-878058-52-5	$16.95 USA/$21.95 Canada
WordPerfect For Windows For Dummies™	by Margaret Levine Young & David C. Kay	1-56884-032-2	$16.95 USA/$21.95 Canada

Fun, Fast, & Cheap!

1/26/95

CorelDRAW! 5 For Dummies™ Quick Reference
by Raymond E. Werner

ISBN: 1-56884-952-4
$9.99 USA/$12.99 Canada

Windows "X" For Dummies™ Quick Reference, 3rd Edition
by Greg Harvey

ISBN: 1-56884-964-8
$9.99 USA/$12.99 Canada

Word For Windows 6 For Dummies™ Quick Reference
by George Lynch

ISBN: 1-56884-095-0
$8.95 USA/$12.95 Canada

WordPerfect For DOS For Dummies™ Quick Reference
by Greg Harvey

ISBN: 1-56884-009-8
$8.95 USA/$11.95 Canada

Title	Author	ISBN	Price
DATABASE			
Access 2 For Dummies™ Quick Reference	by Stuart A. Stuple	1-56884-167-1	$8.95 USA/$11.95 Canada
dBASE 5 For DOS For Dummies™ Quick Reference	by Barry Sosinsky	1-56884-954-0	$9.99 USA/$12.99 Canada
dBASE 5 For Windows For Dummies™ Quick Reference	by Stuart J. Stuple	1-56884-953-2	$9.99 USA/$12.99 Canada
Paradox 5 For Windows For Dummies™ Quick Reference	by Scott Palmer	1-56884-960-5	$9.99 USA/$12.99 Canada
DESKTOP PUBLISHING / ILLUSTRATION/GRAPHICS			
Harvard Graphics 3 For Windows For Dummies™ Quick Reference	by Raymond E. Werner	1-56884-962-1	$9.99 USA/$12.99 Canada
FINANCE / PERSONAL FINANCE			
Quicken 4 For Windows For Dummies™ Quick Reference	by Stephen L. Nelson	1-56884-950-8	$9.95 USA/$12.95 Canada
GROUPWARE / INTEGRATED			
Microsoft Office 4 For Windows For Dummies™ Quick Reference	by Doug Lowe	1-56884-958-3	$9.99 USA/$12.99 Canada
Microsoft Works For Windows 3 For Dummies™ Quick Reference	by Michael Partington	1-56884-959-1	$9.99 USA/$12.99 Canada
INTERNET / COMMUNICATIONS / NETWORKING			
The Internet For Dummies™ Quick Reference	by John R. Levine	1-56884-168-X	$8.95 USA/$11.95 Canada
MACINTOSH			
Macintosh System 7.5 For Dummies™ Quick Reference	by Stuart J. Stuple	1-56884-956-7	$9.99 USA/$12.99 Canada
OPERATING SYSTEMS / DOS			
DOS For Dummies® Quick Reference	by Greg Harvey	1-56884-007-1	$8.95 USA/$11.95 Canada
UNIX			
UNIX For Dummies™ Quick Reference	by Margaret Levine Young & John R. Levine	1-56884-094-2	$8.95 USA/$11.95 Canada
WINDOWS			
Windows 3.1 For Dummies™ Quick Reference, 2nd Edition	by Greg Harvey	1-56884-951-6	$8.95 USA/$11.95 Canada
PRESENTATION / AUTOCAD			
AutoCAD For Dummies™ Quick Reference	by Ellen Finkelstein	1-56884-198-1	$9.95 USA/$12.95 Canada
SPREADSHEET			
1-2-3 For Dummies™ Quick Reference	by John Walkenbach	1-56884-027-6	$8.95 USA/$11.95 Canada
1-2-3 For Windows 5 For Dummies™ Quick Reference	by John Walkenbach	1-56884-957-5	$9.95 USA/$12.95 Canada
Excel For Windows For Dummies™ Quick Reference, 2nd Edition	by John Walkenbach	1-56884-096-9	$8.95 USA/$11.95 Canada
Quattro Pro 6 For Windows For Dummies™ Quick Reference	by Stuart A. Stuple	1-56884-172-8	$9.95 USA/$12.95 Canada
WORD PROCESSING			
Word For Windows 6 For Dummies™ Quick Reference	by George Lynch	1-56884-095-0	$8.95 USA/$11.95 Canada
WordPerfect For Windows For Dummies™ Quick Reference	by Greg Harvey	1-56884-039-X	$8.95 USA/$11.95 Canada

ORDER FORM

IDG BOOKS

Order Center: **(800) 762-2974** *(8 a.m.–6 p.m., EST, weekdays)*

12/20/94

Quantity	ISBN	Title	Price	Total

Shipping & Handling Charges

	Description	First book	Each additional book	Total
Domestic	Normal	$4.50	$1.50	$
	Two Day Air	$8.50	$2.50	$
	Overnight	$18.00	$3.00	$
International	Surface	$8.00	$8.00	$
	Airmail	$16.00	$16.00	$
	DHL Air	$17.00	$17.00	$

*For large quantities call for shipping & handling charges.
**Prices are subject to change without notice.

Ship to:

Name _____

Company _____

Address _____

City/State/Zip _____

Daytime Phone _____

Payment: ☐ Check to IDG Books (US Funds Only)

☐ VISA   ☐ MasterCard   ☐ American Express

Card # _____ Expires _____

Signature _____

Subtotal _____

CA residents add applicable sales tax _____

IN, MA, and MD residents add 5% sales tax _____

IL residents add 6.25% sales tax _____

RI residents add 7% sales tax _____

TX residents add 8.25% sales tax _____

Shipping _____

Total _____

Please send this order form to:

IDG Books Worldwide
7260 Shadeland Station, Suite 100
Indianapolis, IN 46256

Allow up to 3 weeks for delivery.
Thank you!